WOOD

WOOD

THE WORLD OF
WOODWORK AND CARVING

BRYAN SENTANCE

with 815 illustrations, 634 in colour

Thames & Hudson

ONE

TWO

THREE

FOUR

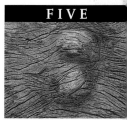

FIVE

SIX

SEVEN

PAGE 1: Wooden hanging decorations, India.
PAGE 2: Carved door, Kohistan, Pakistan.
PAGE 3: Totem, ancestor figure, Angola.
PAGE 5: Japanese *netsuke* rabbits carved from close-grained boxwood.
PAGE 6, ABOVE, RIGHT: Tuareg box embellished with metal and bone, Morocco.
BELOW, LEFT: Ojibway model snowshoes, Great Lakes, North America.
BELOW, RIGHT: Intarsia landscape, Italy.
PAGE 7, ABOVE, LEFT: Turned and painted bowl, Khokhloma, Russia.
MIDDLE RIGHT: *Retablo*, wooden box with potato paste figures, Peru.
BELOW, LEFT: Flat-pattern carved Rabari chest, Gujarat, India.

Designed by David Fordham

First published in the United Kingdom in 2003 by Thames & Hudson Ltd,
181A High Holborn, London WC1V 7QX

www.thamesandhudson.com

© 2003 Thames & Hudson Ltd, London

British Library Cataloguing-in-Publication Data
A catalogue record for this book is available from the British Library

ISBN 0-500-51120-9

Printed and bound in Singapore by C. S. Graphics

Dedication

FOR POLLY

'I am but mad north-north west: when the wind is southerly, I know a hawk from a handsaw.'
HAMLET, PRINCE OF DENMARK
Act 2, scene 2
WILLIAM SHAKESPEARE

CONTENTS

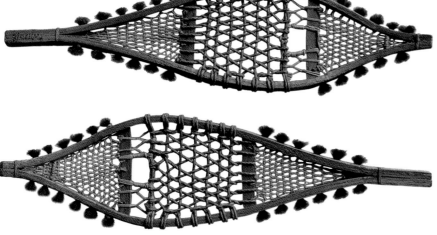

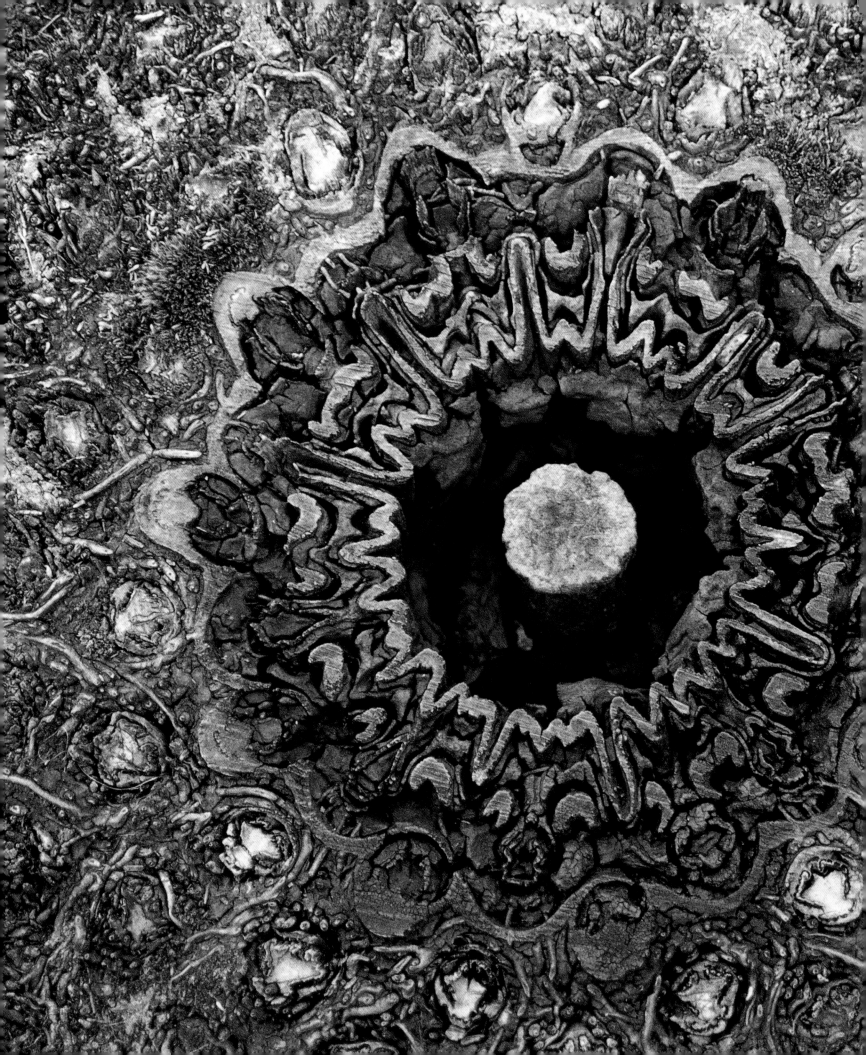

INTRODUCTION

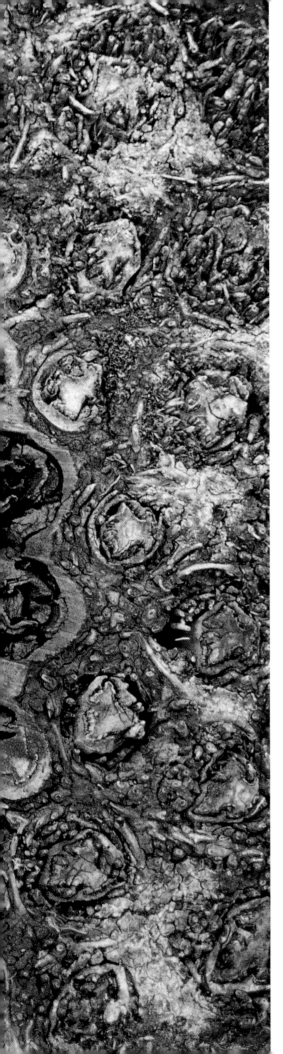

ABOVE, LEFT: *Nineteenth-century carving of the god Garuda from Tamil Nadu, India.*
ABOVE, CENTRE: *Dogon granary door carved in relief, Mali.*
ABOVE, RIGHT: *Carved oak cherub on an English house in Lavenham, Suffolk.*

LEFT: *Cross section of a tree fern.*
ABOVE, LEFT: *Dan mask from the Ivory Coast or Nigeria.*
ABOVE, RIGHT: *Fijian chip-carved kava bowl.*
RIGHT: *Low-relief carved ebony from India.*

INTRODUCTION

SINCE PREHISTORIC times wood has provided fire, shelter, tools, weapons and all manner of implements and containers. In many parts of the world newborn infants are placed in wooden cradles and the dead are laid to rest in wooden coffins. Some of the world's most significant inventions – the wheel, the printed page and the first computer, the abacus – were developed using wood. From trees comes food to eat, medicine to heal and dyestuffs to decorate.

ABOVE, RIGHT: *Gnarled hornbeam tree in Hatfield Forest, Essex, England, an ancient woodland that has been managed and coppiced since the Iron Age.*

RIGHT: *A Viking ship carved on a memorial stone in Gotland, Sweden. Much of our knowledge of historical woodwork has been acquired by studying such artefacts which have lasted long after the wood itself has decayed.*

ABOVE: *Preserved wood from Flag Fen in Cambridgeshire, England. Submerged in bog, timbers like this have remained intact for about 3,000 years, giving valuable information about the Bronze Age site.*

BELOW: *This felled tree on the Isle of Mull in Scotland has only been exposed to the elements for a few years, but has already started to decay.*

ARCHAEOLOGY

THE OLDEST evidence of prehistoric woodworking is a yew spear discovered at Clacton in England which is believed to be about 250,000 years old. It survived because it was preserved in wet ground. Vegetable fibres normally rot away when exposed to air and moisture, but when they are protected from either the fibres may remain intact indefinitely and so the oldest pieces of wood have survived in extremely wet, airless conditions or in very dry environments. For this reason it has been possible to gather a great deal of information from the following sites: a Bronze Age village buried in the boggy soil of Flag Fen in Cambridgeshire, England; Pazyryk in the Altai, southern Siberia, where the frozen remains of pits lined with logs and log coffins with wooden pillows, dating from 400 BC, were discovered; the Okeechobee Basin in Florida where a burial platform (1st millennium BC) with carved wooden totem posts was found; and the ancient cliff-dwellings of the Anasazi in the arid American South-west.

The conditions that have preserved these ancient relics must be replicated or, once put on display in a museum, they will turn to peat or dust. Timber preserved by moisture must either be kept damp or have the fluid replaced by a preservative such as polyethylene glycol.

DATING WOOD

THE DIFFICULT task of dating objects was made considerably easier by the radiocarbon technique developed after the Second World War (1939–45). Organic material contains Carbon 14, a radioactive isotope which decays gradually after death, and by measuring the traces remaining it is possible to estimate how long ago a material died.

The accuracy of carbon dating was fine tuned with the help of ancient trees using a system known as dendrochronology. Each year a tree's cambium layer produces a new growth ring and these can be counted to see how long a tree has lived. The layers vary from year to year in size and composition, but are the same for all the trees of one species in any given area. By examining and matching the patterns recorded by trees, both alive and long dead, a sequence going back thousands of years into the past can be recorded. Inspecting the rings of living and fallen Bristlecone pines, growing in the mountains of western North America, has made it possible to record a sequence extending back for 9,000 years.

TOP RIGHT; AND ABOVE RIGHT: *Reconstruction of a Bronze Age house at Flag Fen, Cambridgeshire, England; reconstruction of a crannog on Loch Tay in Scotland, originally built around 50BC. The layout and construction technique employed in both these buildings have been surmised from post holes, preserved fragments of wood, and by studying the architecture of traditional peoples in the developing world.*

RIGHT: *'Odysseus and the Sirens', after an illustration on a Greek painted vase.*

TOP LEFT: *Reconstructions of maple wood cups, based mainly on tiny wood fragments with metal fittings around the necks, from the 7th-century Sutton Hoo ship burial, England.*

ABOVE: *A reconstruction of an Anglo-Saxon thatched timber building clad with boards of riven oak at West Stow in Suffolk, England.*

WORKING WITH LITTLE EVIDENCE

THERE ARE times when the wood itself has decayed completely and archaeologists have to interpret vestigial imprints or remains such as metal fixings that have survived. Although all that remained of the hull of the Sutton Hoo ship in Suffolk, England (a royal burial from AD 625) was a large imprint and rows of the rivets that had once held the planks together, there was sufficient detail to enable reconstruction of the size, shape and construction techniques employed by the Saxons during the 7th century. At other times assumptions may be made and conclusions drawn by comparing fragmentary evidence with the products of surviving cultures who continue to use ancient, traditional ways of working.

THE HISTORY OF TREES

THREE HUNDRED million years ago a large part of the Earth's land masses was covered in forests. Their remains have been preserved as coal and fossils so that we now know that there were no trees, but giant horsetails and club-mosses up to 45 m (150 ft) tall. Neither plant exists on such a scale today, but tree ferns and the palm-like cycads, which evolved soon afterwards, still thrive in the tropical and sub-tropical regions of the southern hemisphere.

ABOVE: *Tree ferns, an ancient tree-like plant found in the southern hemisphere, formerly employed by the indigenous Maori in New Zealand.*

BELOW: *Fan-shaped leaves of a ginkgo sapling, probably a descendant of the first true tree.*

ABOVE, RIGHT: *Fossils of a 340-million-year-old specimen of* Telangium affine *from Scotland.*

RIGHT: Metasequoia glyptostroboides, *the dawn redwood, thriving in the University Botanic Gardens in Cambridge, England.*

THE FIRST TREE

TRUE TREES are tall plants that support themselves on a woody trunk by means of a tough substance called lignin. Earlier plants multiplied by producing spores which were distributed by the wind, but true trees reproduce sexually – they have male and female parts.

The Ginkgo tree, *Ginkgo biloba*, was probably the first true tree. Sometimes called the 'maidenhair tree' because of its resemblance to the maidenhair fern, it has survived virtually unchanged for 200 million years. Although fossils show that it was once distributed over much of the northern hemisphere – it was common in the London area 30 million years ago – the only wild survivors are to be found in the mountains of China. It is a very beautiful, tall tree with fan-shaped leaves that turn golden yellow before they fall, so many specimens have been nurtured in the precincts of Buddhist temples in the East and in botanic gardens and country estates in the West.

CONIFERS

NARROW-LEAVED, cone-bearing trees had evolved 140 million years ago. The leaves or 'needles' contained chemicals that repressed germination and growth as they fell on the forest floor, allowing coniferous forest to dominate the northern hemisphere. Among these trees were the redwoods, the largest living species ever to grow on the planet. One of the oldest species, *Metasequoia glyptostroboides*, the dawn redwood, once known only through fossils, was believed extinct until specimens were discovered in 1941 growing in the Chinese Xitianmu Mountains.

Broad-leaved trees

Certain species have evolved to suit hotter conditions, but coniferous trees generally prefer cooler temperatures and are now to be found mostly in a band around the top of the northern land masses or on high ground. As the ice melted at the end of the last Ice Age 12,000 years ago conditions were no longer suitable and the conifers gradually retreated as new species, which had evolved nearer the equator and were more suited to the warmer, wetter climate, colonized the land. The newcomers had larger leaves which dropped as they became dormant in the cold weather. These broad-leaved trees usually grow slowly, producing denser, harder wood.

Left: *Broad-leaved woodland in Hatfield Forest, Essex, England. Woods like this once covered most of Europe.*

Including the devastations of fire, flood and ice the single most powerful influence on trees has been man. Since the Stone Age forests and jungles have been cleared so other crops could be planted. Some species have been cultivated at the expense of others. The techniques of harvesting employed by our forefathers were not always sustainable, but there appeared to be a seemingly endless supply of raw materials. Only now is it clear just how much damage has been done. Trees provide life itself.

The Tree of Life

One of the most potent and widespread of all symbols is the Tree of Life. Carved on wood and on stone, woven or embroidered onto textiles, painted in pigments and dyes, in virtually every culture and religion, in diverse guises, covered in a variety of foliage, the Tree of Life appears representing the dynamic life force of the whole of the manifested cosmos. This is typified by the Tibetan concept of the Universe at the heart of which grows a giant tree with six branches. Its roots reach down into the depths of the Underworld, its trunk is in the land of the living and its branches stretch up to heaven, to the realms of the gods. This image appears in many other distant cultures including that of the Norsemen who believed a giant ash tree called Yggdrasil stood at the centre of creation holding all the parts of the Universe in their place. The myths of the Tolowa Native Americans of northern California relate how the first thing made by the Creator was a redwood tree and that, at the first sunrise, the tracks of all the future creatures were to be discovered on the ground around it. In Australia the stories of the Aborigines tell how the World Tree supports the sky and has the stars lodged in its branches.

Above: *Mixed forest in Finland. The harsher climate of the northern regions of Europe, Asia and the Americas dictates landscapes dominated by birches and conifers. The inhabitants of these forests once depended on the trees for building materials, food, clothes and many of the other essentials for survival.*

Right: *Drawing of embroidery, from Hazarajat in Afghanistan, depicting a stylized Tree of Life motif.*

THE FIRST PEOPLE

IN LOCALITIES dominated by forest or jungle the creation of both the Universe and man is often associated with trees. The Norsemen, for instance, believed that Ask, the first man, and Embla, the first woman, were carved by the gods, Odin, Vili and Ve, from driftwood washed up on the seashore. In the Admiralty Islands, in the Pacific Ocean, the first man was also carved from a tree, while in Tonga mankind grew from shoots on the World Tree.

According to the Bible, at the centre of the Garden of Eden the Tree of the Knowledge of Good and Evil grew. Eating the forbidden fruit of this tree, Adam and Eve were cursed to death and damnation. Christ redeemed mankind by dying on the cross which was purportedly made from the wood of the very same tree. In Christian iconography the fruit of the tree is an apple, but an Irish myth tells how the hero Finn gained wisdom by eating a salmon that had swallowed the fruits of the Tree of Knowledge, a hazel that overhung its pool, and so received the name 'Mac Cool' which in Gaelic means 'son of the hazel'.

LEFT: *A carved chair, from the Swat Valley in Pakistan, with turned walnut legs and cedar backrest. The pre-Islamic symbols include a solar motif, while the central column represents the Tree of Life.*

TOP RIGHT: *Craftsmen all over the world depict Tree-of-Life motifs on their work. Here, a Hindu needlewoman, from Saurasthra, India, has worked the motif in appliqué.*

RIGHT: *The Tree of the Knowledge of Good and Evil stood at the heart of the Garden of Eden as illustrated in this 16th-century woodcut.*

TREE SPIRITS

IN CULTURES all around the world, untainted by industrial philosophies, trees are thought to be sentient beings or the abode of spirits, sometimes malevolent but often benevolent. In Japan they are haunted by ghosts, in Russia by the Rusalka who lured maidens to a watery death, in Ancient Greece oaks were the homes of dryads and hamadryads, nymphs who guarded their trees with axes, and in Ireland hawthorns were associated with fairies and cutting one down is still considered to court disaster. Thorn trees in the British Isles were once commonly found with strips of cloth tied around their twigs as votive offerings.

RIGHT: *The ancient yew tree in the church yard at Fortingall in Scotland. Although difficult to prove, some estimates put the age of this tree at around 9,000 years old, which would make it the oldest tree in the world.*

BELOW, LEFT: *A woodcut by Albrecht Dürer. The wood of the Tree of Knowledge of Good and Evil, according to legend, was subsequently used for the cross upon which Christ was crucified.*

Groves of old trees became centres of worship before the first temples, churches or cathedrals were built. The name of the ancient Druids was taken from *duir*, which means oak tree. Ancient peoples would go into the groves, lay their hands upon the trees and invoke their help, hence, to this day, to turn aside misfortune, people still say 'touch wood'. Many British church yards contain yew trees far older than the church itself as early missionaries picked their sites strategically to harness the power of old beliefs in the tree's immortality. The old yew in the church yard at Fortingall in Scotland had already been standing for thousands of years when St Columba landed on the Hebridean shore of Iona in the 6th century.

NEAR LEFT: *Tree-of-Life motif carved in shallow relief on a ceremonial board for hanging a kris, a Javanese sword. Scandinavian carvings also depict deer gnawing at the tree trunk.*

BELOW: *Early tree-like plants in an illustration from a children's encyclopedia showing an artist's impression of life 300 million years ago.*

A MATTER OF LIFE AND DEATH

TREES ARE not just a symbol or a raw material and the Tree of Life is an image that is both metaphorical and literal. Trees provide a habitat for other plants and a huge range of mammals, reptiles, birds, insects and even amphibians such as the tree frogs of the Amazon jungle. Their fallen trunks become tons of humus which enrich the soil. They anchor the soil and prevent erosion washing it away to leave a sterile land that would produce no food. But most of all trees feed off sunlight, turning carbon dioxide into breathable oxygen. Every day a single beech tree gives off enough oxygen to supply the needs of ten people. Without trees life as we know it would cease to exist.

LIFE & REMAINS OF THE CARBONIFEROUS AGE

THE LUXURIANT VEGETATION OF THE CARBONIFEROUS AGE—FERNS, MOSSES, HORSETAILS, AND SOME OF THE ANIMAL LIFE OF THE PERIOD, INCLUDING AN ARCHEGOSAURUS AND A FISH

LEFT: *On Polynesian islands such as Samoa hardwood clubs were the major weapon. Replicas are still made for tourists, but stocks of suitable woods have dwindled as agriculture and the cultivation of coconut palms have taken over the land.*

BELOW: *Lumberjacks sawing up a kauri tree with a cross-cut saw. The massive kauri tree, native to the northern end of New Zealand, was an important source of timber for the Maoris.*

ENDANGERED CULTURE

BEFORE THE first Europeans reached Easter Island in 1722, the inhabitants had already been responsible for an ecological disaster. In their compulsion to transport and erect the fantastic stone heads, for which the island is now so famous, they had chopped down every available tree, causing the extinction of the native *toromiro* tree. No longer able to build boats, they were unable to fish and as they could not grow sufficient food on the poor soil the island infrastructure collapsed, their culture crumbled and the population dwindled.

LEFT: *Early 18th-century Moai kavakava figure, from Easter Island, representing a deified ancestral being. Carved from now extinct toromiro wood, they were wrapped in bark cloth and stored in the rafters.*

BELOW: *Monkey puzzle tree in Kilmartin Glen, Scotland. European landowners planted large numbers in the 19th century.*

RIGHT: *Harvesting cork from oak trees in Portugal, an industry losing viability as plastic corks become widely utilized.*

ENDANGERED SPECIES

THE MONKEY puzzle tree, *Araucaria araucana*, is considered so sacred in south central Chile that one local people named themselves the Pehuenche, which means 'the people of the monkey puzzles'. Now they are fighting to protect it from illegal logging by timber dealers who covet its tall, straight trunk. A tree that has existed for more than 200 million years could one day soon only be found in the gardens of Europe. The monkey puzzle is just one endangered tree species on a list that now runs to more than eight thousand.

RIGHT: *Wood from some of the world's thousands of endangered trees. From left to right, bubinga from Gabon and Cameroon; padouk from the Andaman Islands; Brazilian mahogany; purpleheart from Central America; Indian rosewood; satinwood from Sri Lanka; teak from Burma; afromosia from West Africa.*

BELOW: *Swidden agriculture in late 19th-century Finland, also known evocatively as 'slash and burn'. This technique reduces forest and leaves exposed soil that is easily eroded and leached of goodness, resulting in land where little can grow.*

RIGHT: *Felled and sawn kauri trees being jacked onto trucks in the forests of northern New Zealand. Only pockets of forest remain – today, most of the land is used for sheep farming.*

BELOW: *Sawn logs awaiting shipping on the quayside at Ardrishaig, Scotland. This timber comes from sustainable forest managed by the Forestry Commission, but has largely replaced indigenous species with fast-growing softwoods.*

Hardwood trees, in particular, are valuable and have been overlogged, but in order to fell and transport one valuable hardwood tree roads and clearings may be made involving the clearing and burning of thousands of other trees, some of which might themselves otherwise have grown into valuable giants. Often there is no replanting scheme to provide wood for future generations, but only a lifeless habitat where the soil erodes and countless species of plants and animals die out.

Since *homo sapiens* first broke the soil with a stick to plant a seed or root man has been slashing and burning his way across the world, clearing land for the cultivation of crops and to provide grazing land for herds. As the population continues to grow more and more building land is needed, but more and more pollution is being created and changes are occurring in the climate. Virgin tropical rainforest is now disappearing at a rate equivalent to an area the size of a football pitch every two seconds.

The future

I N ORDER to prevent the eradication of tree species forestry techniques must take a more responsible approach with more selective felling and the replanting of sustainable forest. Organizations now exist that monitor logging – anything approved by the Forestry Stewardship Council has not caused irreparable damage. If woodworkers use recycled timber or find less threatened woods and the general public recycle their newspapers then the need for felling fresh forest for paper pulp is reduced. There are now campaigns for better international legislation to curb the destruction of the rainforests and on a local level individuals can foster the cultivation of indigenous species in their streets and gardens. At the end of the book there is a list of organizations that offer information about the purchase of responsibly produced timber or the planting, cultivation and conservation of trees or woods.

ABOVE, LEFT: *Carving by the author using a piece of recycled Andaman padouk, an endangered species of hardwood.*

ABOVE, RIGHT: *New Zealand's kauri tree can live for 3,000 years. Extensive logging has left few mature specimens and only one per cent of ancient kauri forests now survive. Tane Mahuta, the largest living specimen, is only 2,000 years old.*

LEFT: *Logs of fir, a fast growing softwood, cultivated in central Scotland.*

RIGHT: *Cross section of a felled softwood showing the widely spaced grain typical of fast-growing trees.*

ABOUT THIS BOOK

I HAVE ALWAYS loved making things and the material that I return to time and again is wood. As a small boy, growing up near the sea, I spent many hours beachcombing, dragging home pieces of grotesquely shaped driftwood which were frequently borrowed for still lifes by local artists, both amateur and professional. Sometimes I would cut into them and be enthralled by the relationship I found there, for as I carved away, the wood would have its say, arguing and persuading me that it would only allow me to use my tools in a certain way. This form of work is not without its difficulties as I try to impose my will, but as we cooperate, the wood and I, the process becomes both stimulating and reassuring, and I feel as if it shares with me something of its yielding strength.

Craftsmen all over the world have experienced this communion and the form and style of their work has been dictated by the qualities of the timber that they use, as well as the culture upon which they draw. By presenting examples of woodwork from diverse societies side by side I hope to give the reader greater comprehension of the manual techniques of working wood and also a little insight into the sophistication of the craftsmanship of societies too often dismissed as primitive. I hope that, like Albrecht Dürer viewing the first artefacts imported from the Americas, the reader will marvel 'at the subtle genius of men in distant lands'.

ABOVE: *Carved torsos at the Neka Palace in Ubud, Bali. Traditionally, Balinese carving has been closely related to religion, but the tourist trade has provided work for a whole new generation of woodworkers using both traditional and innovative styles.*

BELOW: *Elephants from India and Myanmar. Today, both the real elephants and the ebony from which these were carved are seriously at risk.*

THE RAW MATERIAL

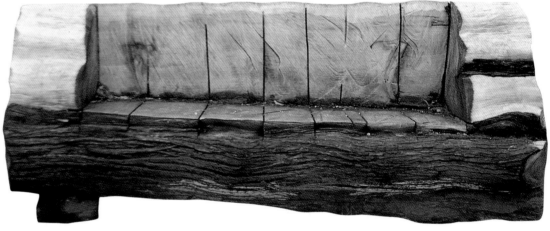

FAR LEFT: *Cross section of Scots pine.*

TOP LEFT: *Mexican carved gourd.*

TOP RIGHT: *Japanese* netsuke *rabbits carved from close-grained boxwood.*

ABOVE, RIGHT: *The roots of a Moroccan thuja tree, valued for its interesting grain.*

ABOVE: *A bench carved from a tree trunk using a chain saw, Britain.*

LEFT: *Yugoslavian bowl decorated in typical fashion with chip-carved patterns.*

THE RAW MATERIAL

TREES ARE the longest-living and largest organisms on Earth. Forests and jungles have become shrunken enclaves, but once they covered vast tracts of land, including much of what is now the Sahara Desert in Africa. Wildwood with scattered clearings, which supported flowers and grasses, stretched from Finland to Italy. As early as 500 BC half the wildwood in Britain had disappeared, cleared by settlers and eaten by their herds, but man has not been the only cause of deforestation. Since the dinosaurs walked the Earth, forests and jungles have swollen and shrunk, pioneers in the empty wilderness left by retreating glaciers, eaten into extinction by herbivores, buried under the sands of deserts. Millions of years ago Antarctica was covered with tropical forest lost as the shifting of the Earth's axis turned a once tropical zone into a polar ice cap. Man may not be the only culprit, but the balance is now in man's hands – the choice is between economic gain and the ecological balance of the planet.

ABOVE: *The even, widely space growth rings typical of coniferous trees. Fir trees are grown extensively for their tall, straight trunks.*

BELOW: *Stacks of jack fruit wood, nangkar, awaiting transportation, central Bali.*

BELOW, LEFT: *The bark of* Platanus x hispanica, *the London plane.*

BELOW, RIGHT: *The bark of* Eucalyptus macarthurii.

HOW TREES GROW

TREES BELONG to the division of the plant kingdom known as spermatophyte or seed-bearing plants. A tree seed puts roots down into the ground and thrusts a stem upwards, lifting its leaves towards the sun. New growth occurs around the trunk or bole in the cambium layer which produces two types of cell. On the inside are the sapwood or xylem cells that form tubes from the root to the crown of the tree. As the sun causes moisture on the leaves to evaporate, nutrient-rich water is sucked up from the roots where it has been absorbed by osmosis from the surrounding soil. The green chlorophyll in the leaves absorbs carbon dioxide while exposed to sunlight and produces food sugars through the process of photosynthesis. This food is distributed to other parts of the tree via the phloem cells on the outer edge of the cambium. As new cambium layers are produced each year the old xylem cells die off in the heartwood of the tree, while the old phloem cells become crusty outer bark and eventually flake off.

RIGHT: *Banyan tree at Petchaburi in Thailand. Using aerial roots, a single banyan tree can spread out to form a whole grove on its own, providing welcome shade. The Buddha achieved enlightenment beneath just such a tree.*

ABOVE: *An Iban warrior in Sarawak collecting the poisonous sap of the ipoh tree to coat the darts of his blow pipe. Other types of trees are tapped in the same way in order to collect natural sugars for maple syrup, latex for rubber and palm sap for wine.*

BELOW: *Chinese cork carving. The light, spongy outer bark of* Quercus suber, *the cork oak, can be harvested to provide floatation aids, bottle stoppers and even flooring.*

THE USES OF TREES

AN ASTOUNDING range of products is harvested from trees. Bark provides cork, cloth, medicines such as aspirin and quinine, and the chemicals used for tanning leather; sap and resin are collected for adhesives, rubber, poison and sugary syrup; fruits and nuts are used as food, spices, dyes and even provide the fluffy capoc formerly used to stuff life jackets; roots are split and woven into baskets and traps; shoots and leaves flavour food and thatch homes, as well as being made into hats and textiles; blossom enchants with beautiful colours and fragrances, and also provides valuable medicines. The timber cut from the trunks and branches is perhaps the most widely used of all construction materials exploited in every walk of life, and wood pulp is the world's main source of paper. Trees that died millions of years ago are still useful – their wood is the source of fossil fuels and their resin is the origin of amber.

RIGHT: *An Ainu man, from northern Japan, wearing the traditional appliquéd costume made from a textile woven from shredded elm bark. Shredded bark fabrics were also used on the North American Pacific coast, while in the Pacific, Central Africa and Latin America cloth is still made by beating out sheets of bark from trees such as the paper mulberry,* Broussonetia papyrifera, *or the fig,* Ficus natalensis.

23

SOFTWOODS

A S FAR as the woodworker is concerned, wood belongs to one of two categories, softwoods or hardwoods. This can cause some confusion as some hardwoods are very soft while some softwoods, such as yew, are very hard. Technically, softwoods come from the botanical group *Gymnospermae*, which can be translated as 'plants with exposed seeds'. They have no flowers, but develop their seeds in cones and are therefore also referred to as cone bearing or coniferous. Most softwood trees are evergreen, keeping their needle-like leaves through the winter, but some such as the larch are deciduous, replacing their fallen needles in the spring. Conifer woods are dark places where both sound and undergrowth are suppressed by layers of fallen needles.

Most softwoods are fast growing. With a single leading stem and branching side shoots, they typically form a tall conical shape. The epitome of this is the Norway spruce, which, since the 19th century, has been grown commercially for Christmas trees.

The tallest and oldest

M ANY softwoods achieve a considerable size, but the largest are the redwoods growing in Oregon and California in North America. The biggest of all is the giant redwood, *Sequoiadendron giganteum*. For bulk, nothing can match the General Sherman, the largest living object on Earth, which can be found in the Sequoia National Park in California. It is about 2,700 years old, measures roughly 95 m (311 ft) in height, 17.6 m (25 ft) in diameter at chest height and is estimated to weigh about 1.2 million kg (2.7 million lbs). Even taller, although less bulky and only 1,500 years old, is a coast redwood, *Sequoia sempervirens*, growing in Redwood National Park in California. It is 112 m (368 ft) tall and is known simply as Tall Tree. With the possible exception of wind, redwoods can stand anything that nature throws at them, including fire. Left in peace, they could carry on growing taller and taller for centuries to come.

Another extraordinary conifer, the bristlecone pine, grows in the White Mountains of California. It is not a vigorous giant, but a gnarled and twisted survivor. Eking out its existence in an environment of extremes, the bristlecone grows very slowly, exuding resins that protect it from the climate and prevent the loss of water through evaporation. Dendrochronology has shown the oldest tree, the Methuselah tree, to be 4,700 years old. Incredibly, there may be an older tree still. In Scotland, in the churchyard at Fortingall there is an ancient yew tree. The heart of the tree has rotted away, so ring counting is not possible, but, basing calculations on the tree's girth and the growing habits of yews, some believe this tree may be 9,000 years old.

The uses of softwoods

B ECAUSE they are generally fast growing, softwoods are relatively quick and cheap to farm which makes them the most widely used woods commercially. Their tall, straight trunks

have the advantage of length, but their widely spaced growth rings make the wood, on the whole, easily splintered and unsuitable for high-quality cabinetmaking, although it has been used extensively in the construction of the traditional furniture of Scandinavia. However, softwoods, such as cedar and sandalwood, which exude fragrant resins, are highly sought after for making clothes chests or religious images. The slower-growing softwoods – for instance, yew – are much harder and can be used in the same way as hardwoods.

OPPOSITE, FAR LEFT: *Knots caused by branching in a plank of spruce wood.*

OPPOSITE, TOP LEFT: *The gnarled stems of the ancient yew at Fortingall in Scotland.*

OPPOSITE, MIDDLE: *Piñon pine growing in the arid landscape of northern Arizona, North America.*

OPPOSITE, BELOW, LEFT: *The giant redwood, a native of western North America.*

OPPOSITE, BELOW, RIGHT: *Cones of softwood trees* – Pinus x holofordiana *(left and centre);* Atlas cedar, Cedrus atlanticus *(right).*

LEFT: *A poupou, panel, in the boathouse at Waitangi, New Zealand, carved from kauri wood.*

ABOVE: *French Canadian lumberjacks sitting on the stump of a freshly felled conifer.*

RIGHT: *Indian carving of the goddess Saraswati; made in Mysore from fragrant sandalwood.*

HARDWOODS

THE HARDWOOD grouping includes not only the hardest woods such as *Lignum vitae*, a native of the West Indies, Venezuela and Colombia, and ebony, which grows in India and South-East Asia, but also the softest, balsa, which is a major export from Ecuador because of its lightness. Technically, hardwood trees belong to the botanical group of flowering plants called *Angiospermae* which, after their flowers have been fertilized, produce fruits or nuts. Hardwoods have broad leaves as opposed to needles. In general, broad-leaved evergreens thrive in the tropics and the southern hemisphere, while in the temperate regions of the northern hemisphere broad-leaved trees are usually deciduous, losing their leaves in the autumn as part of their strategy to survive the cold winters.

As a hardwood tree grows it constantly forks and divides into smaller and smaller branches, producing a spreading form rather than the conical shape typical of softwoods.

ABOVE: *English oak showing the classic spreading form typical of hardwood trees.*

LEFT: *Leaves from hardwood trees. The smaller is from the field maple,* Acer campestris, *the larger from the London plane,* Platanus x hispanica.

The qualities of hardwoods

HARDWOODS are usually slower growing than softwoods and may take three times as long to reach maturity. As they produce less new wood each year their growth rings are closer together and the fibres between are more densely packed, which makes the wood denser and less likely to splinter. As a result, hardwood has greater structural integrity than softwood and will last longer without treatment and is less prone to insect damage. The range of density and hardness between one wood and another relates to the speed of its growth and also to the thickness of the walls of individual cells or fibres. However, because hardwood takes longer to reach a size viable for felling, its timber is more expensive and now that demand has outstripped the speed at which replacements can grow many of the hardwood species, particularly those growing in the tropics such as ebony and teak, are seriously threatened with extinction.

ABOVE; AND BELOW, LEFT: *Mahogany being hauled by mules in Mexico; an elephant hauling teak logs in Myanmar.*

BELOW: *A sycamore tree,* Acer pseudoplatanus, *which is commonly wider than it is tall.*

Uses

HARDWOODS are not only more durable than softwoods, but offer a much greater range of weight, hardness, figure and colour and can therefore be put to a

variety of uses, depending on the qualities required. The strength and stability of woods such as walnut and mahogany, which are not prone to warping, makes them ideal for accurate joinery and furniture construction. The expense of using hardwoods with beautiful colour and figuring can be alleviated by slicing them into veneers, used to clad a carcass of cheaper timber or to add decorative details.

Because of their loose grain, softwoods are only suitable for shallow carving, while many hardwoods can be finely carved in great detail. Oak has always been popular in northern Europe, but it was surpassed in the 17th century by the delicacy that could be achieved with walnut, limewood and the timber of imported hardwoods blessed with a dense, even grain. Hardwoods are normally chosen for outdoor furniture, buildings and boats as they can survive the elements for longer with little or no preservation.

Balsa, the lightest of woods, is popular for model making, but is also used for insulation, notably in the walls of aeroplanes where weight is a prime consideration.

ABOVE, LEFT: *On a block of oak lie veneers of, from left to right, sweet chestnut, sapele, elm, and sycamore (above, right) and walnut (below, right).*

TOP RIGHT: *One of the many 16th- and 17th-century oak-framed buildings in the Suffolk town of Lavenham, England.*

RIGHT: *A sun carved by the author from oak, the most commonly carved wood in English vernacular decoration.*

BELOW: *An armadillo carved in Ecuador from balsa, the lightest of all hardwoods.*

TROPICAL PLANTS

THE TROPICAL regions of the world are home to many valuable species of hardwood trees, but the hot and wet conditions also encourage the rapid growth of a multitude of other plants. Some reach more than 30 m (100 ft) in height and grow faster than one metre (3 ft) a day. Of these large vigorous plants most support themselves by climbing up taller vegetation, but a few are rigid enough to support their own upright posture.

THIS PAGE, CLOCKWISE FROM ABOVE: *Coconut palms on the coast of Upolu, Samoa; hair slide carved on Bali from a piece of coconut shell; turned bowl, from Java, with the spotty grain typical of wood from the coconut palm trunk; Balinese spoon with a coconut-shell bowl and trunk-wood handle; coconut wood Javanese spoon.*

Palms

TECHNICALLY, palms are not trees, but monocotyledonous flowering plants. Typically, they are tall with a single straight trunk providing wood hard enough to be carved or turned into many useful objects. Dark vessels running through the lighter

coloured wood create a distinctive grain pattern that appears streaky when cut longitudinally and spotty when cut across the trunk. In Ancient Egypt the wood of date and dom palms was cut into planks and also used for the columns and joists of buildings as it still is in North Africa today. Large quantities of coconut wood are exported from Sulawesi in Indonesia for use as structural members in building projects in Bali and other parts of Indonesia where the trees are cultivated for their fruit.

The sea-borne fruit of the coconut has been widely scattered by the world's oceans and the tough shell is frequently used as a receptacle and cut into bowls and

LEFT: *An incised bamboo medicine pot with a carved hardwood lid and base, Lombok, Indonesia. Hollow bamboo culms make ideal containers, requiring only the minimum of carving or joinery.*

ABOVE: *The roof of a restaurant in Lovina, north Bali, constructed with a coconut wood frame covered with bamboo.*

RIGHT: Arundo donax *reed ceiling supported on beams of date palm wood, Taourirte, Morocco.*

BELOW: *Bamboo in the hills of northern Thailand.*

BOTTOM: *A Japanese water dipper made from simply jointed pieces of bamboo.*

spoons. The shell is marked with three spots and the name coconut is derived from the Spanish or Portuguese coco, which means a grinning face. In Samoa they tell how Tuna, a young Fijian, fell in love with a Samoan girl named Sina whose angry brothers decided to kill him. Before he died, Tuna promised Sina that a tree would grow from his grave. The tree was the coconut and every time Sina lifted a fruit to drink she found herself kissing the lips of her lover.

Bamboos

THE bamboo is technically a member of the grass family, but the high lignin content gives it enormous tensile strength. In Africa and Asia it is common to see a building under construction enveloped in a scaffolding not of steel but of bamboo. A thicket of bamboo was the only thing to withstand the atom bomb dropped on Hiroshima in Japan during the Second World War.

Bamboos grow fast and tall, providing a ready source of material to craftsmen in every continent except Europe and the Antarctic. Its tubular form, divided at intervals by nodes, is ideal for the manufacture of containers and musical instruments. The uses of bamboo are countless – it has been employed to make anything from boats to buildings, from furniture to flutes, from ladders to ladles, from plumbing to paint brushes, and from walls to weapons. Split lengthwise into slats, bamboos are often woven together to make wall panels. When split finely they can be woven into all manner of baskets and mats. Bamboos have a wide variety of colour and markings, but when dry most are reduced to the same golden yellow that eventually weathers to a dull grey.

Gourds

THE woody shells of the dried fruits of gourds, members of the squash family, are widely used as containers and, especially in sub-Saharan Africa and Latin America, are often carved and engraved with the same techniques used by woodworkers.

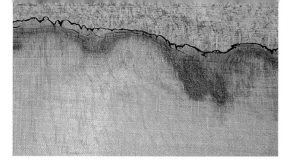

GRAIN

THE WAY in which a tree develops from one year to the next influences the way its fibres mesh together, affecting the texture and density of its wood and therefore its workability. The decorative effects produced are correctly referred to as figuring.

Growth rings

EACH year a tree grows a new cambium layer revealed in cross section as a set of concentric rings and longitudinally as a set of more or less parallel lines. Early or springwood grows quickly to produce a pale colour, while the late or summerwood grows more slowly and shows as the darker section of the annual ring. Fast-growing spruce produces widely spaced rings, while slow-growing box has more densely packed rings. Whatever the species, when the weather is favourable a tree will grow faster and produce wider spaced rings and so the spacing varies from one year to the next and from season to season, creating an irregular pattern. Growth may well be faster on one side if the tree is growing on a hill or in a windy situation and then the rings will be asymmetric. Tropical hardwoods enjoy a continuous period of growth uninterrupted by the seasons and may have no conspicuous rings.

Density

THE texture of wood is dictated by the size of hollow cells used for transporting sap, the thickness of the walls of the cells and the way they are distributed. Timber with a marked contrast in its distribution of early and latewood (ring porous) is harder to work and finish than timber with evenly distributed pores (diffuse porous). The finest workmanship can be produced using wood with a close, even grain as it is less likely to splinter. The ideal wood for the carver is lime (*Tilia sp.*), a diffuse porous hardwood with thin cell walls which is therefore both even and soft. Close-grained woods with thick cell walls are heavy – for instance, *Lignum*

vitae which weighs 76 lbs per cubic foot (1,216 kg per cubic metre). Dense, heavy woods are hardwearing and will take a high polish. They are ideal for cogs, pulleys, mallets or bowling balls and can also be sliced finely for use as decorative veneers.

Figuring

STRAIGHT trees produce grain with a straight figure, while gnarled and twisted specimens produce a wavy pattern. Where a branch or twig grows out from the main stem, the parallel lines will be forced to bulge to accommodate it. When a tree is pollarded it produces a swollen burr from which a large number of shoots sprout. A section through one of these reveals a complex pattern resembling fine rain drops hitting a puddle. On a wood such as oak one may also be able to see the pattern of medullary rays, used to carry nutrients horizontally, at right angles to the grain.

The angle at which timber is cut will show different figuring. For instance, a radial quarter-sawn cut will reveal a pattern of parallel lines, but a tangential plain-sawn cut will show marbled figuring. Woods with the most attractive figuring, sliced thinly with a variety of angled cuts to produce a range of effects, are frequently used as veneers.

Rot and insect damage are the enemy of the woodworker, but turners often seek out and exploit spalted wood in which dark spidery lines, once known as 'fairy writing', caused by the early stages of decay, creep across the wood.

OPPOSITE, TOP LEFT: *Early 20th-century bowling balls made from* Lignum vitae.

OPPOSITE, ABOVE, RIGHT: *'Fairy writing', a pattern in beech wood caused by early stages of decay.*

OPPOSITE, FAR LEFT: *Bulging burrs on the trunk of a maple.*

OPPOSITE, CENTRE: *The Hindu god Rama carved from kopalang wood, Mas, Bali.*

OPPOSITE, BELOW, RIGHT: *A lacquered Chinese cupboard constructed from dramatically grained jichi (tiger wood).*

BELOW, LEFT: *Moroccan pot and bowls turned from thuja root in Essaouira.*

BELOW, RIGHT: *Cross section of softwood showing the regular spacing of growth rings and the contrast in colour between sapwood and heartwood.*

ABOVE: *Veneers with decorative figuring, from left, Australian silky oak or prickly ash (*Cardwellia sublimis*); West African zebrawood (*Microberlinia brazzavillensis*); pollarded English oak (*Quercus robur*); and Sussex oak (*Quercus petraea*) from Europe and North Africa.*

BELOW: *Decorative turned vase exploiting the attractive figuring created by a burr.*

COLOUR

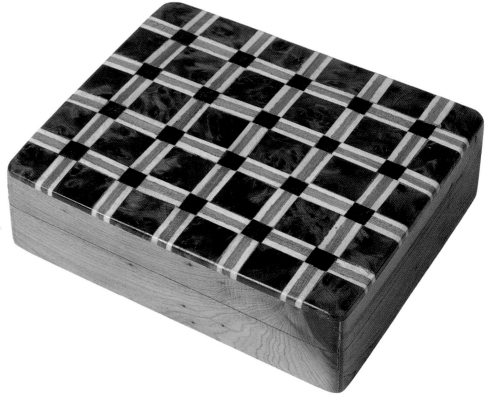

For millennia, woodworkers have depended on the range of colour naturally available in wood and, since the Ancient Egyptians began importing stocks of black ebony from Punt, a mysterious land somewhere in tropical Africa, a very profitable trade has grown up to satisfy this demand. In the 17th century tastes in furniture among the European elite became increasingly elaborate, incorporating veneering and marquetry, and the demand for exotic woods plied merchants with gold as they returned from voyages to the tropics, the holds of their ships lined with timber as ballast. A wonderful spectrum of colours appeared on European shores: padouk from the Indian Ocean, greenheart from the Americas, bubinga from darkest Africa.

The development of synthetic aniline dyes in the 19th century produced a wide range of pigments which made it possible to tint pale wood virtually any colour, but these unnatural colourings lack the warmth and mellowness of natural wood.

BELOW: *Naturally coloured veneer, top, from left to right, makore (cherry mahogany) from West Africa; ayan (Nigerian satinwood) from Nigeria, Ivory Coast and Cameroon; San Domingan rosewood; bottom, from left to right, purpleheart or amaranthe violetwood from Central America; Brazilian mahogany from Central and South America; padouk from the Andaman Islands.*

ABOVE, RIGHT: *Section of horse chestnut showing the contrasting colours of sapwood and heartwood. The dead heartwood is darkened by trapped organic chemicals.*

BELOW: *Moroccan marquetry box made in Essaouira, exploiting the natural colours of cedar, thuja, lemonwood and ebony.*

Natural colour

The conditions in which a tree grows – the type of soil in which it has its roots, the amount of sunshine it receives and the supply of water – have a profound effect on the colour of its wood. The colour of most timber is somewhere between pale yellow to brown. Tropical hardwoods have the densest wood and therefore the most concentrated colour, while the fast-growing softwoods of the northern hemisphere are generally pale.

Colour dulls with time and wood exposed to the elements fades to grey or white, although beneath the surface the colour remains strong for much longer. Once a piece of timber has been polished or varnished its colour will appear richer and so untreated wood can be assessed simply by rubbing with a wet finger.

General colour

The range of colours available in hardwood is surprising. Here are just a few examples. Pale or whitish woods

ABOVE: *Type of tobacco pipe used by the Zulu and Xhosa in South Africa. In southern Africa many tribal groups associate tobacco smoking with the spirit world or fertility and pipes are often carefully shaped and carved. Here, the aesthetically pleasing colouring is created by contrasting sapwood and heartwood.*

RIGHT: *Flying duck carved by Wichi Indians from the Chaco in northern Argentina from cow bone and naturally coloured woods dominated by green palo santo wood. The cultural identity of the forest-dwelling Wichi, threatened by agriculture, is now supported by the sale of wood carvings.*

include lime, sycamore and paper birch; yellow is obtained from satinwood and tulipwood; green is provided by greenheart and palo santo; for red, Andaman padouk and Honduras mahogany; purple comes from bubinga and purpleheart; brown woods include walnut, aphromosia and teak, and among the black woods are ebony, *Lignum vitae* and wenge.

The more colourful softwoods tend to be the reds and include yew, rimu, sequoia and western red cedar.

Secondary colour

THE new growth of sapwood at a tree's circumference is comparatively pale, the colour gradually becoming darker or richer over the years as it becomes heartwood at the tree's core due to the organic chemicals that become trapped in the dead wood. In some instances the change is so abrupt that it may look as if the wood of two completely different trees has been stuck together. A prime example is ebony with its black heartwood and yellow sapwood. Other examples include brazilwood which has orange-red heartwood and contrasting pale sapwood, and pecan hickory with a reddish brown heartwood and white sapwood.

The growth rings of some trees may also be coloured differently which produces a streaky effect, particularly noticeable in the dramatically striped zebrawood.

BELOW, LEFT: *Mortar and pestle turned on a lathe by Freddy Gilson. The laburnum wood has strongly contrasted sapwood and heartwood.*

BELOW, RIGHT: *A turned candlestick made from dramatically coloured purpleheart wood. Like many other woods with a strong colour or distinctive figure, purpleheart has been over exploited and is now on the endangered list.*

COPPICING AND FORESTRY

THE IBAN of Sarawak, like many other forest-dwelling folk, were once entirely dependent on the providence of the natural world and believed the arboreal spirits should be treated with great respect. A blow pipe was placed beside a selected tree as a warning and after it had been felled offerings were made to the tree's spirit on a hand-woven textile spread over the stump. If rituals of this kind were neglected, accidents were likely to happen.

ABOVE; AND BELOW: *Clothes pegs made by gypsies in England. Many country crafts employ freshly felled, green (unseasoned) wood as a raw material; vigorous new growth on pollarded willows in Cambridgeshire, England.*

Coppicing

DURING the Iron Age men began to manage their woodland systematically, so that wood of the right size and shape was produced. This sustainable approach involved coppicing appropriate broad-leafed trees such as hazel, willow and ash. By cutting it off just above the ground with an axe or billhook, a tree is stimulated into pushing up a number of new stems from the stool or stump. In North America the Pima of southern Arizona achieved the regeneration of their willows by setting fire to the old wood. Depending on the requirements of the grower and the vigour of the tree, these stems can be harvested after ten years or so and the tree cut back once again. In 1964 DNA finger printing of a copse of small-leaved limes (*tilia cordata*) in Westonbirt Arboretum in Gloucestershire, England, showed that a 14.5 m (48 ft) diameter ring was actually one tree that had been coppiced for much of its life – possibly 6,000 years.

Tree felling

FIRE or bark stripping has been used to weaken a tree before felling – by the Maoris in New Zealand, for instance – but the felling technique is virtually universal. An undercut, or birdsmouth, is made on the side of the tree facing the direction of fall and then a larger cut is made from the back, slightly higher up. If this is done with an axe or a cross-cut saw wedges are inserted behind the saw to stop the weight of the tree pressing down and jamming it. With the bulk of its thickness cut away, the tree falls. Side branches are trimmed off and the trunk hauled away.

ABOVE: *Timber! Another kauri falls in New Zealand.*

BELOW: *A 'Manchester' chair made from coppiced alder, England. Because of its water-resistant properties, alder was extensively used for the building of the Manchester Ship Canal. The resulting coppices were subsequently employed as a source of wood for chair building.*

Woodland crafts

CRAFTSMEN are still active in woodlands all over the world, turning newly coppiced and felled timber into baskets, hurdles, chair legs, bowls, clogs, rakes, brooms and cricket bats. Made from green (unseasoned) wood, these objects are inclined to warp or change shape as they dry, a factor allowed for by good craftsmen. Other workers are still busy making charcoal or stripping bark, particularly from oaks, which is rich in tannin used for curing leather. Today, Japanese craftsmen continue to make folk art (*mingei*) objects from freshly felled wood.

Forestry

As the Earth's population grew the demand for timber increased and it became clear to early conservationists such as the American President Theodore Roosevelt that indiscriminate logging was leaving barren devastation. Enlightened nations now aim for a sustainable system that will ensure supplies of wood for future generations by planting, harvesting and replanting in rotation, a system most economically viable with fast-growing softwoods.

ABOVE, LEFT; AND ABOVE, RIGHT: *Plantation of young conifers in South Lanarkshire, Scotland; hazel coppice in Hatfield Forest, Essex, England.*

RIGHT: *Transporting timber by river in British Columbia, Canada.*

BELOW, LEFT: *A British 19th-century gate maker beside the shack in which he lived while working with timber from the neighbouring woodland.*

BELOW, RIGHT: *Dutch clogs. Many woodland craftsmen, such as the makers of Dutch clogs, were semi itinerant, setting up their workshops near a coppice of a suitable wood, a lifestyle encountered as far away as Japan and India, as well as in surviving hunter-gatherer groups the world over.*

TIMBER AND LUMBER

FOR POLES, piles and spars processing is minimal, requiring little more than the stripping of bark and the lopping of branches, while in some projects, such as dugout canoe construction, work may begin immediately on a felled trunk. Before use by craftsmen, however, most timber (a general purpose term for wood intended for carpentry, joinery or carving) is usually cut or split into manageable planks and blocks known in North America as lumber.

Splitting

THE simplest technique for making planks is splitting or riving. Small sections of timber can be cleft with an axe or a froe (a blade struck with a mallet). This is ideal for making roofing shingles, but large trunks need splitting with wedges struck with a heavy mallet or beetle. Strategic positioning of the wedges decides whether the split is axial, producing a plank triangular in section, or tangential, producing a plank with parallel faces. In Alaska in North America and British Columbia in Canada the indigenous peoples used to split boards from the living cedars, with a stone maul and yew wedges, leaving the massive trees to live on. After splitting, planks were generally smoothed with an adze.

TOP: *Chinese sawyers cutting planks with a frame saw.*

ABOVE: *Oaks split with mallet and wedges.*

RIGHT: *Cutting beams with a frame saw, Ethiopia.*

BELOW: MEDIEVAL WOODCUT OF NOAH'S SONS TRIMMING PLANKS WITH AXES.

Sawing

PLANKS can be made more accurately with a saw. As this usually takes place in a saw mill, the process is known as milling. Modern saw mills use powerful band saws and circular saws for processing logs, but in many developing countries the task continues to be accomplished with a frame saw or pit saw. The latter technique could still be watched in England well into the 20th century and is the origin of the surname sawyer. The log was positioned over a pit and cut with a long, tapering two-man saw. The senior man stood on top guiding the blade, while his unfortunate mate stood in the pit, pulling the saw while sawdust and lubricating oil showered upon him.

Pit-and-frame sawing cut 'through and through', but with modern machinery

other cuts are possible such as 'quarter sawn', which produces boards less prone to warping.

Seasoning

AS wood dries it shrinks unevenly which causes it to warp. To minimize this, boards are seasoned in controlled conditions. Stacked with 'stickers' between the planks to allow the circulation of air, if left outdoors wood takes a year to dry for every inch of thickness, but in a kiln it may only take a matter of days.

Man-made boards

SINCE the 1850s man-made alternatives to solid wood boards have been developed which, although less attractive than solid wood, are less likely to warp and are considerably cheaper. Plywood is constructed from sheets of veneer laid with the grain in alternating directions, a technique explored by both the Egyptians and Romans. Blockboard is a tough version

Above: Timber stacked for drying in the kiln at the Abbey St Bathans Sawmill, Duns, Berwickshire, Scotland. While seasoning in the open may take several years, the controlled atmosphere of the kiln can reduce the process to a few days.

Below, left: The Kenmore Hotel on Tayside, Scotland. Unsawn softwood tree trunks are a common feature of Scottish traditional architecture and are also to be found in many other forested parts of northern Europe.

Below: *Reconstruction of an Anglo-Saxon building at West Stow, Suffolk, England.*

Bottom: *Man-made boards. From the top, two pieces of plywood, the alternating layers set at right angles for strength; blockboard which is constructed from strips of solid wood sandwiched between veneer; chipboard made from shredded wood chips bonded together.*

with strips of solid wood in the centre. Particle boards and fibre boards are the cheapest, but lack strength since they are made from bonded chips or sawdust. Increasingly popular with woodworkers is medium-density fibreboard (MDF), which contains fibres bonded with synthetic resins.

THROUGH AND
THROUGH SAWN

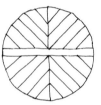

QUARTER SAWN

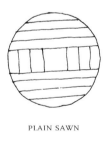

PLAIN SAWN

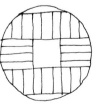

COMMERCIAL
QUARTER SAWN

CARVING AND SHAPING WOOD

FAR LEFT: *Limewood carving by Grinling Gibbons, Petworth House, England.*
TOP LEFT: *Norwegian softwood mugs.*
TOP RIGHT: *Incised Irish bog oak pig.*
LEFT: *Low-relief carving, Temne, Sierra Leone.*
ABOVE: *Haida bentwood grease dish, British Columbia.*
RIGHT: *Moroccan screen with* moushrabiya *pegs.*
BELOW: *Chip-carved slit drum, Lali, Cook Islands.*

CARVING AND SHAPING WOOD

A MAORI MYTH tells us how a man called Rua, whose son had offended Tangaroa, the god of the sea, stole the art of woodcarving from the gods. Searching for his son, Rua found that he had been turned into a carved figure (*tekoteko*) on the front of Tangaroa's underwater home, a magical building with talking statues. He rescued his son, stole some of the carvings from the porch and escaped. Rua taught the secrets of woodcarving to his fellow men, but alas the carvings were dumb.

EARLY CARVINGS

THE HISTORICAL beginnings of woodworking are conjectural as wood is such an ephemeral material. However, artefacts in stone, bone or antler surviving from the last Ice Age were engraved and modified with stone tools to enhance the form of animals suggested by the natural shape of the material. Implements, arms and magical objects were certainly worked in autonomous pieces long before joinery was practised.

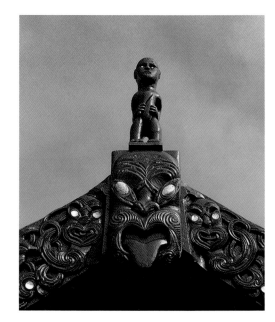

ABOVE, LEFT: *Yoruba stool carved in a single piece, Nigeria.*

ABOVE, RIGHT: *Maori* tekoteko, *carved figure, on the roof of a* pataka, *storehouse, in Rotorua, New Zealand.*

Where suitable timber is available, many objects are traditionally carved from a single block of wood and so in those places carving has become more advanced than joinery. Examples from Africa alone include stools, headrests, cosmetic boxes, ladders, doors, coffins, clubs, shields and dugout canoes. In many cultures it is considered magically advantageous to work with a single block as the spiritual energy inherent in the tree remains more concentrated.

ABOVE: *Design on a Peruvian vase of the Chimu Period (1300–1463) which depicts weavers in a room where the roof is supported by forked branches.*

LEFT: *Group of carved figures from Nagaland, north-east India.*

RIGHT: *Twisting fibres into rope in Mexico, using a frame of naturally forked timber.*

Natural shapes

THE SIMPLEST and strongest woodwork takes advantage of the natural shape of the timber. Bends, forks and holes can all be exploited in many ways. Even on a large scale such as the building of cruck houses or wooden ships greater structural integrity can be achieved by using one piece of timber that has grown into the right shape rather than several smaller pieces joined together. The former might of the British navy was directly related to the availability of naturally curved wood, needing the minimum of shaping and joining, obtained from ancient oak trees growing in old English parkland. To this end, it was considered the patriotic duty of landowning gentlemen to plant oaks on their land.

TWO

ABOVE, LEFT: *Decorative barge boards on a house in Kilmartin Glen, Argyle. Many Scottish buildings are decorated with similar boards shaped mainly with a saw.*

LEFT: *A low-relief carving on a door by an Ifugao woodworker in Banue, Philippines. The figure has been made to stand out by cutting away the surrounding background.*

RIGHT: *Part of the wooden façade of a house, typical of those found in Gujarat, north-west India. The extensive flat-pattern and low-relief carving is complemented by numerous projections.*

BELOW, RIGHT: *An old couple in Guernsey a hundred years ago. Only limited shaping has been required to turn the organic bifurcation of a branch into a pitchfork and to provide a pair of effective walking sticks.*

Finding the form within

TO BE able to cut pieces away from a block of wood successfully and end up with a satisfactory carving, whether its purpose be mundane or sublime, the carver needs sharp tools, suitable timber and an understanding of the structure of his raw material. Once cut away, chunks of wood cannot be reattached and so a carver must clearly visualize the completed work before beginning and then stick to his plan, deviating only when the structure of the timber dictates. The finest carvings are accomplished with hardwoods as these generally split less easily than softwoods and are also available in a wider range of colour and figuring. The almost ethereal, lacelike work of Grinling Gibbons (1648–1720), one of the greatest British wood carvers of all time, was accomplished with soft, but close-grained, lime.

SAWN AND PIERCED SHAPES

THE USE of saws and drills to cut a board or plank into an interesting shape may serve as a preliminary to elaborate carving, but may also be an autonomous process in which two-dimensional designs are produced. The shaping of edges is a simple matter, but elaborate shapes can never be fully independent as structural integrity demands that all the parts of a design must be joined together just like the sections of a stencil. An exception is the ever-popular jigsaw puzzle, in which all the intricate pieces are completely separate so that they can be jumbled up or assembled at will.

Technique

ONCE a design has been marked out on a flat piece of wood, cuts are made along the lines with a saw fitted with a narrow blade as this can be manoeuvred more easily. The fine blades of the fret saw allow the cutting of the tightest curves, but are more inclined to snap and are therefore designed so that the blades can be changed easily. While the fret saw can access nearly 30 cm (12 in.) into a board because of its deep bow, coping saws and frame saws cannot reach so far, but are equipped with blades that can be turned in the frame to allow abrupt changes of direction; they also have thicker blades, so they can be used to shape thicker timbers. Another option is the pad saw, keyhole or compass saw which is equipped with a handle at one end only and therefore has unlimited access.

Cutting waste from the edge is a simple matter, but the removal of wood from the middle first demands the drilling of a hole. The saw is then dismantled, the blade passed through the hole and the saw reassembled. It is also possible to drill a number of small holes close together and then connect them with a small file.

Light and ventilation

DOORS, shutters and even furniture may be perforated to allow the passage of light and air. In England in the Middle Ages 'livery' cupboards with pierced openings, such as the famous 'Prince Arthur's Cupboard', were used for the storage of food. Similarly, in China traditional food cupboards are often equipped with a ventilated section at the bottom to hold chickens.

Privacy

IN hot lands where ventilation is essential, but privacy is preferred, for example in the segregation or 'purdah' of women, a compromise is achieved with elaborate screens often created by piercing and sawing.

Decoration

SAWN wood is often used to decorate furniture and buildings. In Europe 'barge boards' fitted to the gables of buildings are frequently decorated with simple shapes, but in South-East Asia they may be elaborate and enhanced with paint and gilding.

TOP; AND LEFT: *Sawn patterns on the boardwalk at Pahia harbour, Bay of Islands, New Zealand; balconies with sawn arches, Dacca, Bangladesh.*

BELOW LEFT; AND BELOW, RIGHT: *Fretwork grill made of* nangkar *(jack fruit) wood, Kapal, Bali; sawn detailing on a temple near Chiang Mai, Thailand.*

ABOVE: *Oak tracery common to many English churches since the 19th century.*

LEFT: *Jigsaw puzzle made in Sri Lanka.*

FAR RIGHT: *Maori canoe's finely carved stern post.*

BELOW, RIGHT: *English Edwardian plywood box with fretwork details.*

ABOVE: *'PRINCE ARTHUR'S CUPBOARD', A LIVERY CUPBOARD MADE IN ENGLAND IN THE MIDDLE AGES.*

Fretwork

THE craft of fretwork acquires its name from its resemblance to an openwork fret or lattice. Panels of thin wood are cut with a saw and then mounted on furniture such as boxes or pianos or it serves as a cheap substitute for relief carving. It reached the height of its popularity in Britain and North America during the 19th century when it was taken up by many amateur woodworkers.

INCISING AND STAMPING

S INCE THE dawn of time man has scratched his mark onto any conceivable surface, whether marking a spear with magical symbols to ensure it never misses its mark or defacing buildings with lewd or salacious graffiti. Any pointed object will serve as a 'pen', but the finer the point, the more precisely the message can be expressed. As cutting curves is much harder, carved scripts are mostly composed of straight lines. In Celtic Ireland, for example, the opening lines of poems were recorded on wands of yew wood using *ogham*, a script based on groups of straight lines scratched at various angles; the Vikings frequently inscribed their weapons with spells, written in angular runes, to ensure success in battle.

Scratching

S CRATCHING through the surface of a piece of wood reveals the contrasting colour of the unexposed wood beneath or is shown up by the shadows in the grooves. This effect can be enhanced in two ways. An artificial surface can be made with a layer of pigment, so a scratch will reveal the colour of the wood beneath. Alternatively, the wood may be scratched first and then coated with a layer of pigment. When the pigment is wiped off a residue remains behind to reveal the pattern. In Indonesia and Papua New Guinea this technique is used to scratch delicate patterns onto bamboo tubes used by men to hold tobacco, lime or blowpipe

ABOVE, LEFT: *Precise lines etched into a bullroarer by Australian Aborigines. Whirled around the head on a string, the bullroarer vibrates with a loud hum.*

ABOVE: *The head of an ancestor figure on the poutokamanawa (central post) of the Maori Meeting House in Waitangi, New Zealand. The tattoos are cut with a fine V gouge.*

FAR LEFT: *Indian walking sticks bought in Simla, Himachal Pradesh. Patterns have been crudely scratched through applied pigment to reveal the natural colour beneath.*

NEAR LEFT: *A maze-like design cut into the surface of a cotton gin made in Timor, Indonesia.*

pressure is employed. Short, sharp knocks with the mallet are restrained by the hand holding the chisel, making greater control possible. Maori carving, for instance, is full of complex zigzags and spirals.

Stamping

A HARD object laid against a wooden surface and struck sharply will leave a dent. Any handy metal object can be exploited. For instance, lengths of metal pipe can be struck at right angles to the surface to produce circles or at an angle to produce crescents. A number of these stamps can be arranged into a complex pattern. Other designs such as triangles or stars may be made or bought and since the development of techniques for casting moveable type craftsmen have often stamped their names on their tools.

darts. A similar technique once common in Hungary involved the enhancement of etched lines on chairs and boxes by filling them with either oily soot or coloured sealing wax.

The same kind of effect can be achieved by drawing on the surface with a red-hot instrument. This method, known as pyroengraving or pyrography, creates a groove and colours it at the same time. The grain of the wood does not affect the movement of the point so much and a steady hand can produce elaborate patterns and drawings in this way.

Cutting grooves

U SING a V- or U-shaped tool to cut a groove is not as simple as it sounds because at some point the cut will be against the grain and may easily split the wood. However, using a smooth, dense grain and sharp tools, patterns of great complexity can be achieved such as the 'hae hae' lines of Maori carvings in totara or mere wood. Surprisingly, incising lines is easier when the chisel is tapped with a light mallet rather than when hand

TOP: *Tent peg with incised and chip-carved designs fashioned by Tuareg nomads in Morocco.*

ABOVE: *A simple Indian hinged nutcracker with stamped scale pattern.*

NEAR RIGHT: *Bamboo lime pots with incised patterns filled with pigment, Timor, Indonesia.*

FAR RIGHT: *Stamping fine details onto a carving at the woodcarvers' cooperative in Mas, Bali.*

45

CHIP CARVING

Requiring only two or three tools, chip carving is a simple technique used most often in the creation of geometric patterns. It receives its name from the way in which patterns are cut out one chip at a time. Designs are repetitive and therefore require patience rather than imagination in their execution. Decoration on furniture has been carried out in England using this method since the 13th century and became particularly popular in the 16th century. It is also a very widespread form of carving which can be found, with regional variations, all over Europe, Asia, Africa and the Pacific. In West Africa, among the Nupe, Igbo and Yoruba, for example, designs can be on a large scale, employing patterns found also in body and wall painting, while the style in Zanzibar has more in common with the geometric designs used in north-west India and Central Asia, probably because of the strong trade links across the Indian Ocean. In Fiji, Samoa and other Polynesian countries the designs are repetitive, but cut much more shallowly.

Tools and materials

Chip-carved decoration was once common on oak furniture, but the ideal materials for this technique are fine-grained woods such as pear or sycamore, which can be cut cleanly with crisp angles. A lack of figuring ensures that the pattern of grain will not detract from the carved pattern.

Many craftsmen choose to work solely with a skew chisel which has a cutting edge set at 60 degrees so that it cuts with a smooth slicing action. Whole sets of short-bladed knives have been produced for chip carving, although only two are usually necessary – a stabbing knife with the sharpened edge at the end of the blade and a cutting knife with the edge along the side of the blade. Other tools for making difficult cuts have often been ground to suit the needs of a specific craftsman.

Marking out the patterns

What makes most chip-carved work so distinctive is the designs themselves. Even using only a limited vocabulary of shapes – squares, triangles and circles – an extensive treasury of arrangements is possible, all of which need to be marked out carefully before cutting can commence. For patterns composed of triangular and square units

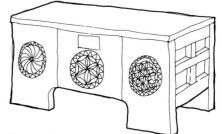

ABOVE: DRAWING OF A CLAMP-FRONTED OAK CHEST WITH CHIP-CARVED MOTIFS MADE IN ENGLAND DURING THE 13TH CENTURY.

ABOVE, LEFT: *A chip-carved picture frame. In Britain and Germany during the late 19th and early 20th centuries patterns with a floral inspiration were carved on all kinds of objects, from frames and platters to shelving and tables. The prolific carvers of the Balkans have always preferred more geometric designs.*

FAR LEFT: *Wooden chip-carved lime or medicine pot with an elaborate stopper made in Timor or Sumba in eastern Indonesia.*

LEFT: *A chip-carved 'Welsh spinning chair' made by an employee of the Gillow company of furniture makers based in Preston, Lancashire, England.*

precise measuring along carefully ruled lines is necessary, while patterns of interlocking circles or pentagons are marked out in lines scratched with a pair of dividers or drawn with a pencil and pair of compasses.

Cutting the design

Each triangle cut is actually removed as a series of chips that leave an inverted pyramid. To accomplish this, a line is marked from each point of the triangle to the middle and a stabbing cut is made along each line which is deepest at the middle. This removes the risk of subsequent cuts splitting the wood. Next, slicing cuts are made from the perimeter towards the stabbed line to remove the chips. Further cuts may be made to deepen or tidy up the shape. The principle is the same for any shape cut.

Above: *Solid wood door carved by Nupe craftsmen in northern Nigeria.*

Above, right: *Relief panel with chip-carved details outside the Tumi shop in Oxford, England.*

Above, far right: Poupou *panel depicting a Maori ancestor figure, Waitangi, New Zealand.*

Right: *Detail of a chip-carved panel from the Swat Valley in north-west Pakistan.*

FLAT-PATTERN CARVING

A FLAT-PATTERN carving is in essence a two-dimensional design revealed by working in three dimensions. Where a graphic artist would create a design of positive and negative shapes by using blocks of black and white or contrasting colours, the woodworker is forced to cut back the negative shapes and reveal the pattern with the assistance of light and shade. Even greater contrast is achieved when the negative shapes are completely removed by drilling or sawing.

Techniques

DECORATION may be carved on a finished piece, as is the case in most of Africa where many objects are cut from a solid block, but it is a more widespread practice to create the designs on flat boards cut to shape before assembly. A pattern from a well-known repertoire of motifs may be drawn freehand onto the surface, but one-off designs or those copied from other sources may require the aid of templates, stencils or simple mathematics.

Vertical cuts are made along the drawn lines, followed by sloping cuts towards them on the negative side of the line. In some cultural groups such as the tribal Gonds of Orissa in eastern India work may cease at this point, giving the impression of an image sunk into the background, but generally, with the edges clearly defined, the waste wood in the negative areas is cut away to an even depth. The quantity of wood removed is to some extent limited by the thickness of the board being carved, but the lower the background, the greater the contrast with the positive pattern. The clarity of the pattern will also benefit from crisp cutting with sharp tools and may be emphasized with slight undercutting. Details may subsequently be added to the surface with the aid of scribed lines, stamping or shallow carving.

Uses

FLAT-PATTERN carving is frequently employed for decorating softwoods with fibres too splintery for high-relief work and so the technique is widespread,

OPPOSITE, CLOCKWISE FROM ABOVE, LEFT: *A flat-pattern carving of a palm wine tapper from Sierra Leone where the makers of blocks for printing textiles are now using their traditional techniques to make souvenirs for tourists; panel of a granary door, from Mali, carved with images probably intended to deter rats; detail of the pattern on an English oak writing desk made in the 17th or 18th century; door with carved panels made by Gonds, a tribal people living in Orissa, India.*

for instance, on the pine furniture of Scandinavia and the cedar of Central Asia and the Himalayas. As the decorated surface does not protrude this technique is commonly found on chests, chairs and other furniture, as well as on the structural members of buildings. In the valleys of Nuristan in Afghanistan and adjoining Swat-Kohistan in Pakistan's North-west Frontier Province carvers have become adept at working the plentiful stocks of deodar (Himalayan cedar) using it, lavishly decorated, for everything from mosques to medicine spoons. Patterns are generally geometric, abstract or stylized, but include calligraphy, flowers, foliage or animals and may be juxtaposed with chip-carved motifs.

The same skills are employed universally in the manufacture of stamps and printing blocks which require a clearly defined raised surface. In Sierra Leone the makers of wooden blocks used for decorating textiles have turned their skill at flat-pattern carving to making relief panels illustrated with scenes of traditional life to sell to tourists.

ABOVE: *A 17th-century carved chest panel from Nuristan, eastern Afghanistan. Nuristani woodwork contains many motifs, such as solar discs and rams' horns, a legacy of the pre-Islamic past.*

LEFT: *Chair, from the Swat Valley in northern Pakistan, with turned walnut legs and cedar back. Softwoods such as cedar are ideal for flat carving.*

ABOVE: *A flat carved panel, once part of the front of a chest, made by tribal artisans in northern India. The patterns of abstract foliage have been made more delicate by the addition of incised grooves.*

RELIEF CARVING

CARVING IN relief is a technique intended to create a three-dimensional effect on a flat surface by cutting back the background and rounding the projecting forms. Craftsmen in southern Europe focused on relief work in stone, but in the north the focus was on wood. Hardwoods with an even grain are preferred as detailed, delicate work is possible. In England and other parts of northern Europe the medium was most often oak, but the most exquisite carving was achieved during the 17th and 18th centuries in walnut, box or limewood in the hands of such masters as Grinling Gibbons. By way of contrast, carving in softwood is generally limited to fairly low relief. The effect of relief carving is enhanced by harnessing light and shade, creating the illusion of depth by undercutting certain parts of the work to cast strong shadows around them.

Although relief carvers are now solitary or confined to small establishments, often specializing in restoration work for churches, at the height of the taste for the Baroque and Rococo thriving workshops in the West often employed dozens of craftsmen chiselling industriously at sensuous swags festooned with flora and fauna.

Low relief

THE term bas relief, derived from the Italian *basso rilievo*, means low relief and is applied to work in which figures and forms project less than half their true proportion from the background. Carving in low relief was employed by the Ancient Egyptians who sometimes overlaid the wood with gold. It became increasingly popular in medieval Europe for the decoration of furniture, especially with the development of panelled construction. Originating in Flanders, the most frequently employed motif in the 15th century was *faltwerk* or 'linenfold', a design still popular today, which resembles the rippling surface of folded cloth.

High relief

HIGH relief appears to stand out prominently and the foreground may include figures carved virtually in the round. The effect may be enhanced with artificial perspectives and by fixing together a number of boards (a technique referred to as laminating) to increase the actual depth. Many superb carvings, depicting the Crucifixion and other religious scenes, were executed for use in churches and cathedrals as a *reredos* to stand behind the altar table, sometimes employing designs based on engravings of paintings by established masters. The design was traced onto wood by rubbing coloured powder through pinpricks in the engraving (pouncing) or by coating the

back of the paper with oily chalk and using it much like carbon paper. High-relief carvings are also employed by both Buddhists and Hindus and in localized animist and ancestor worshipping cults. Among the most notable are the panels of gods, flowers and animals carved in Tamil Nadu to decorate the towering wooden temple cars or *thers* that are pulled in procession through the streets of southern India.

OPPOSITE, TOP: *House wall panel carved in high relief, Nias Island off the west coast of Sumatra.*

OPPOSITE, CENTRE: *A lintel from north Bengal, India. The low-relief carving depicts Rama and Sita in a scene from the Hindu epic* Ramayana.

OPPOSITE, BOTTOM: *A balcony front from Gujarat, north-west India, where the homes of the wealthy are encrusted with relief-carved wood.*

ABOVE: *Detail of an elaborately carved, painted and gilded door at the Neka Palace in Ubud, Bali.*

RIGHT: *The Hindu god Vishnu as Rama on a panel from a south Indian temple cart.*

INSET: *An old warrior standing beside the carved house panel of a Maori meeting house in New Zealand. The rich carving on Maori meeting houses is a symbol of cultural identity and the link with the ancestors.*

INTAGLIO CARVING

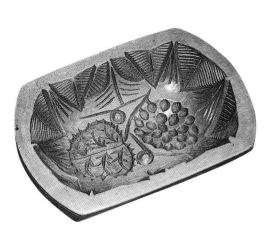

INTAGLIO IS an Italian word meaning an engraved or incised design. The term is now most often used for carving sunk below the surface, the opposite of relief – a footprint rather than the foot itself. Intaglio is a means to an end, generally intended to impress a positive raised image onto a soft surface. Working in negative places considerable demands on the skill and imagination of the craftsman.

Seals

THE use of intaglio carving can be traced back to the Sumerian civilization in Mesopotamia. The first writing system, cuneiform, was developed there more than 5,000 years ago , probably as an accounting system, employing marks impressed into clay tablets with a wedge-shaped reed. As only the elite could write, personal ownership was indicated by rolling a cylindrical seal across the clay. These pieces of steatite were carved with scenes of gods, heroes and worshippers that were revealed on the tablets in relief. Vast numbers of square intaglio seals were found in the ruins of the Indus Valley civilization (2500–1700 BC), often depicting bulls and as yet undeciphered lettering.

Food moulds

SEAL carving has generally been restricted to stone or ivory, but the same principle has been applied to the use of wood for moulds frequently involved in the production of food. In England in the 16th century gingerbread biscuits were stamped with a mould. In France, up until the 19th century, a confection sold at fairs was melusine, also made of gingerbread, with a human head and serpent's tail depicting the eponymous heroine of an

FAR LEFT: *Cake mould made for the Straits Chinese colony in north Java.*

ABOVE: *A 19th-century Welsh mould for flumery, a pudding made by boiling wheat in milk and seasoning with cinnamon and sugar.*

BELOW, LEFT: *A mould for sweets eaten in Jordan at the Muslim festival of Id ul Fitr.*

BELOW, CENTRE: *Javanese mould for making sweetmeats.*

BELOW, RIGHT: *Chinese cake mould shaped like a peach, a symbol of longevity.*

STEATITE INTAGLIO SEAL, INDUS VALLEY CIVILIZATION.

old legend, the ancestress of the Counts of Poitiers. All around the world wooden moulds and stamps continue to be used in the shaping of puddings, sweets, cakes and butter, especially for the creation of festive food such as the flower-stamped moon cake, a delight enjoyed during the traditional Chinese August viewing of the moon and at the Vietnamese autumn festival, Trung Thu.

THE IMPRINT OF AN
ASSYRIAN CYLINDER SEAL.

RIGHT: *A Maltese watercolour mounted in a frame encrusted with elaborate scrolling patterns formed in sections from gesso shaped in a hardwood mould. Although carving the mould is a specialized craft, mouldings can subsequently be turned out in large numbers very economically.*

BELOW: *A Scottish beech wood mould for stamping out round pats of butter impressed with a raised motif. The pat is cut out, stamped and ejected with this simple device.*

Mouldings

A PECULIARLY English use of moulds is restricted to a small corner of East Anglia. Here, the traditional craft of pargeting involves decorating newly plastered buildings with combed patterns or the embossed shapes of animals, symbols and scrollwork formed from plaster in a wooden mould. In Europe moulded plasterwork was used from the mid-16th century to embellish friezes and ceilings, but it was not until the 18th and 19th centuries that this technique was applied to furniture and picture frames. Until then scrolls and decorative motifs had been laboriously carved by hand, but from then on finely carved moulds of box, rosewood or beech were used to cast shapes in glue and sawdust, plaster or gesso which, once attached and painted or gilded, appeared to be an integral part of the structure.

TWO

ABOVE: CARVED
AND PAINTED HEAD
OF TUTANKHAMUN,
EGYPT, 1330 BC.

CARVING IN THE ROUND

Carving in three dimensions that can be viewed from every side is said to be 'in the round'. Although today the term is most often applied to sculpture, it could also be applied to the carving of blocks of solid wood into utensils and objects, including spoons, boxes and furniture, and is used to create both the tiny *netsuke* Japanese toggles and the colossal totem poles of the indigenous peoples of the American North-west.

Technique

Sections may be joined together, but it is preferable, wherever possible, to work from one solid block. The ideal wood for carving in the round is close grained as greater detail and more elaborate shapes can be achieved with less risk of breakage and it also has subdued figuring so that it will not distract from the form. Grain with a fancy figure is only desirable if it can be exploited to emphasize the shape or texture of the work.

First the shape is roughed out by removing waste with a large tool such as an adze, axe or saw before more careful cutting begins with chisels and gouges driven with a mallet. In Africa and Polynesia most work is carried out with the adze, but as work becomes finer, smaller and smaller tools are employed and the mallet is put aside in favour of the precise control of the hand alone. The carver constantly changes his viewpoint to check the shape is right from every angle and also to allow light and shade to reveal the subtleties of the curved surface.

Today, the natural appearance of wood, with a waxed or varnished finish, is fashionable, but for thousands of years carvings intended for the religious use of Christians, Hindus and Buddhists were normally painted, gilded or wrapped in textiles.

The origins of carving

The earliest carvings known, dating back to the Upper Palaeolithic period (37,000 to 11,000 years ago) belong to two categories. Some were functional objects such as spear throwers, but others were small objects of worked stone, ivory or bone which seem to have been suggested by the original shape of the material such as the swelling curves of a stone or the bifurcation of an antler. They generally represented animals or fertility figures and were probably votive or talismanic – intended to promote good luck, fertility and success in the hunt. Care lavished on the creation of a tool or weapon was considered to enhance its effectiveness and in cultures, such as that of the Inuit in the Arctic, with no 'art' as such, many wonderful objects were once made. The Maori, the Vikings, the people of the Hindu Kush in Afghanistan and Pakistan and many others once lavished a great deal of care on the carving of the main structural members of their homes and considered this imbued them with the power of their ancestors.

OPPOSITE, FAR LEFT: *Carving of St Joseph, made before 1820 for a Christian community in India.*

OPPOSITE, LEFT: *Stylized caricature of an orthodox Jew, Krakow, Poland.*

OPPOSITE, CENTRE: *Lord Krishna's sister Subhadra, a carved image from Bengal, India.*

OPPOSITE, RIGHT: *A Batak female figure, from north Sumatra, carved from hard thorn tree wood.*

ABOVE, RIGHT: *Chair carved in one piece from wood common among the Gurage and Jimma peoples of Ethiopia.*

RIGHT: *Japanese* netsuke; *these miniature masterpieces are used as toggles on waist sashes.*

Virtually all sculpture continued to be functional or was intended for religious use until the concept of 'art for art's sake' developed in Renaissance Europe. Since then the greatest change has been global tourism and the carvers of distant lands, such as the master carvers of Bali who once worked exclusively on religious subjects, have turned their hands to carving souvenirs. Purists might say this has debased an art form, but, as well as unfettering the imagination of artists, it has kept traditional skills alive and put food in the mouths of craftsmen and their families.

TURNING

CARVING NORMALLY demands that a chisel or gouge be pushed into or across a stationary piece of wood. By using a lathe, the situation is reversed and the spinning wood moves against a tool supported against a rest. To provide adequate leverage, tools with extra long handles are best. Turning may be the only process involved, as is usually the case with bowls, dishes and pots, but at other times the article turned may be further shaped or carved. Many turned items are destined to become components of larger structures such as chairs which may be assembled in another workshop.

Bodgers

WOODTURNERS around the world are often itinerant such as the English bodger. Until the middle of the 20th century bodgers could still be found working in British woods, notably in the High Wycombe area. They would set up a workshop in a stand of trees they had purchased and then cut a larch or ash sapling and fix it to the structure to provide the power for a pole lathe. Timber, usually elm or beech, was felled, sawn into suitable lengths and then split into billets. On a shave horse the billets were trimmed with a draw knife until they were more or less round in section. Once fixed on the revolving lathe, the billet was skilfully shaved into shape with a chisel. Bodgers turned out legs and stretchers for use in the construction of 'stickback' chairs. The completed chairs were sold at the market in Windsor and so became known as 'Windsor' chairs. Traditional Japanese craftsmen set up shop in much the same way, turning bowls for lacquering and regional variations of the *kokeshi* doll.

Turning between centres

FOR thousands of years it has been the practice to fix the wood to be turned between two points. The turner stands beside the lathe, steadies his tool on the rest, and cuts shavings from the upper part as the wood revolves towards him. Turning between two centres is ideal for producing objects that are longer than they are wide, such as chair legs, candlesticks or the handles for tools.

Turning on a face plate

THIS is the best method for producing bowls, dishes and platters that are wider than they are high, and need turning on the face as well as on the side. On modern powered machines the lathe is generally fitted at the drive end with a plate to which a block of wood can be attached either with screws or by clamping in a chuck. For face-plate turning the rest is

TOP: *A turned and painted spice box from Jalalabad in eastern Afghanistan. With the passage of time, the lids of turned items, such as this, often cease to fit tightly due to the uneven contraction across and with the grain.*

ABOVE: *Set of Russian nesting* matrioshka *dolls, turned from limewood in Lipyetsk Polkhov and painted in Semyenov.*

RIGHT: *Farm yard animals made in Germany using the hoop-turning technique on the face plate of a lathe.*

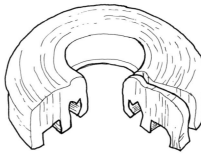

ABOVE: INDIVIDUAL ELEPHANTS BEING SPLIT FROM A TURNED HOOP.

ABOVE: Early 20th-century English boxwood chessmen. Turning has created a convention of simply differentiated, stylized forms. Only the knight's head is made separately.

ABOVE, RIGHT: Mike Wickham turning a form from a piece of wood fitted into a chuck on the face plate of the lathe. The adjustable tool rest has been swung round for support.

moved as required when the turner is working on the outside or cutting into the face.

Turned articles

Some turned items require further work such as splitting or carving. An interesting example is the hoop-turned animals and figures that have been made in south-east Germany for the last 300 years. A section of softwood log is turned on the face plate into a ring with a predetermined arrangement of curves and notches. Once removed from the lathe, the ring is split radially with a knife and hammer into as many as 170 pieces, each of which is revealed as a miniature elephant, horse, cow or tree. Once finished and painted, these toys are exported all over the world.

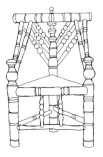

'THROWN' CHAIR MADE FROM TURNED COMPONENTS, ENGLAND, 16TH CENTURY.

LEFT: Nepalese milk bottle; Tibetan tsampa bowl for eating barley meal mixed with butter tea; and an English goblet of spalted beech with an ebony finial.

BELOW: Turning between two centres with the tool rest parallel to the work.

BENDING

IN CURVED work weak points occur where the grain is short or where joints have been introduced, but when timber is bent into shape the grain runs the whole length and structural integrity is ensured, thereby allowing the creation of elaborate flowing shapes. Techniques for bending wood have existed since prehistoric times, although early man used heat to help him straighten rather than bend his arrows. For walking sticks, craftsmen have often bent and bound wood while still alive and green so that it will grow into the shape without being weakened by the stress of stretching and compression.

Kerfs

THE thinner a piece of wood, the easier it is to bend. By cutting grooves or 'kerfs' into a thicker piece of timber this too becomes easier to bend. This technique is suitable for forming curved surfaces such as plinths and columns for furniture which will only be visible from the outer, uncut side.

Steaming

WOOD is most elastic when freshly cut and still green. Bending seasoned wood is made easier by imitating this state and soaking it. The best results are achieved by shutting the timber in an airtight pipe or chest connected to a drum of water heated to boiling point to provide a constant supply of steam. Exposure to the

LEFT: *Bento-bako*, A JAPANESE BENTWOOD LUNCHBOX.

Opposite, top: *A bentwood chair, the first mass-produced furniture.*

Opposite, centre: *Tibetan bentwood box used for storing butter and a cherry wood Shaker-style 'nice' box with copper rivets and swallowtails.*

Opposite, inset: *Bentwood frame sieves for sale in a Russian street.*

Above: *An Egyptian* mazhar *made from skin stretched over a bentwood frame.*

Right: *Kerf-bent box made in British Columbia.*

Below: *Replica of a laminated Roman birch-wood shield dating from the 1st century* AD.

steam should last about an hour for every 25 mm (1 in.) of thickness. Bending must take place within minutes of withdrawal while the wood is pliable. It must be bent into the desired shape, bound or clamped in position and left to dry out and set for anything between an hour and a week, according to the type of wood used.

Steam is used to bend parts of all manner of products including boats, yurts, walking sticks and round or oval boxes. Among the most elegant of these are the cherry-wood boxes made by the Shaker communities in the 19th century in North America. In the 1870s in Austria Michael Thonet applied the same methods to furniture construction and came up with curvilinear bentwood café chairs and rockers, the first mass-produced furniture.

Kerf-bent boxes

THE major furniture item of the American North-west coast is the cedar box built by indigenous peoples such as the Haida, Kwakiutl and Tshimshian. Carved or painted with totemic symbols, they have many different uses, from food containers to coffins. The four sides are made from a single plank kerfed in three places with a bent knife, softened by steaming over a pit of hot rocks doused with water and pegged or sewn together at the final corner.

Lamination

A THIN sheet of wood is easiest to bend, but when a series of other sheets are bent and glued to it in layers or laminations a curved surface with considerable strength is formed. Laminated forms were made popular by European furniture designers in the 1930s, but the technique had also been exploited thousands of years previously by the Roman Army whose legionaries were equipped with shields constructed from laminated sheets of steam-bent birch wood stuck together with animal glue.

59

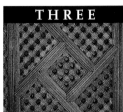

JOINERY

THREE

LEFT: *Detail of a* moushrabiya *screen, Medersa ben Youssef, Marrakesh, Morocco.*

ABOVE, LEFT: *Stick chair with adze seat, Cambridgeshire, England.*

ABOVE, RIGHT: *Rabari chest with tongue and groove panels, Gujarat, India.*

RIGHT: *Large pail, from the Czech Republic, made from butted staves.*

BELOW, LEFT: *Replica of a box with rudimentary joints, Suffolk, England.*

FAR RIGHT: *Rush-seated chair from the Greek island of Lemnos.*

JOINERY

THE BUILDING of the ark is the first craft mentioned in the Old Testament of the Bible and Noah is regarded in Jewish, Christian and Islamic myth as the first craftsman and therefore the patron of woodworkers. Flood myths exist in many cultures and suggest that boat-building skills may date back to before the end of the last Ice Age. The remains of houses, built before 5000 BC, with sophisticated joinery have been discovered in the Yangtse valley in China and techniques have changed little in millennia. In the amazing death pits of Ur in Iraq, which date from about 2,500 BC, there were a number of artefacts constructed with complex joinery techniques, while Egyptian tomb goods displayed a mastery of tongue and groove, mortise and tenon, butt and mitre joints. In other parts of Africa timber has always been plentiful and most items are traditionally carved from a single block, but in Egypt the indigenous trees produced wood in small sizes, forcing craftsmen to develop techniques for joining them into larger pieces.

ABOVE: *Interlocking screen, Mezquita Cathedral, Cordoba, Spain.*

BELOW, LEFT; AND BOTTOM LEFT: *Navajo brush arbour, Arizona, North America; oak lych-gate with pegged joints, Limpsfield, Surrey, England.*

PRIMITIVE JOINTS

QUICK, TEMPORARY joints have been constructed since time immemorial by simply resting one piece of timber into a natural fork in another. The separate members can also be attached by lashing them tightly together with sinew or plant fibre, or with a peg or nail. For a stronger, more permanent joint the wood must be cut into shapes that will interlock securely. The development of the most refined joinery is closely related to the introduction of metal tools that made accurate cutting and shaping possible.

THREE

TYPES OF JOINT

IN BOTH East and West an extensive repertoire of joint-making techniques has been developed, but inventive woodworkers may still improvise when a specific task demands a unique solution. Local conditions and needs may dictate the focus on particular types of joinery. For instance, the post and lintel structure used in Chinese wooden buildings to form a frame supporting the roof requires a large number of long beams and so splicing joints to increase the length of timber available is particularly important. Joints can be categorized in a number of ways. In the West it is normally by the method of construction – joints either fit up against each other, across each other or into each other. In the East the distinction is based on function – joints are either used to splice two members together lengthwise or to connect them at an angle.

ABOVE: *Roof at the entrance to the Chui Eng free school for Hokkien boys in Singapore, built in 1854.*

TOP RIGHT: *Drawing of an Egyptian chair or bed leg, from the 8th or 7th century BC, with sockets cut for mortise and tenon joints to hold the side members, just as they are today in many parts of Africa and Asia.*

NEAR RIGHT: *The roof framework at the Mission in Santa Barbara, California, North America. A dovetail joint locks the beams in the centre.*

FAR RIGHT: *Constructing boats with overlapping planks in medieval Scandinavia, after a woodcut by Olaus Magnus.*

BOTTOM RIGHT: *The Pagoda and Golden Hall of the Horyu-ji Temple in Nara, Japan, the oldest surviving free-standing wooden structure in the world today despite the rigours of weather and the onslaught of earthquakes for thirteen centuries.*

OPPOSITE, BELOW, RIGHT: *Jointless bridge arch supported by the pressure of its own weight, the Old Rectory, East Ruston, Norfolk, England.*

JAPANESE JOINERY

IN EARTHQUAKE-PRONE Japan wood rather than stone has been the architectural *prima materia* for thousands of years due to its shock absorbency and the timber's resistance to insect and fungal damage. Japanese toolmakers developed fine chisels and thinner saws that cut on the draw stroke, thus making it possible to cut timber very accurately. Stimulated by the introduction of Chinese and Korean joint-making techniques by Buddhist missionaries in the late 6th century, Japanese craftsmen developed a huge vocabulary of precision joinery. Despite the unstable landscape, Japan boasts the largest wooden structure in the world, the Todai-ji Temple in Nara, and the oldest surviving free-standing wooden structure, the Golden Hall of the Horyu-ji Temple in Nara built in AD 679.

FIXINGS AND FASTENINGS

The craft of cutting joints requires time, care and the appropriate tools, and so the makeshift woodwork of people on the move or in a hurry often depends more on the materials to hand, for instance, creepers that will serve for bindings or wooden off cuts that can be trimmed quickly into pegs. These same techniques may also be used to add strength to a cut joint.

Lashing and sewing

The use of rope or twine to secure wooden members was once wide-spread in the construction of temporary shelters or implements as well as the building of permanent houses, bridges and boats. In Samoa the traditional house, the *fale*, has a structure of solid poles driven into the ground with roof members tied on using a system of decorative lashing with sinnet, a tough twine made from coconut fibre. The panels of Maori buildings are tied to a solid frame, while the *waka*, or war canoe, is traditionally made from a hollowed out tree to which the prow, stern, sides and fittings are all tied, so that it can be dismantled easily for storage or repairs.

On the American North-west Coast kerf-bent boxes made from a single plank are secured at the final corner with pegs or by sewing with spruce root through pre-drilled holes. A similar technique is employed to secure bent-wood or bamboo boxes, sieves, strainers and steamers in many parts of Europe, Africa and Asia.

Pegs, nails and screws

A wooden peg, also called a 'treenail' or 'trunnel', driven through two pre-drilled wooden members can be seen in much of the oldest surviving woodwork, such as the 7th-century Horyu-ji Temple

ABOVE, LEFT; AND ABOVE: *Beams lashed with sinnet, Samoa; watch tower of lashed poles, Taiwan.*

BELOW, LEFT; AND BELOW, RIGHT: *Panels lashed to a Maori storehouse, New Zealand, 1906; lashed and socketed bamboo chair, Bali.*

TOP RIGHT: *The fastenings for the outrigger of
a dugout canoe secured with a wooden peg and
lashed twine, Lovina, northern Bali.*

RIGHT: *Carved gunwales lashed to the sides of the
world's largest dugout canoe, Ngatokimatawhaorua.
The prow, stern post and gunwales of Maori
canoes,* waka, *can be detached for separate storage.*

in Nara in Japan or Wells Cathedral in England, begun in the 12th century. Wooden pegs are still common since they are virtually invisible and do not rust and discolour the work as nails and screws can.

The nail comes in a variety of shapes and sizes. Some of the iron nails used by the Roman army when assembling the pre-fabricated wooden sections of their camps were as long as 46 cm (18 in.), while brass pins used to attach the fittings of trinket boxes may be less than 5 mm ($^{1}/_{4}$ in.). Metal screws were found in the lava-filled streets of Pompeii in Italy, but, owing to the labour-intensive demands of their manufacture, did not become a common fixing until the development of technology in the industrial escalation in the mid-18th century led to their mass production.

Glue

ADHESIVES are traditionally made from natural resources such as tree resin, bitumen or melted horns and hooves. These substances must be heated to melt them down to a consistency that can be spread easily and therefore have the advantage that, should repairs or restoration be necessary, they can be unstuck with boiling water without damaging the wood. Many modern synthetic glues have enormous strength, set quickly and are waterproof, but unfortunately cannot be dissolved to allow for reconditioning. Glue generally requires time to set and so clamping is necessary to prevent the separate parts moving. Modern contact adhesives have the advantage of instant adhesion, but no correction is possible if alignment is not accurate the first time.

BELOW, LEFT; AND BELOW, CENTRE: *Screens
from Haryana, India. The one on the left has
a carved mortise and tenon frame, and the
diagonal lattice is reinforced with metal rivets.
The 17th-century screen in the centre provides
privacy for women in purdah. The frame and
lattice are reinforced with metal.*

BELOW, RIGHT: *Balinese coconut-wood roof.
The structure is fastened with modern metal bolts.*

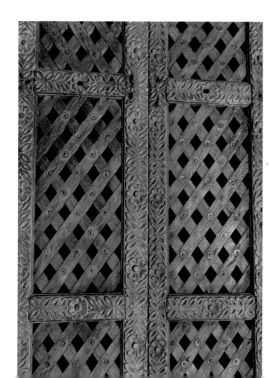

END TO END

To ensure strength it was essential that some parts of wooden ships, such as the sternpost and wing transoms, should be made from single baulks of timber, but other parts, such as the keel, could be made from several lengths fitted together which made it feasible to build enormous vessels capable of carrying 100 guns. Woodworkers all over the world with ambitions that stretch beyond the natural length of the timber available have had to confront the problem of creating a joint to serve this purpose efficiently.

Sewing

The indigenous timber of Ancient Egypt was only available in irregular shapes and sizes. To overcome this difficulty furniture, boats or coffins were all constructed like patchwork from many small pieces of wood sewn together with halfa grass ropes. Similar techniques were used in California in North America, and when the Spanish conquerors arrived in the 17th century they named the area the Bay of Carpenteria because of the industrious canoe-making of the Californian Chumash. The canoes or *tomols* were constructed from planks, shaped from driftwood with clamshell adzes and chert knives, which were sewn together with milkweed fibre. The largest dugout canoe ever built, *Ngatokimatawhaorua*

('the adzes which shaped it twice'), was built by Maoris in 1940. The 35 m (115 ft) hull was made from the trunks of three massive kauri trees simply jointed and sewn together with phormium fibre.

Bundling and reinforcing

The American Declaration of Independence in 1776 deprived the British navy of the tall New England pines that had previously furnished them with masts, and shipwrights were forced to adopt the French system of composite masts of several timbers jointed together and reinforced with iron bands. Single lengths of bamboo or timber can be lashed together for greater length, but, when staggered and fastened together in a bundle, length and strength are combined. Several pieces running parallel can be bolted together in much the same way, a technique

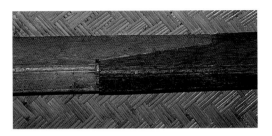

ABOVE, LEFT: *Ship building in progress in Essaouira, Morocco. Several lengths of timber are bolted together in staggered joints to lengthen the ribs of the hull.*

TOP RIGHT: *A simple scarf joint connecting two lengths of coconut wood in the roof of a building in northern Bali.*

ABOVE: *A lapped scarf joint in the framework of a building in Argyll and Bute, Scotland, made from green (unseasoned) oak.*

LEFT: *Lengths of track from a Brio toy train set, made in Sweden. The simple interlocking joints are easily connected by small children.*

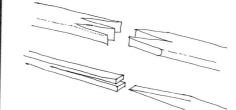

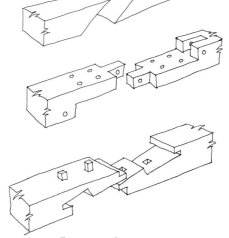

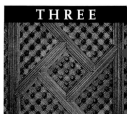

ABOVE: JOINING
SECTIONS OF A BOW
AND OF AN ARROW.

LEFT: *Scarf joints in chopsticks from Thailand.*

TOP: *Decorative scarf joint in a billiard cue.*

BELOW, RIGHT: *The largest wooden structure in the world, the Todai-ji Temple, Nara, Japan, its great size requiring many scarf joints.*

FROM TOP: SIMPLE SCARF JOINT;
15TH- OR 16TH-CENTURY ENGLISH
JOINT; JAPANESE RABBETED
OBLIQUE SCARF JOINT, *OKKAKE-DAISEN-TSUGI.*

THREE

still widely employed in architecture and shipbuilding.

Scarf and splices

WHEN a carpentered joint is used to connect two pieces of timber longitudinally it is known as a scarf. Techniques may involve halving, notching or inter-locking, the crucial factor being that as large a surface area as possible of each member makes contact with the other. There is a long history of scarf joinery in the architecture of the Far East where long roof members are used despite a lack of long timber, and in the construction of European tithe barns. Generally, scarfs are strengthened with bolts or dowels, but those employed for the keels of English warships also incorporated a slanting tongue and groove.

Yew, the best wood for bows, is unfortunately often gnarled and suitable lengths are hard to come by. In England during the Victorian era sportsmen solved this problem by splicing two lengths together with a zigzag 'fishtail' joint glued and subsequently bound with linen. This method is also used when building furniture from rubberwood which is only available in short pieces. Simple spliced joints, in which a single tongue projects into a notch in the other member, are used to attach the handles to cricket bats and the 'footings' to arrows, while a more decorative version is employed to attach the contrastingly coloured handle to billiard cues.

EDGE TO EDGE

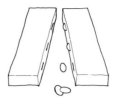

WHEN TIMBER is not available in sufficient widths it becomes necessary to use several separate boards laid edge to edge. Table tops and the panels of doors and furniture may demand the joining of several boards, while walls, roofs, ceilings, floors and the shell of boats may require a large number. The oldest-known surviving wooden structure in the world – a chamber with wooden panelling buried under a mountain of earth – is the tomb of the legendary Phrygian king Midas at Gordion in Turkey, which was constructed in about 700 BC.

THREE

Butt joints

THE simplest joints are made when two pieces of timber neatly butt up against each other, but even with the application of glue this creates a weak join and some form of reinforcement is necessary. A simple, virtually invisible solution is to bang double-headed nails into the butting edge of one board and then hammer a second board onto the protruding points. A more professional version is to drill sets of matching holes into which short lengths of dowel can be fitted, while modern joiners may now use machine tools to cut slots into which compressed beechwood 'biscuits' are fitted.

When boat builders butt planks together the construction of the boat is called 'carvel'. Soft fibres must be hammered into the cracks to prevent leaks, a process known as caulking.

Featheredge

THE earliest planks were made by splitting tree trunks into lengths using a mallet and wedges. Repeatedly splitting these along the radius of the grain produced a number of thin planks with a triangular section. These were poor for butt joints, but ideal for overlapping. The modern machine-cut version, called featheredge, is still widely used for fencing and cladding buildings. In England timber cladding is referred to as weatherboard and in North America it is known as clapboard.

The Vikings pioneered the technique of building robust boats with riveted overlapping planks and many seaworthy

vessels are still constructed in this way. Boats of this type are said to be 'clinker built' because the riveting is accomplished by clinching (bending over) soft nails.

Shiplap

A MORE efficient overlap, producing a flatter finished surface, is shiplap. On each board the surface is trimmed down on one edge and the underneath trimmed on the other so that when two boards are butted up one fits snugly over the other. Shiplap is used for cladding buildings and also for interior wall panelling.

Tongue and groove

To make this efficient, invisible joint, the edge of one member has a groove cut along its length to house the tongue that protrudes from the edge of the other. Individually cut tongue and groove joints are used worldwide in the construction of furniture, while pre-cut tongue and groove boards are used extensively for flooring and wall panelling.

OPPOSITE, CENTRE: *A moveable chicken house clad with featheredge boards, England.*

OPPOSITE, BOTTOM: *A painted ceiling in the El Glaoui Kasbah in Taourirte, Morocco.*

TOP; AND ABOVE, NEAR RIGHT: *Shiplap beach huts at Southwold on the Suffolk coast, England; reconstruction of Anglo-Saxon shiplap made from split oak planks, West Stow, Suffolk, England.*

ABOVE, FAR RIGHT: *Carved cedar wood chest from the Swat Valley in Pakistan. The panels slot into grooves in the mortise and tenon framework. The panel on the right slides out to provide access.*

RIGHT, CENTRE: *A wooden bread container, shaped like a tagine pot, Marrakesh, Morocco. The conical lid is made of butt-jointed slats.*

FAR RIGHT: *Anglo-Saxon tongue and groove joints made from split oak planks.*

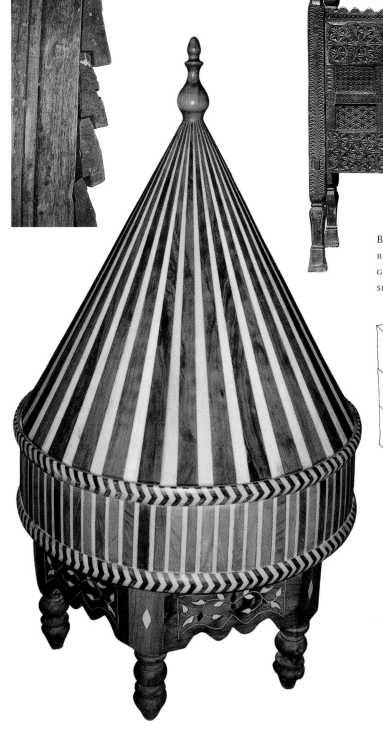

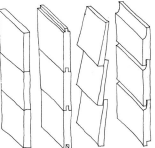

BELOW, FROM LEFT TO RIGHT: BUTT JOINTS; TONGUE AND GROOVE; FEATHEREDGE; SHIPLAP.

OVERLAPPING JOINTS

A NUMBER of techniques are used to secure components that cross each other, obliquely or at right angles, depending on the strength required as well as the materials and equipment available. For constructing log cabins the accumulated weight of the building presses down on joints cut into whole logs. Bamboo structures are most often securely lashed with split rattan or other plant fibres. Screws, nails or bolts are employed for crude joints, while flimsy lattices and trellises are generally secured with just a rivet or staple.

Lashings

LASHING is the quickest method of fastening two members together and, tied tightly, can be surprisingly strong. While a hunting party equipped with nothing more than a large knife can swiftly build a temporary shelter using materials gathered on site, Asian construction workers have no qualms about the strength of scaffolding made from lashed bamboo. A good lashing is made by winding the binding around the members in both directions and then pulling the binding tight with extra 'frapping' turns.

Tied with care, a lashing can be decorative as well as strong as can still be seen on Polynesian buildings where massive timbers are beautifully lashed with two cords of different colours.

Halving joints

WHEN two pieces of solid timber of equal thickness cross, halving joints are utilized. If half the thickness is cut away from each the two will lock together to form a joint no thicker than a single piece. Two vertical cuts are made with a saw – the space between is the width of the members, and the waste is then removed with a chisel. Joints cut into the glazing bars of windows are more complicated, requiring further cuts into their moulded sections to allow a neat fit. Halving joints may also be used to form a relatively strong T-shaped join.

With members of different thickness, wood need only be cut away from the thicker to make a 'lap' for the thinner to sit in, forming a flush joint. This is a variation of the lap joint also used for corner construction.

TOP; AND ABOVE: *'The Gordian knot', a wooden puzzle; plaster figure on a mahogany crucifix incorporating a cross halving joint, Malta.*

BELOW, LEFT: *Lashed bamboo fence in the Majorelle Gardens, Marrakesh, Morocco.*

BELOW, RIGHT: *A cross halving joint on a garden gate in Suffolk, England.*

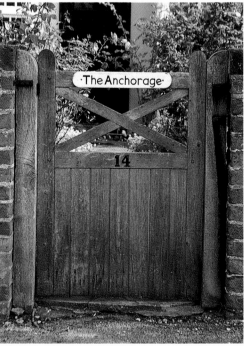

LEFT AND BELOW: DRAWINGS, CLOCKWISE, FROM TOP LEFT, OBLIQUE LAP; JAPANESE COGGED LAP (*WATARI AGO*); CORNER HALVING; CROSS HALVING; T HALVING.

Log cabin joints

AMONG the most dramatic uses of overlapping joints is the log cabin style of architecture taken to North America by emigrants from northern Europe, but also found in Korean and Japanese barn construction. Simple joints, often a straightforward curved 'cradle', were popular as they could be cut with no more than an axe and therefore a solid, weather-proof house could be erected quite quickly. Many variations can be used, some notched on one side, some notched on both.

Artesonado

THE Islamic fondness for geometric pattern was sometimes applied with style to panelling and to ceilings. Rather than simple boards, the *artesonado* ceilings of North Africa and southern Spain, a land occupied by the Moors for hundreds of years, are made from interlocked beams of cedar wood, apparently interlaced to create a pattern of polygons and stars. The spaces between the structural sections may be further embellished with carving or painting.

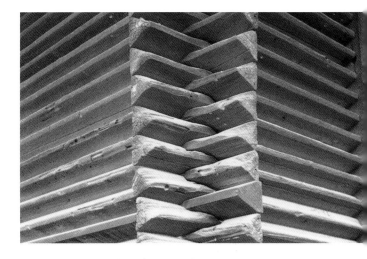

ABOVE, LEFT: *Green oak oblique lap joint pinned with wooden pegs known as treenails or trunnels.*

TOP RIGHT: *Welsh gout stool with cross halving.*

LEFT: Artesonado *ceiling in the Alhambra, Granada, Spain.*

ABOVE, RIGHT: *Log-cabin joints used to assemble a sacred repository in the Japanese temple complex at Nara. This building was probably built by Korean craftsmen in the 7th century.*

RIGHT: *English girl guides at a camp in the 1920s, building a 'gadget' with lashed staves.*

SLOTS AND SOCKETS

T HE T-SHAPED joints produced by fitting the end of one piece of wood into a hole in another are strong and are therefore found all over the globe. Glue, dowels, nails or wedges may be used for extra security, but in China, where rapid changes in humidity and temperature cause frequent expansion and contraction, it is necessary to make an allowance for the movement of the wood and so craftsmen have become expert at cutting mortise and tenon joints secured purely by the tight fit. This means that Chinese furniture is very stable, but can easily be dismantled if needed.

Sockets

M AKING a hole in one piece of wood with a drill or auger and trimming another, either with a drawknife or on a lathe, to plug into the socket can make simple, but effective, joints. Often used by woodland craftsmen working with green wood, the technique was perfected by the makers of 'stick' chairs, which are constructed by plugging the legs into the underside of the seat and the back and arms into the top. The Windsor chair is the ultimate stick chair, widely imitated because of its simple design which makes it cheap, elegant, light and strong.

Housing joints

I N the construction of shelving and frameworks wider joints need to receive boards or planks. Housings or dados are made from shallow grooves or slots the same width as the plank or board by cutting two parallel kerfs across the grain with a saw before removing the waste with a chisel or router.

Mortise and tenon joints

A MORTISE, or mortice, is a rectangular slot or recess, cut along the grain, into which the end of a piece of timber can be fitted. Perhaps the most common joint of them all is the mortise and tenon joint. The tenon is made by cutting away wood from each side of one member to leave a tongue about a third of its thickness. The mortise into which it will fit may be cut entirely with a chisel or alternately waste may first be removed by drilling a series of

holes before trimming with the chisel. For accuracy, a mortise is cut to only half its depth from one side and then the wood is turned over and work completed from the other. This type of joint can be adapted for many purposes and for timber in different combinations of thickness or width. Mortise and tenon joints have a large glueing area which makes them very strong, but even greater strength can be achieved by driving wedges into the end of the tenon, causing it to splay out.

TOP LEFT: *Cutting mortises at Bo, Sierra Leone.*

LEFT, MIDDLE: *Housing and through housing joints in coconut wood, Ubud, Bali.*

BOTTOM LEFT: *A 'Windsor' chair constructed by pushing turned 'sticks' into sockets.*

BELOW: *Through housing joints, Singaraja, Bali. The wedges force a shallow housing the horizontal beam upwards, locking it into the mortise.*

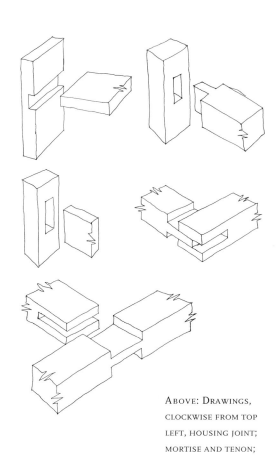

Bridle joints

Used for similar functions, the bridle joint is the 'negative' version of the mortise and tenon. Instead of cutting wood from the sides to form a tongue, wood is cut from the centre to form a pair of 'jaws'. A housing is then cut on either side of the other member to leave one third of the wood which, when the two sections are fitted together, slots into the other like the bit into a horse's mouth. As so much of the wood is cut away bridle joints lack strength and are therefore only used in the construction of lighter frameworks.

ABOVE: DRAWINGS, CLOCKWISE FROM TOP LEFT, HOUSING JOINT; MORTISE AND TENON; CORNER BRIDLE; T BRIDLE; MORTISE.

BELOW, LEFT: *Window frame, from Kashmir, assembled with mortise and tenon joints, those at the corners incorporating mitres.*

ABOVE: *Housing and butt joints on a copy of a Japanese bridge at Logan Gardens, Dumfries and Galloway, Scotland.*

BELOW, RIGHT: *A Chinese horseshoe chair made from rosewood and constructed with joints that fit so snugly that no nails or glue are required.*

THREE

CORNERS

ABOVE: *The neatly fitting mitred corner of a chip-carved picture frame made in the late 19th century.*

I N MOST structures the corners take the majority of the stress and so joints with strength and rigidity are essential. Variations on mortise and tenon, bridle or halving joints may be employed, but certain joints, such as the dovetail, are used specifically for this purpose.

Butt

B UTTING the end of one structural member up against the other makes the simplest form of corner joint, but – with no form of interlock – glue, pins or some other fixing are necessary. This technique lacks any strength and is, therefore, only used on quickly constructed work that will be subjected to minimal strain.

Lap

S TRONGER than the butt joint, although it still requires gluing or pinning, the lap or rebate joint is often used in box and drawer construction. A rebate is cut on the inside face of one member and the other

74

RIGHT: *A box inlaid with pieces of shell fitted with a sliding lid; made on the Indonesian island of Lombok. The sides are joined with mitred joints and butted onto the base.*

OPPOSITE, BELOW: *Afghan carpenter's cedar wood tool box decorated with chip carving and incised patterns. An assortment of joints, including laps, butts and mitres, have been used as a demonstration of the owner's skill at his trade.*

member is butted up into it. This is ideal for jobs such as fixing drawers as the end grain of the sides can be hidden behind the lap cut into the drawer front, thus presenting an uninterrupted surface.

Mitre

WHEN joints are mitred the ends of both members are cut at 45 degrees so that, butted together, they will form a right angle. This creates an 'invisible' joint as the end grain of both members is concealed from view. Accurate joins demand careful marking or the assistance of a mitre box. Mitres are often used in combination with butt or lap joints, but need reinforcement.

Reinforcements

GLUEING, pinning or dowelling may all be employed to secure weak joints, but in ancient times it was common practice to tie separate parts together with cords or thongs laced through pre-drilled holes, a method still followed today by the makers of kerf-bent boxes in the American North-west. Extra strength can also be ensured by attaching both members to a block of wood on the inside of the corner.

Combs and dovetails

THE comb joint in which the ends of both members are cut with square 'teeth' imitates the joining of the hands by interlocking the fingers. A well-cut comb joint, tapped into position with a wooden mallet, can be strong enough without the use of glue or pins, but pales into insignificance beside the dovetail joint, the touchstone of the cabinet maker's art. The wedge-shaped tails and pins that form

the dovetails require fastidious marking, precise sawing and the careful chiselling away of waste wood. The finished product is both attractive and extremely strong, the interlocked wedges binding securely together to resist forces pulling against the joint.

A number of variations of comb or dovetail joints are possible, incorporating mitres or rebates which may completely conceal the mechanics of the joint. The principle was utilized by the builders of the Tomb of Mausolus in Halicarnassos (360–350 BC), one of the Seven Wonders of the World, a structure held together by insetting metal dovetails into the blocks of stone.

RIGHT: *Lapped dovetail joint at the corner of a drawer from a sideboard.*

BELOW: *A Chinese portable chest of drawers made from highly polished rosewood. The pieces of the carcass are connected with mitred comb joints. Similar chests made in Japan are often reinforced at the corners with metal plates.*

FAR LEFT: *Marquetry, Hakone, Japan.*
ABOVE, LEFT: *Norwegian pyro engraving.*
ABOVE, RIGHT: *North American design worked in straw.*
LEFT: *Chinese feng shui mirror.*
RIGHT: *Lacquered Japanese tea utensils.*

DECORATING AND FINISHING

LEFT: *Moroccan chest covered in hide, metal and bone.*
ABOVE: *Swedish painted horses from Dalarna.*

DECORATING AND FINISHING

THE CRAFTWORK of the Shakers, established in 18th-century North America, has become an icon of simplicity. They applied the philosophy 'beauty rests in simplicity' to their lifestyle and their woodwork, eschewing frivolity, fashion and vanity, eradicating clutter and extraneous adornment, to produce aesthetic objects of great beauty. But even Shaker crafts are not totally devoid of decoration. The rear posts of their chairs were topped with elegant turned finials and their famous bentwood 'nice' boxes were finished with stylish 'swallow tail' joints. They were also not averse to paintwork in restrained colours, as they believed this reflected the way things were coloured in heaven.

Archaeological finds have shown, mainly through the excavation of burial sites, that the most highly prized objects have always been decorated in some form or another, whether with carving, veneering, gilding, or painting. Many items are decorated with a number of different techniques and it is quite common for beautiful carving to be further enhanced with paint or gilding. The human race has a compulsion to decorate and embellish, to 'gild the lily'.

FAR LEFT: *Tobacco pipes of painted stems bought at the souk in Marrakesh, Morocco.*

NEAR LEFT: *A painted dragon on the front of a 17th-century Tibetan chest used to store vestments. Objects with a religious association are frequently given far more decorative attention than those associated with the temporal world.*

BELOW, LEFT: *A beached fishing boat in the Algarve, Portugal. Since ancient times seafarers have given their vessels painted or carved eyes, and heads or figures in the hope that this will help them find the way home safely.*

ABOVE: *Architectural decoration in the form of stylized singa heads made by the Batak in northern Sumatra. The richly carved or painted buildings of Indonesia and South-East Asia display many such ornaments intended to avert the influences of evil spirits.*

OPPOSITE, BELOW, LEFT: *Once the legs of beds and tables have been turned and carved by men it is often the task of women to add the painted details.*

FINISHING

SOME OF the harder, oilier woods such as *Lignum vitae* need very little protection, but most are vulnerable to wear and tear, insect damage or exposure to the weather. Defence is provided with paint, oil, wax or varnish according to the materials available, but the choice may include aesthetic as well as practical considerations as sealing alters the natural colour and lustre of wood. Modern technology and the opening up of global trade have increased the options even in remote regions. Today, in South-East Asia and Africa light-coloured, cheap woods are often disguised with liberal coatings of boot polish to imitate darker, more expensive, hardwoods.

LEFT: *A carved eye and a painted 'Lamb of God' on a Maltese fishing boat.*

RIGHT: *Gilded carving at the entrance to a temple prayer hall, Chiang Mai, Thailand.*

ABOVE: *Didgeridoos for sale at the airport in Sydney, Australia. On display are a mixture of traditional and contemporary designs intended to appeal to tourists. The company selling these products, The Rainbow Serpent, is devoted to helping the indigenous peoples of Australia by marketing genuine handicrafts.*

BELOW, CENTRE: *In Thailand temples are decorated with beautiful gilded carving. A complex of temple buildings sparkles in the sun like a heavenly city.*

BELOW, RIGHT: *In New Zealand, most Maori woodwork is embellished with carving, one notable exception are the swirling patterns, known as* kowhaiwhai, *which can be seen painted on the rafters of meeting houses.*

STYLES AND FUNCTIONS OF DECORATION

DECORATING TECHNIQUES that require expensive materials or years of practice, such as veneering, are most often carried out by professionals and specialists whereas cheap, simple methods, such as painting, may be employed by both professionals and the untutored. Folk styles of painted woodwork, such as Norwegian *rosmalning*, executed by local craftsmen or by amateurs, are most often floral and exude a naïve charm. The work of professionals, frequently accompanied by lavish layers of gold, appears in the homes of the wealthy such as the houses of the Baroque European aristocracy and in places of worship, for instance, in the temples of Thailand and the cathedrals of medieval Europe. During the 20th century an increase in the amount of leisure time made it possible for European and American amateur craftsmen to pursue hobbies in the creative arts, often to a very high standard. Both men and women toiled at fretwork, cabinet making and marquetry, making and decorating beautiful objects for their private use.

The homes and artefacts of those who follow a simple, down to earth lifestyle are covered with motifs ripe with symbolism intended to invoke or placate the mysterious forces of the universe. For most people, decoration is nowadays purely aesthetic as we have become distanced from the spiritual side of life, but, even in an industrial society, the frequency of floral designs shows how nature is brought into the home.

FOUR

Veneers

BELOW, LEFT: *Early 20th-century clock with banding and an inlaid veneer motif.*

BELOW, RIGHT (CLOCKWISE FROM TOP LEFT): *Rotary veneers: bird's eye maple, bubinga, pomelle with 'plum pudding figure'; classic veneers: rosewood, satinwood, walnut; sliced veneers: aspen, white birch, ash, castello.*

THE MOST beautiful woods, prized for their colour or figuring, are often the most expensive because of their rarity, the cost of importing them from far-off tropical lands or the freakish circumstances of their growth. To reduce costs and make the wood go further they can be sliced into thin sheets called veneers which may then be stuck on to a thicker piece of cheaper wood to disguise it, a practice described by the Roman author Pliny as 'bestowing upon the more common woods a bark of a higher price'. Veneers have been used for thousands of years since the Egyptians began importing ebony, at great expense, from tropical Africa.

Cutting veneers

For centuries the easiest way to cut veneers of even thickness was with the aid of a multiple-bladed frame saw operated by two men. In the 19th century this was replaced by the circular saw, but in the 20th century it became common practice to use a sharp blade to slice off veneers only a few millimetres thick. The cutting process is facilitated by first soaking the wood in water.

A variety of figuring is made available by the choice of angle at which the veneer is cut, revealing different views of the growth rings. For example, veneer sliced tangentially, known as flat-sliced or crown-cut veneer, has an attractive marbled appearance. When quarter-cut, a slice is taken from the outside of a log towards the centre close to the radius to produce a pattern of near-parallel lines. Using a rotary cut and turning the whole log against the blade will spirally cut long sheets of veneer with wild irregular patterning, which are generally used for facing plywood. One of the most attractive types of veneer has a spotted figure, acquired by cutting across burrs on a tree trunk.

Colouring

WOODS are normally chosen for their beautiful grain or colours and the best work exploits the subtleties of

carefully selected wood, although costs are sometimes reduced by dyeing cheap veneer to imitate expensive timbers or to create a colour not found in nature. Subtleties of tonal graduation can be artificially produced by dipping a piece of veneer in hot sand and scorching parts of it.

FOUR

Veneering

CUSTOMARILY, veneer is stuck to a wooden base with heated animal glue. A smooth and secure finish is achieved by pressing down with a veneer hammer to force out any air bubbles or excess glue. As the glue can be softened once more with the application of heat, for example with an electric iron, it is possible to make repairs to damaged work.

Uses

SHEETS of veneer such as walnut or satinwood are commonly used to disguise the carcass of a piece of furniture made from cheaper wood, a skill perfected by cabinet makers in the 17th century and shamelessly indulged by European craftsmen of the 18th century. Ornamentation with inlay and marquetry also employs sheets of veneer and for several hundred years ready-made inlay motifs and bandings have been made up by specialist craftsmen to satisfy the demand.

CUTTING VENEERS (FROM TOP): BURR, QUARTER CUT, ROTARY CUT, FLAT SLICED.

81

MARQUETRY

MARQUETRY IS the woodworker's version of mosaic, featuring a pattern of tessellating shapes laid out on the surface of a piece of wood. The Royal Standard of Ur is an early example made in Mesopotamia about 5,000 years ago which consists of a wooden box, possibly the sounding board for a lyre, overlaid with scenes from contemporary life fitted together from pieces of shell, lapis lazuli and red limestone. The Ancient Egyptians also decorated many items with marquetry patterns in ivory, ebony and painted calcite.

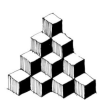

ABOVE: A PARQUETRY OPTICAL ILLUSION, WITH THREE DIFFERENT-COLOURED WOODS.

FOUR

Marquetry and parquet

GEOMETRIC wood marquetry continues to flourish in the Middle East and North Africa – it reached as far as India and Andalusia in Spain with the spread of Islam, a religion that abhors images, but encourages pattern. The technique has changed very little except bone and plastic are now often used as substitutes for rare and expensive materials such as ivory and imported hardwood veneers.

After the repulse of the Moors from Spain in the late 15th century, many craftsmen remained behind and developed the distinctive geometric Mudejar style, but under Christianity which allowed figurative work marquetry became more representational. Pictorial marquetry, referred to as intarsia work, reached its peak during the Renaissance of the 15th and 16th centuries when the choir stalls of Italian churches and cathedrals were decorated with realistic perspective and landscape scenes, often designed by great artists such as Uccello and Piero della Francesca.

Parquetry

FOR many people the term parquet is synonymous with woodblock flooring, but it actually refers to geometric patterns made from symmetrically shaped pieces of veneer. It is possible to create *trompe l'oeil* effects such as three-dimensional cubes, but most patterns are built up from strips of veneer of contrasting colours laid alternately and taped together. A series of cuts is then made at right angles to produce a new strip of alternating colours. This is then pushed along so that the staggering produces a chequered pattern. With continued slicing and staggering, either at right angles or diagonally, a virtually endless number of designs can be created.

ABOVE: *A Spanish craftsman in Granada gluing down slices of* taracea *(sliced end grain). The regularly shaped pieces will be tessellated to cover the entire surface of the table.*

BELOW, LEFT: *Small Moroccan box made in Mers Sultan, south of Casablanca, decorated with bone and mother of pearl set in resin.*

BELOW, RIGHT: *English Tunbridgeware box, 19th century. Using the end-grain technique, many identical items could be turned out very quickly.*

End-grain marquetry

SOME time around the 9th century AD craftsmen in Syria perfected a technique which made it possible to mass produce marquetry and inlay. A selection of 80 cm (31 in.) rods – triangular, rectangular, rhomboid or hexagonal in section – are first glued together in

a bundle and clamped in a wooden casing. When the glue has set the bundle is sawn across the grain into hundreds of identical slices each only a millimetre thick. These can be glued onto the surface of a box or table, covering the surface much more quickly than with an individual tessera. Under the name Tunbridgeware, geometric and pictorial work using the same technique became popular in England during the 1820s for decorating tables, boxes and trinkets.

Mother of pearl and other types of shell have irregular shapes and do not come in 80 cm (31 in.) lengths so cannot be sliced in this way. They must be cut individually by hand and prices for work incorporating shell rise dramatically according to the amount used.

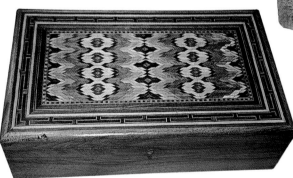

ABOVE: *Box decorated in parquetry, a technique that lends itself to all manner of optical effects and illusions.*

ABOVE, RIGHT: *Chest of drawers decorated with a patchwork of symmetrical patterns worked in marquetry from Hakone, Kanagawa Prefecture, Japan. Any individual piece could contain up to fifty different patterns.*

RIGHT: *A marquetry box made in Damascus, Syria, during the late 19th century. The motifs are constructed using the end-grain technique which was developed in Damascus a thousand years earlier.*

83

Inlay

Unlike marquetry, where pieces of veneer are glued to the surface of a piece of timber, inlay is the craft of insetting shapes into recesses cut into the background. The Ancient Egyptians made a great deal of inlaid furniture, particularly enjoying the contrast between ebony and ivory, while in India ivory traders had supplied the needs of craftsmen since the days of Mohenjodaro 4,000 years earlier. Shell inlay had reached a high standard in China, exploiting the opalescent lustre of mother of pearl for the wings of butterflies and the petals of flowers, long before it spread to Korea and Japan in the 7th century AD. During the 16th century, at their bases in India and Japan, Portuguese traders enthusiastically bought and commissioned all manner of goods in a fusion of European shapes and the well-established local decorative techniques including lacquer and ivory or shell inlay. The marquetry and inlay techniques of North Africa were also influential and with the expansion of world trade, making exotic timber more readily available, cabinet making in Europe took off in a blaze of pattern and colour.

The process

The simplest method of insetting a shape is to cut the motif to be inlaid first, lay it on the background and draw around it. This outline can then be cut with a knife or chisel and the waste removed, making a recess slightly shallower than the inlay. An alternative is to cut the recess first and then make a template for the inlay by taking a paper rubbing of the recess. The inlay can then be glued in place and clamped until dry, when the surface will be levelled by sanding.

The effort involved in inlay work can be greatly eased by purchasing ready-made motifs, traditionally featuring flowers and shells. Simple strips of pale boxwood or black ebony, now more often imitated with dyed wood, are known as 'stringing' when set into the surface to define borders. More elaborate 'bandings' for borders are composed from veneers of several colours assembled in stripes, diamonds or herringbone designs.

FOUR

Shell, ivory and bone

Tortoise shell is made from plates of the carapace of turtles softened in boiling water until they can be flattened or bent. First used in the Far East, it was widely employed in northern Europe during the 17th century, often in combination with brass, copper or pewter. Ivory was once frequently used in inlay work, although costs could be cut by using bone, a material that does not mellow to such an attractive tone. Trade in both ivory and tortoise shell has been made illegal in an attempt to prevent the extinction of elephants and turtles. Today, plastic is used as a substitute for both. Shell is still the major source of inlay in the Pacific, where it is most often set into a dark wood base, but even certain species of shellfish are now under threat and trade in their shells has been banned.

Metal and wire

Shapes cut from sheet metals, such as brass, silver or pewter, may be inlaid in the same way as wood veneer, but thin strips can also be used. Slits are made into a block of wood and strips of brass are then driven into the grooves with a hammer. While this technique can be used to create delicate geometric patterns or even figurative designs, the Western use of strip metal is more or less limited to the delineation of borders.

OPPOSITE, TOP LEFT: *Maori carving of an ancestor figure on a poupou panel in a meeting house, New Zealand.*

OPPOSITE, ABOVE, LEFT: *A Romanian mandolin with an inlaid veneer design around the sound hole.*

OPPOSITE, BELOW, RIGHT; AND INSET: *Carved wood baby carrier, slung on the back, made by the Kenyah or Kayan in Borneo. The dark wood is contrasted with inlaid pieces of conus shell; photograph taken in 1895 when Zanzibar was an important centre for ivory trading.*

RIGHT: *Wooden tray, from Bahrain, inlaid with scrolling patterns made from strips of brass.*

BELOW, LEFT: *A hexagonal box from Essaouira, Morocco. The inlaid geometric pattern is assembled from pieces of cedar, lemonwood, ebony and mother-of-pearl shell.*

BELOW, RIGHT: *Bowl, from Lombok, inlaid with shell and a Chinese coin.*

FINISHES

WITHOUT PROTECTION, the surface of worked timber becomes dirty and marked with handling, while exposure to sunlight causes the colour to become dull and the figuring to fade. Exposed to the elements, wood will become bleached and the attentions of insects or fungi will eventually cause it to crumble into dust or mould. One of the oldest known techniques of preventing decay, still practised in Asia, involves placing vulnerable objects where they will be permeated by smoke and soot. Fats from cooking also adhere to the surface or may be deliberately rubbed in, resulting in wood with a dark lustre.

Oil and wax

THE easiest method of polishing and sealing wood is the application of oil with a rag or brush. Although olive oil is most suitable for sealing vessels intended for food, tung oil, obtained from the seeds of the Chinese oil tree (*Aleurites cordata*), is the most durable finish and the alternate application and rubbing down of several coats produces a high polish. Danish oil and teak oil are less expensive and quicker drying, while linseed oil is cheap, but dries slowly, darkens the wood and has a strong smell. Oil has the added advantage of soaking deep into the wood, providing more protection than other methods.

Wax polish is applied in several layers with a cloth, allowed to dry and then buffed to create a soft sheen that mellows pleasantly. Traditionally, woodworkers make wax polish from a mixture of beeswax and carnauba wax thinned with turpentine, but ready-made versions are now easily available in a number of colours and tones.

French polish

IT requires time and skill to apply, but French polish (a mixture of shellac, the secretion of an Indian beetle, and alcohol) was considered the king of wood finishes in the 19th century. Achieving the shine is a painstaking process requiring the careful application of up to twenty coats using a soft 'rubber' made from cotton wool wrapped in linen – the rubber is charged with polish and then stroked over the surface with small circular motions. The glass-like shine is unbeatable, but is vulnerable to scratching and is easily stained by water or alcohol.

Varnish

EARLY varnishes were made from tree resin dissolved in alcohol until it was thin enough to spread with a brush. Modern varnishes, employing synthetic resins, are far more transparent, although they may be tinted to taste. Varnish only coats the surface and after some time begins to flake and so periodically it must be stripped off and replaced.

Changing colour

ON occasion, the appearance of timber may be changed to look older or even resemble the wood of another tree. Expensive ebony can be imitated by blackening a pale wood such as ash with soot. Colour, as with cricket bats, can be bleached in ammonia fumes or faded to look old by treating it with lime. In developing countries the most common

OPPOSITE, TOP: *Staining a carving with boot polish in Freetown, Sierra Leone.*

OPPOSITE, ABOVE, LEFT: *Weathered wreck on the north coast of Scotland.*

OPPOSITE, BELOW, LEFT: *The chair of a Dan elder, Ivory Coast, with the patina of constant use.*

OPPOSITE, BELOW, RIGHT: *Peter Barton applying French polish to a hand-made guitar.*

ABOVE, LEFT: *Wooden figure made by an Ewe craftsman in Ghana, polished by years of handling.*

ABOVE, RIGHT: *Tray made from dyed woods in 1915 by a German internee at a camp in the Scottish Borders.*

BELOW, LEFT; AND BELOW, RIGHT: *An unpolished kopalang wood carving made in Mas, Bali; similar carving to the one on the left, but with a generous coating of boot polish.*

way to darken wood today is a generous coating of boot polish.

Whatever the finish applied, handling and exposure to fumes and dirt eventually build up layers of grime and grease. Constant rubbing over the years by fingers, feet or bottoms buffs this up into a desirable unique mellow sheen known as patina.

PAINT

IN MOROCCO there is a saying that a piece of wood is not finished until it has been painted. This attitude still holds true in the Maghrib, but in Europe modern tastes prefer the beauty of natural wood, although in medieval times the carved wooden interiors and statuary of cathedrals were aglow with paint and gilding. Paint and pigment may be used for aesthetic effect or as a medium for symbolic – both spiritual and temporal – colour schemes. It can also be used to protect and preserve the wood it covers.

Preparing the surface

FOR a single colour finish only the minimum of preparation is necessary before a liberal coating of pigment is rubbed in or painted on. In New Zealand most Maori carvings were painted red using a mixture of red ochre and shark-liver oil. To provide a surface suitable for detailed decoration a smooth, non-porous ground is necessary. To achieve this a great deal of sanding is required before the base is sealed with a primer. Prior to the development of modern paints this was often accomplished in Europe and North America with red lead, a substance that filled and sealed the grain, but is no longer favoured because of its toxicity. Since the Renaissance fine furniture has been prepared with coats of gesso, a mixture of fine plaster and rabbit-skin glue, applied in as many as forty layers to create a surface as smooth as porcelain.

Pigments

MOST pigment is obtained from powdered minerals. These range from the virtually ubiquitous ochre, a clay rich in iron oxide, from which we can obtain a number of yellows and reds, to semi-precious stones such as lapis lazuli, found in Afghanistan and Chile, which is the source of ultramarine. Other sources of colour include plant extracts, soot and a few animal products such as sepia, which is derived from cuttlefish ink.

For ease of application, pigment must be dissolved in some form of solution. This might be water, plant juice or oil, such as the sugar-cane juice used by the Iban in Sarawak, spirits, such as turpentine derived from conifers, notably *Pistacia terebinthus*, or fish oil and animal fats such as the bear grease once used by indigenous peoples in North America. Some of the most delicate Italian painting employed tempera in which the pigment was mixed with egg white. Today, modern water-soluble acrylic paints are favoured even in the most far-flung places for their ease of use and bright colours.

Styles

PAINT may be used to colour the sculpted planes of carvings or as

ABOVE, LEFT: *Late 18th-century painted carving of the Virgin and Child in the Portuguese style, acquired in the Christian enclave in Kerala, southern India.*

ABOVE, RIGHT: *Recently painted furniture put out for sale in the labyrinthine souk in Marrakesh, Morocco.*

ABOVE: *Pair of candlesticks from Lima, Peru, painted by Umberto Urquizo in a style more often used for painting on the back of glass.*

LEFT: *A Japanese mask used in the Noh theatre, carved in the 1930s. Before painting, the wood was sealed with a coating of gesso.*

autonomous decoration on a flat surface. The style of this varies enormously with location, culture and tradition, but certain styles stretch beyond such borders. The European floral 'peasant' style is widespread and appears on many items including English narrow boats, Hungarian benches, Tyrolean utensils, Sicilian furniture and Russian domestic ware. The influence may well have travelled west with the first Romany on their exodus from India where echoes can be seen in the painted doors and furniture of Rajasthan.

In Europe poorer quality wood was sometimes painted to simulate the grain of more expensive woods, tortoise shell, or marble. American colonists also employed techniques such as vinegar painting to simulate other materials, often achieving eccentric, but charming effects.

LEFT; AND RIGHT: *Russian painted wooden spoon; painted guardians on the doors of the Temple of Heavenly Happiness in Singapore.*

BELOW, LEFT; AND BELOW, RIGHT: *A Kenyah warrior with a painted shield, Kalimantan; Indian playing card boxes, Puri, Orissa.*

89

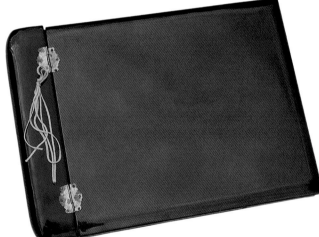

Lacquer

TRUE LACQUER, with its hard, glossy surface and lustrous depths, must be the most glamorous finish ever produced. Primitive methods of lacquering were used to paint wood during the Japanese Jomon culture about 7,000 years ago, but it was Chinese craftsmen who perfected the techniques in the late 3rd century BC during the Han Dynasty. Lacquer was popular for its beautiful finish, but also for its power in deterring insect damage. Later Chinese craftsmen used it as a medium for carving intricate patterns, having first built up hundreds of layers. It was the spread of Buddhism from the 6th century AD on that brought about the dissemination of lacquer from China into Indochina and eventually back to Japan where it was to reach its zenith under the name of *urushi*.

Technique

IN China the raw material for lacquer work is obtained from a variety of the sumac tree, *Rhus vernicifera*, in Japan from the *Rhus verniciflua* and in Indochina from the *rac* tree, *Melanorrhoea usitata*. The tree is slashed and the bleeding sap collected in a cup before being boiled and strained until pure. Lacquer may be applied to any non-porous surface – wood, leather, basketry or metal – as long as all imperfections have been filled and the surface has been scrupulously smoothed. The more layers that are applied, the deeper the eventual sheen will be, but each coat must be allowed to dry and then rubbed down with charcoal or scouring rush before the application of the next. Lacquer is so resilient that many examples, which are over a thousand years old, survive intact.

Japanese lacquerware

IN Japan lacquer was first used on religious sculpture and temple fittings, but by the 10th century it had become popular for personal items such as boxes and sword scabbards. The most characteristic of Japanese styles is *maki-e*, which means 'sprinkled picture' and refers to the technique of sprinkling gold or silver dust into a coat of wet lacquer. Variations of this technique require the application of gold flakes or modelling a pattern out of lacquer mixed with charcoal or clay dust. In the late 16th century the nobility and ruling classes patronized the development of a new style known as Kamakura-bori. This resembles Chinese carved 'Coromandel' lacquer, but is created by carving the pattern onto a base of gingko, ho or

TOP: *Detail of a Japanese Kamakura-bori tray. Firstly, the wood was carved with a set of knives and then coated with layers of* urushi *lacquer coloured black with iron oxide, rubbed down as each coat dried. Towards the end a layer tinted with vermillion was applied and rubbed away from the high points.*

A LACQUERED LID FROM A CHINESE COLONY AT LOLANG, KOREA, 1ST CENTURY AD.

ABOVE: *The deep lustrous sheen of the lacquer cover of a photograph album made in Vietnam.*

RIGHT: *The Straits Chinese or Peranakan occupied colonies all over South-East Asia and produced their own, distinctive craftwork. This box, photographed in Bali, is typical of the figurative designs usually worked in red and black lacquer, often with a touch of gold.*

FOUR

katsura wood before the application of the lacquer.

Japanning

During the 17th and 18th centuries new trading agreements saw the arrival of many Oriental objects in Europe and stimulated the style known as Chinoiserie. Attempting to imitate the sheen of lacquer, craftsmen experimented with Indian 'lac', the gummy secretion of a beetle, *coccus lacca*, also known as shellac. This substance is soluble in alcohol and, tinted with paint, can, in the process known as Japanning, be applied in layers that eventually produce a finish with a passing similarity to true lacquer.

Barniz de Pasto

In the town of Pasto in south-west Colombia an ancient technique for waterproofing is now used to decorate masks and carvings. Resin (barniz) extracted from the seeds of a tree, *Eleagia utilis*, is coloured with dyes and stretched by hand into a thin sheet. Designs are cut out from various colours and, one at a time, stuck, using heat, to the carved wood.

This page, clockwise from top left: *Straits Chinese lacquered wood pot acquired in Yogyakarta, Java; lacquered tray with wood base, Pagan, Myanmar, a great centre for lacquerware; multi-coloured Barniz de Pasto duck from south-west Colombia.*

DRAWING WITH FIRE

RANGING FROM crude scorching to delicate sketching, the art of decorating with fire is known by the evocative title 'pyrography' which comes from the Greek for 'drawing with fire'.

The origins of fire

FIRE is a magical element associated with the sun or the gods and myths abound all around the world about how it was first obtained by mankind. The Ancient Greeks told of how the beneficent titan, Prometheus, stole it from the gods and as a punishment was tied to a mountain top where an eagle came every day to eat his liver. In the American Southwest, the Papago Native American myth relates how many unsuccessful attempts were made to acquire fire from the sun until finally a bat accomplished the task. In the attempt, the poor creature lost all the beautiful feathers with which he had been covered and from then on only showed himself at night time. In Polynesia the great folk hero, Maui, had the good fortune to be given fire by his divine grandmother, while the Persian king, Husheng, fighting off a dragon, observed the sparks made when the stones he was throwing struck a rock.

ABOVE, LEFT: *A painted box with outlines and patterns marked out with a hot point. The border design is inspired by Russian textiles and the main picture is a copy of a 1902 drawing by Ivan Bilibin illustrating the tale of the folk hero Volga.*

ABOVE: *North European bread board decorated with pokerwork. As with carving, it is easier to keep control of one's tools when working with a more densely grained wood. Many traditional designs around the world, whether incised, chip carved or pyro engraved, are based upon the intersecting arcs of a circle.*

OPPOSITE, ABOVE, LEFT: *A carved stool in the shape of a jaguar with scorched spots made by Achuara Indians in the Ecuadorean Amazon.*

OPPOSITE, BELOW, RIGHT: *Pyro-engraved discs of calabash shell from West Africa.*

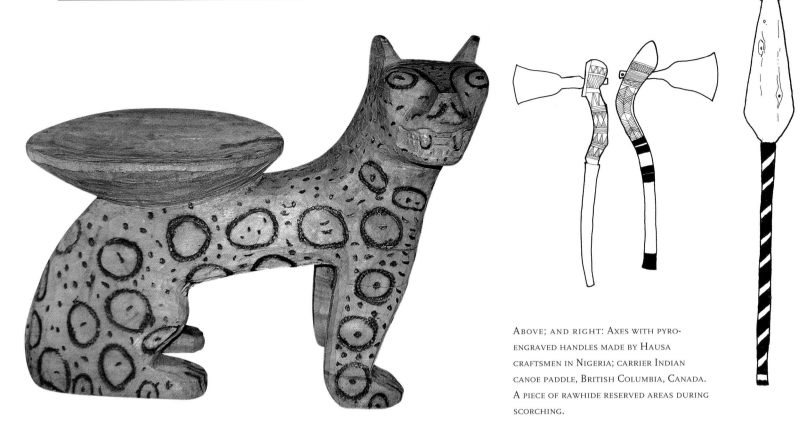

ABOVE; AND RIGHT: AXES WITH PYRO-
ENGRAVED HANDLES MADE BY HAUSA
CRAFTSMEN IN NIGERIA; CARRIER INDIAN
CANOE PADDLE, BRITISH COLUMBIA, CANADA.
A PIECE OF RAWHIDE RESERVED AREAS DURING
SCORCHING.

The historical origins of fire are less certain, but hearths were in use in Hungary and north-west France 350,000 years ago and the evidence of layers of ash, although inconclusive, suggests that there may have been controlled fires in China 500 years earlier.

Scorching

BY carefully holding wood close to glowing embers it is possible to scorch areas without setting fire to them. In North America, tribes as far apart as the Carrier in the North-west and the Cherokee in the South-east employed a distinctive technique in which wet rawhide was wrapped from end to end around a stick. When this was exposed to the fire, the areas between the rawhide were scorched into a dark spiral. The method was used to decorate canoe paddles, ball-game sticks and many other objects.

Pokerwork

A RED-HOT iron is used to brand both animal hide and wood, and its mark can be seen on the packing crates of South American coffee and Swedish car parts. Drawing with a hot tool is referred to as pokerwork or pyro engraving and was once common in both Europe and Africa. A poker is a cumbersome implement and a hot knife or, today, an electric tool resembling a soldering iron are more prevalent. Only a light touch is necessary and a skilled hand can produce work of great delicacy. Once the engraving is completed, further decoration may be added by filling areas with coloured stains or paint.

Gourds and calabashes

THE woody shell of the gourd, a member of the squash family, is an excellent receptacle and is also made into spoons or the sound bowls of musical instruments. In sub-Saharan Africa gourds are known as calabashes and are often decorated with patterns engraved with a hot knife. In South America, where gourds are known as *mates*, the designs are generally engraved and then shaded with careful scorching.

Metallic finishes

In the opinion of Sigmund Freud, the renowned psychoanalyst, metal, being hard and penetrating, represented masculinity, while wood, being soft and yielding, represented femininity. The faking of metal has gone on since ancient times with the employment of a variety of metals, but particularly gold, which for millennia has been used in the decoration of thrones, crowns, religious images and reliquaries, anything marked out as an object demanding respect or reverence.

Gold

'And they shall make an ark of shittim wood (acacia)... And thou shalt overlay it with pure gold.' (Exodus, 25, x–xi) The construction of the Ark of the Covenant as specified by God to Moses is an ancient example (probably from the 13th century BC) of the association of gold with divinity and royalty. Because of its colour and sheen gold has always been associated with the sun without which there would be no life. To the Ancient Egyptians gold was the flesh of the gods and to the Aztecs it was their sweat. To the more metaphorically minded Buddhists and Christians gold represents the incorruptible and the pure, spiritual light of illumination or enlightenment. Gold is also costly and is therefore associated with wealth, both material and spiritual.

Sheet metal

Large objects fashioned from solid gold are too expensive for all but the richest of potentates, and craftsmen, apparently endowed with a Midas touch, have been required to employ tricks to seemingly turn their work into gold. Detailing, known as ormolu, may be cast from brass or gilt bronze to encrust furniture and decorative objects, but entire objects can be encased in metal beaten into sheets.

Among the grave goods of Tutankhamun (1336–1327 BC) was a wooden shrine to the goddess Nekhbet completely covered in sheets of beaten gold. The art of hammering gold into 'leaf' thinner than paper was known to the Sumerians more than a thousand years earlier and large numbers of gilded artefacts were discovered in the 'Death Pits' of the Royal Cemetery at Ur.

Gilding

An object that has been gilded has the opulent sheen of solid gold, but the process required is comparatively cheap as the sheets of leaf are so thin. Today, the

ABOVE: *Gilded heraldic carving by the author.*

LEFT; AND RIGHT: *Carved and gilded doorway, Neka Palace, Ubud, Bali; gold lacquered altar back, Myanmar.*

ABOVE: *Squares of transfer gold leaf.*

LEFT: *Mirror frame, from Isfahan, Iran, decorated with floral designs on a background of gold paint.*

BELOW, CENTRE: *Gilded sign hanging outside a public house in Lavenham, Suffolk, England.*

BELOW, RIGHT: *A door at Mezquita Cathedral in Cordoba, Spain, clad with sheets of polished brass.*

standard size of gold leaf is 8.5 x 7.6 cm (3³⁄₈ x 3 in.), available in books of twenty-five sheets. The leaves may be 'loose', placed between rouged sheets, or 'transfer', pressed hard enough to adhere to the sheets. Traditionally, a surface is sealed with gesso or red lead and coated with sticky size. After the size has been allowed to dry a sheet of leaf is taken and laid onto it, an easy process with transfer leaf, but hard with loose leaf as it must be picked up with a soft brush, called a tip, charged with static electricity. Once in position, the leaf is gently pressed down with a pad of cotton wool wrapped in silk or fine cotton.

The greed of the Spanish Conquistadors in the 16th century was fired by the legend of El Dorado, 'the golden man', who was smeared with resin and then dusted with powdered gold every morning, washing it off each evening in Lake Guatavita in Colombia. It is possible to make gold paint in the same way by mixing gold dust with gum arabic. Traditionally, this was stored in mussel shells, giving it the name 'shell gold'.

FOUR

THE ANGEL

EMBELLISHMENT

BITS AND pieces may be attached to the surface of a wooden object, with glue, nails, screws or cord, after its construction has been completed. These additions may be functional or purely decorative, but even purely functional fittings can still be crafted with an aesthetic consideration.

Function and decoration

SOME functional additions may be concealed, but others may be exaggerated for the sake of decorative effect. Hinges, for instance, may be discreetly attached to the back or inside of a sewing box, but an oak church door or a strong box would be more likely to have conspicuous locks and hinges designed to make a positive statement of strength and security. Many fittings, such as hinges, handles, knobs, locks and keyhole escutcheons, can be made as required from timber or leather, but metal fittings are normally acquired ready made.

The addition of extraneous detailing may also serve to emphasize the function of an object. Doors and strong boxes, for example, may be covered with studs that enhance the air of solidity and impregnability while, in contrast, jewelry caskets may be embellished with filigree metalwork and even precious stones. Often the materials chosen to decorate an object are imbued with religious or social associations just as, in former times, the eagle feathers attached to the carved tobacco pipe of a warrior on the Plains of

North America attested to their owner's valour, whereas in much of Asia the use of shiny objects is believed to reflect the adverse effects of the 'evil eye'. The patterns and designs employed can also be charged with significance – animal-horn motifs generally suggest virility as can be seen in the frequent depiction of bulls' horns, carved, painted or even actual horns, on the buildings and property of the Toraja people in Sulawesi.

Materials

ATTACHED with nails, screws or bolts, iron, steel and brass are all used in the manufacture of functional fittings such as locks, hinges and reinforcements as well as studs and decorative motifs. Precious metals, for instance, brass and copper,

ABOVE, FROM LEFT TO RIGHT: *British Arts and Crafts photo frame embellished with tooled pewter and semi-precious stones; mask, from Papua New Guinea, decorated with cowrie shells and hair; Kenyah warrior from Borneo.*

BELOW, LEFT: *Tuareg coffer with silver and bone decoration, Morocco.*

OPPOSITE, CLOCKWISE FROM TOP LEFT: *Moroccan cupboard with silver and bone; brass fittings on a Chinese tigerwood cupboard; Tuareg bowl with brass motifs, Morocco.*

and may therefore be selected for their occult power or for their symbolism. The carnelian, for example, is associated with the heart, courage and friendship and in Central Asia is believed to help preserve eyesight.

The colours and textures of bone, ivory and shell contrast attractively with wood. Introduced to Peru from the Philippines in the 17th century, with the striking technique of *mueble enconchado* the entire surface of large pieces of furniture is covered in mother of pearl held together with fillets of silver or ivory.

have been used to embellish religious ceremonial paraphernalia around the world. At the end of the 19th century the Arts and Crafts movement in Britain was responsible for a profusion of objects embellished with copper or pewter, both of which are soft and easily moulded or beaten into shape.

Leather makes good straps and effective hinges, and it is sometimes employed to completely cover boxes. Hides were also once widely used in the covering of wooden shields.

Normally used in combination with metal settings, gems and semi-precious stones are steeped in esoteric meaning

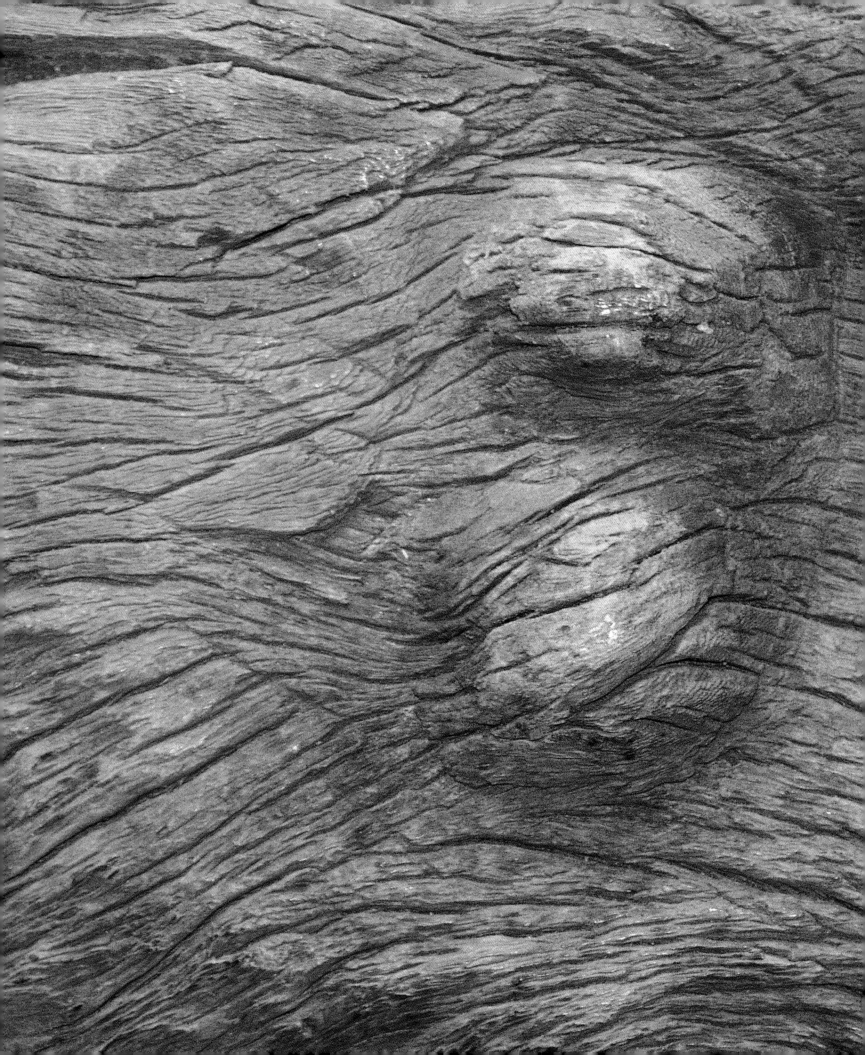

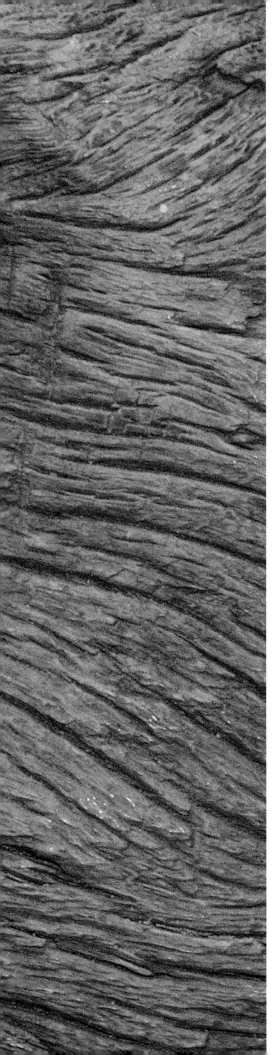

LEFT: *Detail of a Dogon shutter, Mali.*
ABOVE, LEFT: *Chair strung with jute, Rajasthan, India.*
ABOVE, CENTRE: *Stave mug, Romania.*
ABOVE, RIGHT: *Sycamore spoon, Scotland.*
RIGHT: *Replica of an Anglo-Saxon six-board chest.*
BELOW: *Afghan bowl for mixing dough.*

FIVE

WOOD AT WORK

WOOD AT WORK

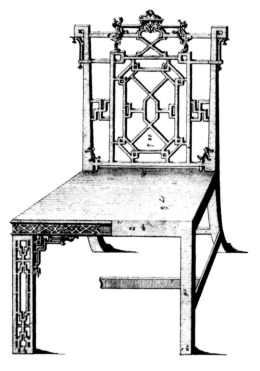

IMBER IS one of the Earth's most widespread resources and has for millennia been exploited as the raw material for countless useful objects – from bridges to buckets, from tables to triremes and from xylophones to yo-yos and zithers. In Britain hand-carved or turned wooden items are collectively known as 'treen', that is 'made from tree'.

The legendary Chinese master craftsman Lu Ban was elevated to the rank of god, but he was depicted as a simple man who would use his skills to solve any problem and then go on his way with no fuss. The names of the craftsmen who have made honest, serviceable objects are generally lost in the mists of time, but in England their legacy survives in the many surnames derived from crafts – carpenter, cooper, wheelwright. Thomas Chippendale, George Hepplewhite and Thomas Sheraton were all 18th-century craftsmen, but they are remembered less for their handiwork than the books of designs they published which established popular styles.

ABOVE, LEFT: *Arts and Crafts biscuit box, England, late 19th century.*

ABOVE, RIGHT: *Illustration of a 'Chinese' chair from 'The Gentleman and Cabinetmaker's Director' by Thomas Chippendale, 1762.*

RIGHT: *The carved handle for a Nepalese butter churn. In mountainous country, where trees are the major resource, all manner of humble tools and utensils are constructed from wood and are often elaborately carved.*

BELOW: *A Macedonian woman doing her washing in a wooden laundry bowl.*

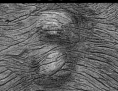

FIVE

AMATEURS AND SPECIALISTS

MANY BEAUTIFUL wooden items are crafted by ordinary people for their own use. Some, like the spoons painstakingly whittled for their sweethearts by ardent Welshmen or the elaborate combs carved by Asante suitors in Ghana, demand a great deal of time and patience, showing the lengths the maker is prepared to go to for the sake of love. Although many woodworking tasks are within the scope of the amateur, others require special tools and a great deal of experience. For instance, the cooper must undergo a long apprenticeship to learn how to manufacture barrels and needs a set of twenty specialist tools including a jointer, heading knife, croze, chiv and beetle.

TOP LEFT; ABOVE, LEFT; AND ABOVE, RIGHT:
*Wooden pattens from the Hindu Kush; sandalwood
'almonds' with Hindu gods, Churu, Rajasthan,
India; door carved by tribal Gonds, Orissa, India.*

BELOW, LEFT; AND RIGHT: *Greenheart gates,
Crinan lock, Scotland; the hull of an old fishing
boat, Mull, Scotland.*

THE RIGHT WOOD FOR THE JOB

THE WOODWORKER is sometimes limited in choice by the types of wood available, but for many tasks while one wood might be totally unsuitable another may be ideal. A tasteless and odourless wood such as sycamore is preferred for carving utensils to be employed with food, while aromatic woods such as sandalwood or camphor are perfect for making drawers, clothes chests and devotional objects. Greenheart wood from Guyana, used to build the gates of the Crinan sea lock in Scotland still functioning two hundred years later, is strong and durable even in sea water, but would make poor mugs as its splinters are poisonous. Apple wood is hard and makes excellent teeth for cogs, but is only available in small sizes. The harder woods can be cut and worked with precision and are used for the best cabinet making (French cabinet makers are known as *ebonistes* after ebony, traditionally their favourite wood). Hardwoods have been traded across the globe for hundreds of years, but they have more often than not been beyond the pocket of the common man who must settle for cheaper local wood. While the English gentleman sat at his rosewood or mahogany desk, the rustic sat at an oak table in a chair of beech or elm.

STICKS

T HE SIMPLEST of all wooden devices is a stick. It can be cut spontaneously to perform any one of a thousand tasks, but can also be easily carried in the hand until needed. People who use sticks on a regular basis tailor them to their needs, making them comfortable to hold and attractive to look at.

Walking sticks

A SIMPLE stick or staff to lean on is a valuable aid for the infirm and for those who must walk for long distances or across difficult terrain, but they have also been employed as an accessory or affectation by gentlemen and dandies. Tall thumb-sticks have a small fork at the top in which the thumb rests, but most, around a metre (3 ft, 3in.) long, are designed to be held in the hand. Some sticks are bent and tied to train them into the right shape while still alive and growing, but most manufactured walking sticks are heated in damp sand and then bent into shape while flexible.

The best British walking sticks require a length cut from coppiced hazel retaining a short piece of the main stem. When inverted, this fork can be shaped into a handle and carved to resemble a favourite animal such as a horse, dog or duck.

Tools

S HARPENED at one end, a stick makes an ideal tool for digging and to this day continues to be one of the major tools of hunter-gatherers such as the Australian Aborigine. Pointed sticks also come in handy as skewers when drying, cooking or serving meat or fish.

Long sticks are an essential piece of equipment for herdsmen, extending their reach by several feet. Long ago European shepherds developed the crook, a stick with a hook on the end which is ideal for catching hold of an errant sheep's leg. The crook might be carved in one piece, but the hook is often made separately from metal or deer antler.

Staff of office

L ARGE or ornate sticks imbue the bearer with an aura of authority and are an essential part of the regalia of kings and religious luminaries and, since the Greek god Hermes first made his snake-entwined caduceus, a rod or staff has often been the symbol of a peacemaker or orator. Carved 'talking sticks' are still used in the Polynesian islands, by the indigenous people of the American North-west and by Maori speechmakers in New Zealand.

ABOVE: Pueblo elder with a silver-topped ebony cane presented by Abraham Lincoln in 1863 as a sign of the recognition of tribal authority, New Mexico, North America.

FAR LEFT: Carved lime spatula used when preparing betel nut, Sepik River, Papua New Guinea.

LEFT: Chinese wood carving of the dome-headed Shou-hsing, the God of Longevity and one of the three Gods of Happiness, usually depicted with a deer, a peach and a gnarled staff.

OPPOSITE, ABOVE, RIGHT: A Hungarian walking stick salesman.

BOTTOM LEFT: THE EGYPTIAN GOD PTAH HOLDING THE 'WAS' STAFF IN HIS HAND, AFTER A PAPYRUS ILLUSTRATION DATING FROM ABOUT 1150 BC.

FIVE

IL MATTO

INCAS PLANTING CORN USING DIGGING STICKS, AFTER A SPANISH 16TH-CENTURY ILLUSTRATION.

'THE FOOL' CARRYING HIS LUGGAGE ON A STICK, AFTER AN ITALIAN TAROT PACK.

Healing and magic

Astaff carved with occult symbols or embellished with magical objects is generally carried by a sorcerer or shaman and used in rituals as a concentrated focus of thaumaturgic power. Smaller sticks decorated with feathers, interwoven 'god's eyes' or paint are stabbed into the Earth by Native Americans, such as the Hopi and Zuni of Arizona and New Mexico or the Huichol of Mexico, to invoke the aid of divine forces in their daily lives. In Colombia sticks about 50 cm (20 in.) long with an animal or human figure carved at one end are held against the stomachs of sick people during the healing ceremonies of the Cholo people.

From left to right: *Batak shaman's magically charged staff, Sumatra; hazel walking stick, Isle of Mull, Scotland; steam-bent furze walking stick; Zulu walking stick; two ball-headed knobkerries or iwisa, South Africa; nail-studded staff of office, West Africa.*

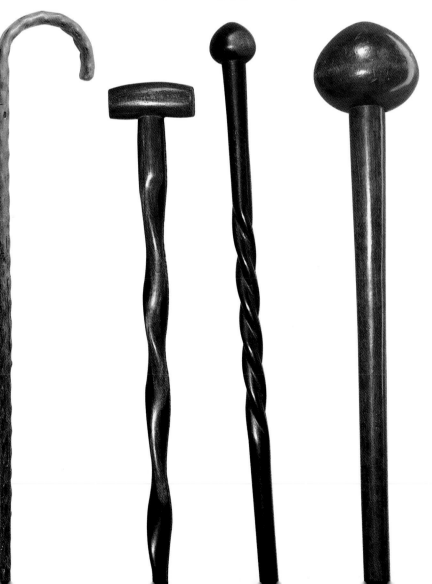

POTS AND BOWLS

Technically speaking, both pots and bowls are rounded containers, a pot is deep rather than broad and a bowl is more or less hemispherical. In practice, the terms are applied to many vessels, including some with lids and many that are cylindrical or even square. In ancient times objects that formed natural cups such as sea shells, gourds, coconuts and even skulls were exploited. As skills developed and crafts evolved people started to exploit available raw materials and to make receptacles from clay, stone, metal and wood.

Carved vessels

The successful hollowing out of a block of wood is most easily accomplished with an adze or a gouge. In the hands of an expert the walls may be quite thin, but often this technique is used to make robust vessels intended for daily use – for kneading dough for bread, for separating the curds and whey while making cheese, or for doing the laundry.

Beautiful, almost spherical, wooden jars, which could have been mistaken for ceramics thrown on a wheel, were made by the Chumash of southern California until the late 19th century. They were cut from green oak and shaped by burning and then rubbing away the charcoal. The finished item was sealed and polished with a mixture of animal fat and red ochre. A few of the surviving specimens have had the rims inlaid with shells and asphaltum.

Many bowls intended for ceremonial use have carved handles or, like the grease dishes of the Haida in British Columbia in Canada, are carved into the shape of an animal or human figure.

Turned containers

To facilitate hollowing, pots and bowls are most often turned when fitted only to the face plate of the lathe, but it is possible to turn a bowl between two centres, leaving a central column that must be cut away with a knife. In their heyday skilled English pole lathe turners could work in this way with a single block

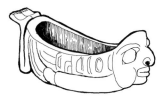

ABOVE: HAIDA FOOD DISH, PROBABLY FOR
GREASE USED AS FLAVOURING, CARVED IN THE
SHAPE OF A MAN, BRITISH COLUMBIA, CANADA.
ON THE AMERICAN NORTH-WEST COAST NEARLY
ALL UTENSILS ARE MADE FROM WOOD OR
BASKETRY AND BOWLS ARE DECORATED
ACCORDING TO THE STATUS OF THE USER.

of elm fixed between between two centres and cut a set of stacking bowls one inside the other. A good turner, such as Japanese craftsmen in Ishikawa whose work is destined for lacquering, can shave a bowl down until the wall is only a few millimetres thick and the wood is translucent.

With the passage of time most wood shrinks, but as the shrinkage is more across the grain than along it – a bowl, originally round, will eventually become oval.

Tableware

In much of the world, although mass-produced metal and ceramic equipment is now the norm, for centuries many of the bowls, dishes and platters used by common people in the preparation and serving of food were made of wood. There was not always much choice, but wood with low odour or taste, such as sycamore, has always been preferred. Although wood usually has a homely charm, in Japan finely turned wooden bowls are sealed

with many coats of lacquer, giving them a delicate appearance as sophisticated as porcelain.

The most popular functional wooden bowl in the modern world has to be the salad bowl. Wood is ideal for this purpose as its natural colours complement the vegetables and the oil in the dressing helps to preserve and polish the wood to a beautiful sheen.

ABOVE: *Heavy pot for storing rice; made from thorn tree wood by Bataks living on Samosir Island in Lake Toba, Sumatra.*

ABOVE, RIGHT: *Turned cylindrical pot painted while on a lathe, Jalalabad, Afghanistan.*

BELOW: *Turned and painted bowl from Khokhloma, Russia, a town famous for its wooden wares.*

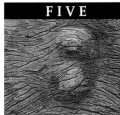

FIVE

OPPOSITE, ABOVE, LEFT, FROM TOP: *Spherical red lacquered pot, Straits Chinese, photographed in Bali; painted 'opium' pot with a small opening, north-west India; 18th-century turned and painted jewelry pots with brass fittings, made in Kerala, southern India.*

OPPOSITE, BOTTOM: *Sycamore salad bowl turned on a lathe on the Isle of Mull, Scotland.*

105

BUCKETS AND BARRELS

ABOVE: *Churning butter, Isle of Wight, England.*

BELOW, LEFT; AND BELOW, RIGHT: *Romanian butter churn made from staves; stave water pail from Jigian, China.*

THERE HAVE been many solutions to the problem of carrying and storing water, including the use of ceramics, skins, gourds and even basketry. At least 5,000 years ago a cunning craftsman realized that, to reduce wastage and create a lighter receptacle, barrels, buckets and drinking vessels could be made from staves, most often of oak or larch, held together with bands of metal or plant fibre. Straight-sided stave buckets are depicted in Egyptian tomb paintings and were later used by the Romans to store wine. The remains of metal bands from barrels were found in England among the treasures of the 7th-century Anglo-Saxon ship burial at Sutton Hoo and also in Scandinavia in the remains of Viking ship burials at Osberg and Gokstad in Norway. It is conceivable that Viking explorers introduced the art of bucket making to the inhabitants of Greenland who were still making beautiful pails decorated with bone and ivory plaques in the last century.

Distribution

TODAY, both buckets and barrels are more often made from plastic or metal, but wood is still preferred for the storage and maturation of wines and spirits because of the taste and aroma imparted by the cask.

Stave tankards continue to be made in Romania, Scandinavia and the Baltic States. They are virtually identical to others discovered during the raising of the wreck of the Mary Rose, an English warship that sank in 1545.

Barrels and buckets are also made and used in the Far East. Fragrant softwoods are employed in the Chinese Province of Jigian to make water pails and 'perfume buckets' which are used to store cosmetics or jewelry.

The cooper's art

THE barrel maker is a specialist craftsman with a set of purpose-made tools. He is known in Britain as a cooper and this is now a common British family name.

Staves of seasoned wood must be trimmed to shape with a drawknife and hollowed on the inside before their edges are smoothed to a bevel by drawing them across the blade of a fixed plane. The barrel can then be 'set up' which involves loosely assembling the staves with an iron

Left; and right: *Giant barrel with a hatch for use outside a restaurant, Singapore; oak wash tub made in Ostra, The Czech Republic, at the Historic Working Village of Bohemian Arts and Crafts.*

Below: *Late 19th-century 'perfume bucket' used to store valuables, Jigian, China. The name refers to the fragrant resinous fir wood from which the bucket is constructed.*

ring around the top and then hammering another ring over them, pulling them into a round shape. At this point a burning brazier is placed inside to heat the staves and make them pliable enough to be bent together and secured by hammering on another ring. To fit the top the end ring is removed, allowing the staves to spring apart sufficiently so that a panel can be fitted into a groove pre cut into the inside of the staves. Finally, the rings, which will have become loose, are replaced with heated ones that will bind the staves tightly together as they shrink.

The word 'barrel' technically refers to a cask with a capacity of 36 gallons, but the techniques are the same for a pin which will hold four and a half gallons, a hogshead holding 54 gallons or a butt holding 108.

FIVE

107

Furniture

I N CULTURES where life is directly linked to the production of food and basic survival, possessions are restricted to a few clothes and essential equipment. People sit on the floor and store their valuables in a limited number of boxes and chests. In pre-colonial New Zealand, for example, the Maori carved beautiful boxes and panels for their buildings, but had no furniture at all. The frantic lifestyle of industrial societies, on the other hand, has generated an excessive quantity of clutter, both psychological and material. With only a few exceptions, wood has always been the preferred material for furniture, although cheap modern items are often constructed from chipboard covered with a thin veneer of wood or synthetic fibre.

LEFT: *A Chinese rosewood side table. In well-to-do Chinese homes chairs and tables are kept at the edge of the room and moved whenever they are required.*

ABOVE: *Elegant Chinese kitchen cupboard. The grilled compartment is said to be for keeping live chickens.*

BELOW, LEFT; AND BELOW, RIGHT: *Tansu chest of drawers with lap jointed drawers, Japan; Czechoslovakian women rocking a baby to sleep in a wooden cradle.*

History

E VEN today, especially in more in-accessible places, there are societies whose lifestyle has changed very little in thousands of years. In many parts of Africa, including Ethiopia, Congo and Zimbabwe, tribal people sleep with their heads raised off the ground by a small, carved wooden headrest almost identical to those found in the tombs of the Ancient Egyptian nobility. In general, African woodworkers continue to employ carving rather than joinery skills in the construction of furniture. Other items used by the Egyptian Pharaohs included string beds with mortise and tenon joints just like the *charpoys* of the Indian sub-continent. The Egyptians also made tables and chairs similar to those we use today, but the chest of drawers did not appear in Europe until Roman times.

Jointed furniture

F RAME construction is an economical use of materials and relies on a rigid carcass clad in thinner sheets of wood. Although the skin may be of expensive hardwood, the hidden framework may be jointed together from cheaper timber. The entire structure of open forms where the structural components are exposed must be constructed from decent material.

The greatest leap forward in European furniture construction occurred in the 17th century when the opening up of world

FIVE

trade routes made a large selection of close-grained hardwoods available to craftsmen. This led to the golden age of cabinet making spearheaded by the French *ebonistes*. In China, however, where there was a readily available source of quality hardwoods such as *Hua-li mu* and *Huang-hua-li*, both types of rosewood, complex joinery techniques eschewing the use of nails or glue had been employed since 400 BC and professional cabinet makers had been producing elegant household furniture since the time of the Han Dynasty (206 BC–AD 221).

Solid furniture

In the Amazon rain forest, the jungles of Central Africa, the islands of the Pacific and other places where timber is easily available, joinery was almost unknown before colonial times and the few pieces of furniture were limited to headrests, stools and backrests fashioned from solid blocks. Headrests were common, not only to keep dirt or insects out of the hair and ears, but to safeguard the sanctity of the head. Some of these items exploited the natural growth of roots or branches, while others were carved to shape, often laboriously removing a great deal of waste wood.

ABOVE, LEFT; AND ABOVE, RIGHT: *Wooden chest with carved drawer fronts used by an apothecary in Hyderabad, India for storing medicaments and herbs; tall cupboard with carved panels, north-west India. The pierced doors at the bottom show the influence of Mughal stone and wood jali work.*

RIGHT: *Barber and customer seated on a rope-strung bed or charpoy in India. This design, incorporating stretchers slotted into mortises in the legs, was used to build beds in Ancient Egypt.*

Boxes and chests

MOST OFTEN rectangular, boxes and chests have been used as containers for everything from cosmetics and corn to fish and finery. When covered by a lid, the contents are protected from contamination and prying eyes – the box has become a symbol of secrecy and confinement. According to the Greeks of Classical times, the first woman, Pandora, was unable to suppress her curiosity and opened the sealed box inside which the gods had concealed the spirits and demons of grief, disease, vice, crime and all the pain and suffering from which mankind had, until then, been protected. Fortunately for the stricken Pandora the final spirit in the box was hope. In British Columbia in Canada, the Haida tell how the great trickster, Raven, brought light into the world, stealing it from an old man who kept it hidden in a box inside a box inside a box inside a box...

ABOVE: *A Maori treasure box, carved from totara wood, for storing feathers worn in the hair. Rectangular boxes are usually known as* papahou *and oval ones are called* wakahuia.

ABOVE, RIGHT: *The side of a Coast Tsimshian kerf-bent box, British Columbia, Canada.*

BELOW, LEFT: *Solid six-plank chest made from Himalayan cedar in Nuristan, a mountainous region in eastern Afghanistan.*

BELOW, RIGHT: *A panelled chest made for the home of a Rabari herdsman in Kutch, Gujarat, India.*

Solid boxes

IN parts of the world where there is a super abundance of timber and joinery has not evolved as much as carving, boxes may be made from a solid piece of wood. Boxes used to store special items may be carved into fanciful zoomorphic or anthropomorphic shapes or decorated with ornate patterns. In New Zealand Maori carved boxes range from *papahou* and *wakahuia* used to store the feathers worn in the hair, decorated with fine swirling patterns, to the pot-bellied, human-shaped containers in which the inhabitants of the Northland used to store the bones of their dead.

The six-plank chest

THE simplest form of box or chest is made from six boards, one for each side, one for the top and one for the bottom. Invented thousands of years ago, the six-plank chest was used by the people of Ancient Egypt, was one of the most widely used items of furniture in Europe until the Middle Ages and is still made today in the mountains of Pakistan and Afghanistan. By extending the two end planks down the whole structure can be raised, lifting the bottom away from dirt and damp. Early versions were crudely nailed or pegged together. Saxon and Viking chests were reinforced with bands of metal or leather, but most versions have been assembled using grooves or mortises and have a lid hinged by pegs on the back corners set into holes drilled into the back of the end boards.

The six-plank method has also been used in the manufacture of chairs and beds.

Panelled chests

THE grain of the front and back panels of six-plank chests ran horizontally and was inclined to split. The clamp-fronted chest circumvented this problem by constructing the front and back from three boards joined by tenons or tongue and groove joints, only the centre panel running horizontally. From the 16th century panelled chests became common. They consisted of a framework with the panels set loosely into grooves so that they could swell or shrink without the danger of splitting.

Treasure chests

ALL over the world boxes for the storage of valuables are frequently made with a domed or pyramidal lid. Examples include Indian dowry boxes and 14th-century European money chests with their rounded lids carved from a solid slab of wood.

ABOVE, LEFT: GERMAN-AMERICAN PAINTED PINE MARRIAGE CHEST, PENNSYLVANIA, NORTH AMERICA, 18TH CENTURY.

ABOVE: *Iranian pen box decorated with painting and end-grain marquetry.*

RIGHT: *Trinket box, from Kholui, decorated with a scene from a Russian folk tale.*

BELOW; AND BOTTOM: *Tuareg jewelry coffer decorated with silver and dyed camel bone, Morocco; a dowry box made to hold a bride's jewelry, Rajasthan, India. Indian boxes for valuables frequently have a pitched or domed lid.*

FIVE

STONE CARVING
IN PERSEPOLIS, IRAN,
SHOWING KING
DARIUS SEATED
ON A CHAIR
WITH TURNED
COMPONENTS.

CHAIRS

IN MOST cultures it is customary to rest on some form of seat raised off the cold, dirty ground, and the act of sitting or rising becomes much less demanding on the leg muscles. To sit higher than anyone else is the prerogative of those with the highest status and the thrones of the most elevated can be sumptuous affairs. The feet of kings are often kept clear of the ground on a stool, lest the spiritual power with which they are imbued be allowed to soak into the ground. Until the early Middle Ages the feet of Welsh princes were kept elevated in the lap of a royal foot holder.

Solid seats

THE simplest seating may be no more than a chunk of log. With the attention of an adze, knife or chisels the seat can be shaped to fit the bottom and the overall form carved to suit local styles and taste. In West Africa the art of stool carving reached its zenith with the *nkonnua dwa* stools of the Asante chief, the Asantehene. These may be inlaid with gold and silver or covered with gold leaf but, like most other African stools, are carved from a solid block of wood. Similar stools were used by all and sundry, but certain designs, such as leopards and elephants, were reserved for the chieftain's use alone.

The Klismos chair

CRAFTSMEN had used sophisticated joinery techniques in Dynastic Egypt to construct chairs with elegant legs and backs, but the *klismos* chair produced in Greece during the 5th century BC excelled these. Egyptian chairs were in essence stools with a backrest fitted on top, but the *klismos* was built with sweeping back legs that rose right up to support the backrest. Although this style virtually disappeared in Europe for more than 1,000 years after the fall of the Roman Empire it was the model for the designs of the master cabinet makers of the 17th and 18th centuries. In China chairs built on the same principle have been produced with little interruption since the 4th century BC.

Planks and panels

FURNITURE construction in Europe in the Dark and Middle Ages followed the

ABOVE, LEFT: *Heavy chair carved from a single piece of wood by the Gurage or Jimma, Ethiopia.*

ABOVE: *A wooden throne carved in one piece, but imitating jointed furniture. The figures represent tutelary spirits and culture heroes; Chokwe, Angola.*

LEFT: *Low-seated walnut chair with turned legs and carved back of a type common in the Hindu Kush. The seat is strung with strips of interlaced rawhide, Swat Valley, Pakistan.*

same evolutionary path as the chest. By simply making the back higher, a chest could be used as a chair or settle. The same style of box construction could also be employed to build benches, beds and cradles. Early examples were constructed from planks, while later styles used panelling in a frame. By the 16th century furniture makers had begun to omit the panelling to produce a lighter, less cumbersome structure.

Stick chairs

In existence for thousands of years, the stick chair is basically a stool with 'sticks' for legs slotted into the bottom of the seat and supports for the back and arm rests slotted into the top. This is not a strong form of construction and so a system of 'rails' is employed, slotted horizontally between the legs to keep the structure rigid. Stick chairs were often made by woodland craftsmen from green wood to supply the needs of the local community and continue to be popular in the West in modern country-style kitchens.

ABOVE: *Replica of an Anglo-Saxon chair with dowelled mortise and tenon joints, West Stow Anglo-Saxon Village in Suffolk, England.*

LEFT: *A traditional rush-seated, rail-back chair with turned legs and stretchers made from green ash by John Richardson.*

BELOW: *An imaginative assortment of variations on the basic rush-seated chair, Andalucia, Spain.*

TOP; AND ABOVE: *Pine garden chair held together with wedged tenons, Norfolk, England; Chinese chair made from huang hua li. To withstand changes of temperature and humidity the framework of these chairs is held together without glue, nails or pegs, relying solely on tight fitting joints.*

IMPLEMENTS AND APPARATUS

Wᴛʜ ʀᴀʀᴇ exceptions, such as the Inuit in the Arctic who fashion implements from bone or horn, most peoples employ a huge array of tools and utensils made from wood.

In the home

Iɴ a wooded environment virtually anything can be made from timber and many craftsmen have specialized in making brooms, brushes, rakes, locks and latches.

Stairs and ladders provide access to places out of reach. Primitive steps can easily be made by leaning up a tree trunk with evenly spaced branches or by cutting footholds into a log. Wooden ladders

usually have round rungs socketed into the uprights, whereas stairs have flat treads secured with housing joints.

Items not stored in furniture may be hung, ready to hand, from hooks, hangers, racks or rails, sometimes exploiting natural forks in timber and sometimes shaped as required. To keep floor space clear, American Shaker rooms were fitted with a peg rail from which anything from coats and clocks to chairs and candle holders could be hung.

Many wooden utensils are found in the kitchen and many wooden devices are employed in the manufacture and maintenance of textiles.

Trades and crafts

Sᴘᴇᴄɪᴀʟɪᴢᴇᴅ wooden tools are required not only by wood workers, but by professionals working with many other materials. The cobbler shapes and sews his shoes and boots on a wooden last,

while hat and glove makers stretch their products on wooden moulds. The plumber bends and moulds sheets of lead with wood shaped into smooth blocks and cones. Millers and brewers used wooden spades to shovel grain off a wooden floor into wooden pots or boxes of a measured capacity, or into wooden hoppers and funnels. The traditional post mill is almost completely built from timber with a wooden frame, wooden cladding and wooden machinery. The picturesque thatching on the roofs of cottages of rural England is achieved with a small selection of metal-edged tools and a number of wooden implements. The thatcher carries his reed or straw up his ladder with a yoke made from forked branches, rakes it into place and then dresses it with a wooden comb or legget. Hazel rods and spars, bent double, are used to hold the straw in place and the final decoration of ridge and eaves employs split hazel 'liggers' and cross rods pegged down with more spars. In Polynesia barkcloth is battered out with a wooden mallet, while in West Africa and South America pottery is beaten into shape with a wooden paddle.

In the fields

THE digging stick, still employed by Australian Aboriginals and many other hunter-gatherer societies, was the first tool used to work the soil and short-pointed 'dibbers' remain part of the stock in trade of modern gardeners for planting bulbs or beans. Many agricultural implements, such as pitchforks, were sometimes made from naturally forked timber, but most continue to be made with handles of shock-absorbent woods such as ash or hickory. During the Middle Ages spades for digging were often entirely of wood with just the cutting edge made of metal.

Breaking the soil with a plough was a much more efficient way of cultivating land and 6,000 years ago teams of animals were already being employed to haul them. By using a yoke, the load could be placed on the animals' shoulders, making the optimum use of their strength. Later inventions included the harrow and the wagon, both made from wood.

RIGHT; AND FAR RIGHT: *Hook carved from walnut attached to the beams of a house in Nuristan, Afghanistan; English metal-tipped, ash gardener's dibber for making holes in the soil.*

OPPOSITE, TOP LEFT: *Clothes brush; bears are common in Swiss and southern German woodcarving.*

OPPOSITE, TOP RIGHT; OPPOSITE, CENTRE LEFT; AND OPPOSITE, BOTTOM: *Women of the White Karen outside a building accessed with a ladder cut from logs, Myanmar; wooden door latch at West Stow Anglo-Saxon Village, Suffolk, England; betel-nut mortar and a lamp fuelled with pig fat, Sepik River area, Papua New Guinea.*

ABOVE, LEFT; AND TOP RIGHT: *Carved cedar wood animal yoke from the Swat valley, Pakistan; cultivating land with a wooden plough in the French Alps a hundred years ago.*

BELOW, LEFT; AND BELOW, RIGHT: *Digging with a hinged hoe, Nigeria; Saxted Green windmill, Suffolk, England.*

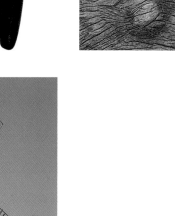

FIVE

Wood and food

T HE GATHERING, harvesting and preparing of foodstuffs often involves a number
of wooden implements and utensils, varying from one region to another
according to the nature of the cuisine.

NEAR LEFT: *Ainu women pounding grain in a
wooden mortar, Hokkaido, Japan.*

Preparation

O NCE collected with rakes and
pitchforks, grains and pulses need
careful sorting to remove stones and dirt.
This is most often achieved with sieves and
riddles with a wire or split-cane mesh set
in a bentwood frame. Grains then need to
be threshed, either with a hinged wooden
flail or by treading underfoot, and then
winnowed to separate the chaff. This
involves tossing the grain into the air with
a basket or shovel so that the wind can
blow away the lighter husks. Making flour
or powder from grain, beans or vegetables
may involve a mill or can be accomplished
at home using a pestle and mortar.
Querns (miniature hand-powered mills)
are generally stone, but in the Himalayas
wooden querns are used to grind spices.

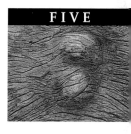

Other vegetables such as manioc, a staple food in tropical America, may be broken down with a large wooden grater, while in Japan ginger is grated on a bamboo device.

The chopping of both meat and vegetables usually takes place on a wooden board. In the Chinese kitchen this may be little more than a section of log strong enough to stand the vigorous hacking of carcasses with a large cleaver. Boards are also used for rolling out pastry such as Turkish baklava and the dough for breads such as Indian chapattis. The same dough may well have been kneaded in a wooden tub. In Russia one side of the board is used for chopping and the other, gaily painted, is displayed when not in use.

Dairy products, made from milk traditionally carried in wooden pails, require sieving and straining and some of the oldest artefacts found in Scottish Iron Age lake dwellings were alder bowls with holes in the bottom for this purpose.

OPPOSITE, BELOW, LEFT: *European wooden kitchen implements – bread board, box wood salt spoon, beech lemon reamer, rolling pin, Scottish spirtle for stirring porridge.*

OPPOSITE, BELOW, RIGHT: *Nepalese wooden quern for grinding spices.*

ABOVE, LEFT; AND ABOVE, RIGHT: *German bread board; wooden milk pots from Uganda, possibly Tutsi.*

LEFT: *Coffee bean mortar, Yemen.*

In some regions milk is churned into butter or cheese in an animal skin bag, but in Europe it is more common to use a wooden vessel of stave construction.

Cooking

T HE fire itself is usually of logs or charcoal and even today in the West the aromatic smell of smoke from woods such as oak is used to preserve and flavour meat, fish and cheese. Over the flames food may be grilled on skewers, a technique popular for cooking salmon in the American Northwest and in Indonesia for cooking satay. A distinctive technique in Chinese cooking is the steaming of dim sum, little packages of vegetables, meat or fish, in bentwood bamboo steamers stacked over water boiling in a wok. The indigenous peoples of British Columbia and Alaska traditionally cook in their beautiful bent-wood boxes, filling them with water which is heated by dropping in red-hot stones.

Serving

W OODEN bowls were once the crockery of common people the world over, accompanied by wooden mugs and wooden spoons, forks or chopsticks. Wooden mats or trivets may protect a table from being scorched by hot pans, but in medieval England slabs of meat were actually served on a wooden plank or 'trencher', giving those with a hearty appetite the epithet 'trencherman'. In Japan sushi and sashimi dishes may be served on a board.

SPOONS

Used in the preparation, serving and eating of food the world over, the spoon has evolved in many forms. In warmer regions simple, but effective, spoons are often made from natural objects such as coconuts and gourds that need very little shaping to fulfil their function, while in cooler forested climes wood was the main option, preferably a wood that did not have a strong taste or smell.

There was a time when everyone carried their own eating implements with them. In the East this was usually a knife, bowl and chopsticks, but in Europe, Africa and the Americas it was predominantly a knife and spoon. The rich might carry spoons made from silver or even gold, but horn or wood were much more common among the masses.

Spoons, scoops and ladles

Basically a bowl with a handle, many spoons are tailor made for a specific purpose. In the Hindu Kush in Afghanistan and Pakistan, where virtually all wood is decorated with carving, they make imaginatively decorated medicine spoons as well as large ladles for serving food. In Europe, for agriculture and industry, large scoops are constructed, sometimes by turning, for doling out grain, pulses or powders, some large enough to blur the distinction between spoon and shovel. The Russian town of Khokhloma, to the east of Moscow, is famous for bowls, spoons and ladles, beautifully painted with striking floral motifs in red, black and gold.

In Asia and parts of Africa stirring may be carried out with a 'paddle' shaped like a spoon, but only hollowed very slightly, if at all.

Ceremonial spoons

Spoons receive more carving and decoration than most other domestic utensils. They are a symbol of the woman's role as the provider of food and therefore her authority at the hearth where meals and hospitality are distributed. Among the Dan people of Liberia and the Ivory Coast eminent women who preside over lavish feasts possess specially carved spoons called *wakemia* or *wunkirmian* decorated with a handle carved into

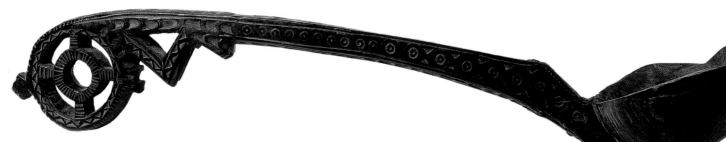

OPPOSITE, LEFT; OPPOSITE, RIGHT; AND
OPPOSITE, BOTTOM: *Dan grain scoop with the
handle carved into a woman's head, Ivory Coast;
Toraja ceremonial spoon used at weddings,
funerals and special occasions, Sulawesi,
Indonesia; ladle with elaborately carved
handle from Nuristan, Afghanistan.*

a woman's head. These serve as a symbol
of the importance of the female role in
society and the women bear the title
wakede or *wunkirle* which means 'spoon
holder'. It is only when a woman is visited
in a dream by the spirit that inhabits such
a spoon that she may take on these duties.

The most famous type of British spoon
is painstakingly carved, particularly in
Wales, by young men demonstrating
their devotion to their sweethearts. These
spoons are usually completely impractical
as they are finely carved with delicate
chains and trapped rolling balls all carved
from a single piece of wood.

Carving a spoon

SPOONS were once made in their
hundreds by craftsmen working in
European woods. The first task was to split
a sycamore log about 30 cm (1 foot) long
into three pieces, each of which was then
trimmed roughly into shape with an axe.
Next the bowl was hollowed out with a
bent knife or spoon-bent gouge and finally
the back was shaped and smoothed using
a spoke-shave held in one hand while the
other steadied the wood. Larger ladles
were hollowed out with a small adze.

ABOVE, FROM TOP TO BOTTOM: *A pair of
Moroccan spoons used for serving soup in the
Jemaa el Fna market, Marrakesh; spoon with
twisted handle made by a member of the Kamba
tribe at the Makindu craftwork cooperative,
Kenya; two painted spoons from Khokhloma,
Russia; coconut-shell spoon, from Thailand,
with a carved handle.*

BELOW: *Hardwood ladle, from the Indonesian
island of Lombok, inlaid with pieces of shell.
The bowl of the ladle is carved into the shape
of a human head with an open mouth. The end
of the handle is a chain, a tricky carving process
which can also be seen on love spoons made
in Wales.*

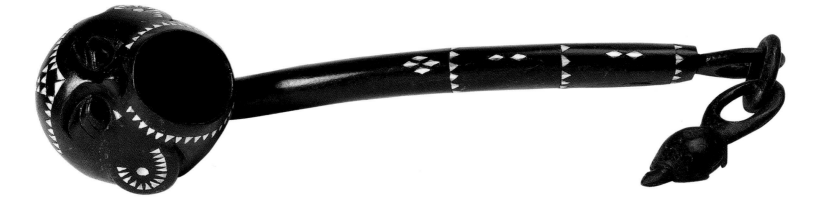

WOOD AND TEXTILES

THE POLYNESIAN settlers of Pacific islands carried with them no source of fibre for making cloth but, with typical resourcefulness, discovered that the inner bark of the paper mulberry tree could be stripped off and beaten out into large sheets that could be wrapped around the body. Barkcloth is also made in South-East Asia, Central Africa and Latin America. Other peoples have woven cloth from the shredded bark of local trees – the Ainu of northern Japan use elm bark and the tribes of the American North-west exploit the plentiful stocks of cedar. In lands with a source of fibres such as wool, cotton or silk wood plays an important part in the preparation of fibres and the manufacture of textiles.

The preparation of fibres

WITH the exception of filaments of silk, most natural fibres are short and need to be spun into yarn. Before it can be spun, wool must be combed or carded so that all the fibres lie in the same direction and this is easily accomplished with a wooden bat covered with tiny spikes, sometimes metal or sometimes made from sections of thorny plants such as the teasel. Cotton must be crushed in a wooden mangle called a gin to crack the seeds and remove impurities before being fluffed up by the vibrations of a bow struck with a mallet. Finally, the fibres can be twisted into yarn. The ancient technique is to attach fibres to a drop spindle weighted with a whorl which is given a twist with the fingers before being allowed to drop slowly to the ground, stretching out the twisting fibres as it falls. The spinning wheel is a mechanized version of the same process, with the turning wheel providing the tension.

made from plastic or metal, were formerly made from bone or wood.

Laundry

ONCE in use, textiles become soiled and need regular cleaning. Down by the river laundry may be beaten with a special bat called a 'calender', while in the wash house it would be rubbed vigorously on a washboard or agitated with a 'posser', a devise resembling a stool on a pole. Washed and rinsed wet laundry is still, even in the modern industrial world, hung on a washing line with clothes pegs, once sold from door to door by gypsies.

LEFT: *Navajo woman using a simple vertical loom, Arizona, North America.*

BELOW, RIGHT: *A foot-powered spinning wheel, China.*

Weaving

LOOMS come in many styles and sizes, but all are designed to make an opening or shed between the warp fibres through which the weft can be passed. The frame of the loom, the shuttle carrying the yarn, the shed sticks, heddles and pulleys that open the shed, the comb and sword used to beat the work tight are all traditionally made of wood.

Making textiles without a loom

THERE are a large number of techniques for making textiles which do not require a loom. Some, such as sprang or twining, are most easily carried out when the work is kept taut on a wooden frame. Others, such as netting, tatting or lace making, require the use of long strands of fibre and to prevent these getting tangled they are wound onto a shuttle or bobbin. The popular crafts of knitting and crochet demand the use of needles and hooks to manipulate the yarn and these, now often

OPPOSITE, RIGHT; OPPOSITE, LEFT; AND OPPOSITE, INSET: *Carved pulley for lifting the heddles on a loom, Cameroon; painted cloth made from a sheet of bark beaten with wooden mallets, Tonga; Samoan girls wearing barkcloth.*

FIVE

LEFT: CHIP-CARVED CALENDER, HUNGARY, 1829.

TECHNOLOGY AND MECHANICS

Wᴏᴏᴅ ᴡᴀꜱ the main material for the construction of mechanical devices from before the invention of the wheel until the refinement of metal-working techniques in the Industrial Revolution when metal became a viable affordable alternative. Even then in Britain in the 18th century the early steam engines designed by Thomas Newcomen and James Watt used beams made from large baulks of timber.

The lever

Uꜱɪɴɢ a pole to shift a heavy weight amplifies the amount of force that can be exerted. The lever is fixed at one point, the fulcrum, near the load and the force is exerted as far away as possible for maximum effect. The Greek genius, Archimedes, claimed that if he had a long enough lever and a place to stand he could move the Earth. This simple principle has been employed for countless purposes including cracking nuts, lifting water into irrigation ditches, known in Egypt as a *shaduf*, and shifting the stones with which the pyramids were built.

The wheel

Tʜᴇʀᴇ is no evidence of precisely when the wheel was invented, although it was in use for moving wagons at least 6,000 years ago. A development of the wooden roller, the first wheels were simply cut

across the width of a tree trunk and were as inefficient as they were heavy, wearing down quickly as the tree's softer sapwood was at the rim. Images dating from 3250 ʙᴄ show how the Sumerians had begun to make wheels from planks, so they were able to put the harder heartwood at the rim. Lighter, spoked wheels appeared in Iran in around 2000 ʙᴄ. Transport, however, was not the only use to which the wheel was put – it had been employed in Egypt for throwing clay pots long before it was used on carts.

Many devices incorporate wheels to reduce friction or transfer drive power. One of the simplest, but most useful, is the pulley – basically a small wheel fitted in a wooden block. The winch or windlass is another form of wheel used to lift or pull by turning a central hub with a rope wrapped around it. Like the lever, the larger the wheel, the greater the force transmitted. Using a windlass 3 metres (10 feet) across, like the one used by the Normans in Peterborough Cathedral in England, a man is able to lift a load ten times his own body weight.

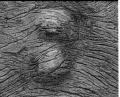

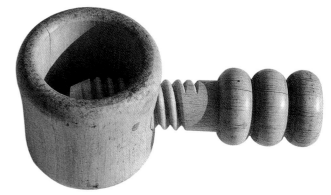

LEFT: *A gin used to remove the seeds from bolls of cotton, Timor. The handle turns rollers that are meshed with spiral worm gears.*

ABOVE: *Nutcracker employing a screw to exert pressure on a nut placed in the cup.*

BELOW, LEFT: *The wheel of the watermill in Killin at the head of Loch Tay, Scotland. With a system of gears and cogs the wheel turns the millstones that are used to grind the flour for the inhabitants of Breadalbane.*

BELOW: *Egyptian carpenter making an Archimedes screw, a simple but effective device for raising water to a higher level for irrigation. The completed screw is cased in a wooden cylinder.*

OPPOSITE, ABOVE, RIGHT; CENTRE; BELOW, LEFT; AND BELOW, RIGHT: *Yugoslavian nutcracker; German nutcracker with jaws operated by a lever in his back; massage rollers; solid cart wheel, California, North America.*

Cogs and gears

B Y fitting teeth into the rims of wheels to make cogs, it is possible to use one to turn another. The teeth of the huge cogs in windmills are often made by slotting teeth of hardwood, such as apple, into mortises in the circumference. When the cogs are of different sizes the speed of their revolutions can be increased or slowed down. This gearing can be used for very precise control and in Germany the Black Forest clocks of the 17th century had movements entirely made from wood. For more than 1,000 years the cumbersome cogs of mills have been used to transfer the energy produced by a wheel turned by water or plodding animals or a sail turned by wind and harness it to provide the power to drive grindstones, bellows, pumps or the driveshafts for machinery.

When a shaped handle is fitted onto a cylinder with a spiral groove and turned it will move up or down the cylinder. This principle was applied to create the wine press in Greece during the 4th century BC and 2,000 years later, with few modifications, the first printing presses.

HUNTING AND FIGHTING

THE OLDEST known wooden artefact is a yew spear, found in England, which dates from about 250,000 years ago. Since then wood has been used in the manufacture of all kinds of arms, some improved with a sharp blade made from flint or metal, but many relying solely on the different properties of the wood itself, its workability, density, flexibility or shock absorbency. Wooden swords were not only children's toys, but were used in practice by the Romans and Japanese Samurai as they are safer than metal. Shields, sometimes covered with metal or hide, are often made from wood. Wooden armour is less common, but peoples of the west coast of North America constructed quite effective suits from rods or slats of cedar and other woods. Wood is also used the world over for the manufacture of the handles and sheaths of weapons.

ABOVE: *Aruac Indians with blowpipe and bow, Brazil.*

BELOW, LEFT; AND BELOW, RIGHT: *Maori with* taiaha *issuing a formal challenge, New Zealand; finely carved Tongan fighting clubs.*

Clubs

SIMPLE but effective, the wooden club is made from dense hardwood, such as Fijian ironwood, *Intsia bijuga*, and may be one- or two-handed. In the Pacific the club was considered the most honourable weapon as it was employed in close hand-to-hand fighting and not in killing from a safe distance. The business end varies in shape and may resemble the ball heads popular among the Native Americans of the eastern woodlands of North America, the saw-toothed edges of Samoa or the wedge found in Amazonia. Those with a large spike on one side were designed to deliver the *coup de grâce*.

Sticks and staffs

A STICK cut from handy vegetation makes a serviceable impromptu two-ended weapon, as does a walking stick or carrying pole, and so martial arts involving sophisticated techniques of stick fighting are largely associated with common folk.

In medieval England contests were popular between exponents of the 1.8 metre (6 ft) quarter staff, while in Japan stick fighting developed into the art of *bojitsu*. One of the classic Maori weapons is the *taiaha*, a beautifully carved staff with a dog-hair tassel fastened near one end.

Projectile weapons

THE spear, with a point of metal, flint or hardened wood, is the archetypal hurled weapon and was once common

everywhere except in the Pacific. Various devices have been developed to increase the power of a spear throw. The Egyptians, Romans and Greeks all wrapped a cord around the butt to achieve this, but in Australasia and the Americas rigid spear throwers are made from wood or bone. These, like the Australian *woomera* and Aztec *atlatl*, are usually wooden sticks with a groove or hook at the rear to fit the butt of the spear, effectively lengthening the thrower's arm by an extra joint.

Throwing sticks have been in use since Egyptian times all over the world. The most celebrated is the boomerang used by Australian Aborigines as a serious hunting weapon, the returning version being no more than a toy.

Darts or arrows may be fired through a blowpipe or with a bow. The compound bow is made by laminating several pieces of wood which makes it flexible, while the self-bow is made from a single piece and depends on the natural lamination of sapwood and heartwood.

LEFT: *Solid wood war shield with carved and painted decoration from Motumotu village, Papua New Guinea (76 cm, 30 in., high).*

BELOW: *Knife with wavy blade carried by farmers on the Indonesian island of Lombok, east of Bali. Both the handle and sheath are made of wood.*

ABOVE: *Afghan flintlock musket, jezail, inlaid with mother of pearl. The firing mechanism was made in England, but the rest of the weapon was made to measure.*

BELOW: *Weapons used by Australian aboriginal peoples. On the left are two boomerangs for hunting. Unlike the famous boomerang that returns to your hand, these are serious implements intended for killing, not play. On the right is a club made from red gum wood decorated with ochre and used by the Wirad Juri tribe.*

FIVE

125

BUILDINGS

THE FIRST buildings that mankind constructed were little more than a roof made from leaves, thatch or hide over a wooden frame. Since then walls and floors have been constructed in many ways using a huge range of materials, but even today the frame of a roof is still generally made from wood.

Log cabins

THE log cabin, hewn from the trees of virgin forest, is a potent symbol of the lusty American pioneer. The technique, employing rudimentary, interlocking, notched joints, was brought by settlers from Germany and Scandinavia where it had been in use since before Roman times. Log construction was also common in Eastern Europe for building both houses and churches, most notably the Church of the Transfiguration at Khizi in northern Russia. This is a fairy tale structure built in 1714 with twenty-two onion-shaped domes.

Until the devastation caused by the Black Death in the 14th century, in Norway logs were sometimes split lengthwise into staves, which were stuck upright into the ground to form the main structural components of buildings. Twenty-five towering stave churches with their shingled roofs survive to this day.

Frame buildings

TIMBER-FRAMED buildings are found throughout the world. Saxon cruck-framed houses, Tudor half-timbered buildings, Fijian bures and the boat-shaped communal houses of Sumatra and Sulawesi are included in this category, but they are in essence all rigid boxes made from substantial timbers that support a roof. The spaces between the timbers have been variously covered or filled with wattle and daub, brick, bamboo matting or wooden planks.

Wooden cladding

KNOWN as weatherboarding in England and clapboarding in North America, the cladding of a frame with overlapping planks is a quick and effective covering for a frame building. This method was taken by the British to New Zealand, New England and other colonies, but plank construction had already been in use for

centuries in the New World by the indigenous peoples of California, British Columbia and the Woodlands of the North-east.

Planks can also be used to cover a roof, but in the forests of northern Europe and North America they have often been cut into tile-shaped shingles. These are easily replaced and can, if required, be used to cover curved surfaces such as the domes of Khizi.

Interiors

WALLS, ceilings, floors, fireplace surrounds and staircases are commonly made of wood and have often been embellished with carving. Structural elements such as brackets, corbels, columns and struts may be elaborately decorated to such an extent that their actual function is forgotten. In England the most boisterous interior woodwork was produced during the Stuart period (1603–1714).

OPPOSITE, LEFT; AND OPPOSITE, ABOVE, RIGHT: *Decorative carved figure on the roof of a building in Sumba, Indonesia; coconut wood skeleton of a shelter in Samoa in the style of a traditional* fale.

OPPOSITE, CENTRE RIGHT; AND OPPOSITE, BOTTOM: *Small tipi made of lashed lodge pole pines covered in buffalo hide belonging to Stoney Indians, Canada; traditional Navajo hogan made from interlocking logs, Canyon de Chelly, Arizona, North America.*

TOP LEFT: *Wooden pagoda at the Temple of Heavenly Happiness, Singapore.*

TOP RIGHT: *One of the many 15th- and 16th-century oak-framed buildings in the Suffolk town of Lavenham, England.*

ABOVE, LEFT: *Stave church,* stavekirke, *built from wooden planks, Borgund, Norway.*

ABOVE, RIGHT: *The Old Custom House in Russell, formerly the capital of New Zealand. This colonial-style timber-clad building, erected in the 1860s, is typical of many in New Zealand and Australia.*

BOTTOM RIGHT: *A traditional wooden house on stilts, providing shade beneath, Cha Am, Thailand.*

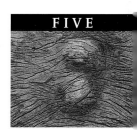

FIVE

Doors

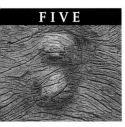

ABOVE: *Beautifully painted doorway in the Norbu Lingka Palace, Lhasa, Tibet.*

BELOW, FROM LEFT TO RIGHT: *Chinese door guardian, Fuk Tak Chi Temple, Singapore; gilded temple door, Chiang Mai, Thailand; elaborately carved doorway, Zanzibar; carved, painted and gilded doorway at the Neka Palace, Ubud, Bali.*

D RENCHED IN symbolism, a doorway is a place of transition, both entrance and exit, a door is a barrier that limits access. On a material level, the transition is between public and private, while on a more arcane level the access is between life and death, between the known and the unknown, between different levels of consciousness. The Celtic word for oak is duir which is also the root for the words door and druid, woodland mystics whose preoccupation was the relation between this world and the other. Some doors are small, providing access into a small nook or cupboard, but others may be massive like the gates to the cities of Mesopotamia.

Security

T HE doorway is seen as a place of both physical and spiritual danger and in many cultures the door and its frame are carved or decorated with signs and sigils or guardian spirits. In India the figure of the god Ganesh is carved over doors, in the Roman world it was the two-headed god Janus, while in Bali the leering face is that of the monstrous Bhoma. In China, where most doors have two leaves, it was traditional to decorate each with the image of one of the heavily armed door gods whose task was to frighten away evil spirits. European superstition would have us believe that neither vampires nor witches can cross a threshold uninvited.

Stout timbers and strong locks provide protection of a physical kind, to keep out unwanted visitors, both human and animal. Additional magical aid may be invoked, as is the case in Mali where the doors of Dogon granaries may incorporate the carving of snakes to deter rats.

The door frame

T HE jambs, vertical members at the sides of the door frame, support a horizontal lintel across the top. When the lintel is load bearing it consists of a stout beam fitted into the structure of the building. Some doorways also have a cross piece at the base. This was used in European barns to prevent grain being lost

the use of sophisticated joinery, usually mortise and tenon or bridle joints, to build a framework of horizontal and vertical members. Panels are fitted into grooves in the frame or held in place with strips of moulding.

LEFT: *Incised and stamped door from a Berber dwelling in the Middle Atlas, Morocco. Berber doors are often decorated with talismanic designs also found in their tattoos.*

BELOW: *The plank doorway and oak frame at the 16th-century De Vere House in Lavenham, Suffolk, England. The building is oak framed with brick infill.*

RIGHT: *A massive 19th-century door from a Batak house on Samosir Island, Lake Toba, Sumatra. The bull is an important sacrificial animal and its head is a common ornament in Batak art. The projections fit into slots in the lintel and threshold to serve as a hinge.*

out of the door during threshing and is therefore known as the threshold. All the parts of the frame may be carved or painted, but most particularly the centre of the lintel. Separate metal hinges are attached to the jambs, although many doors have an integral hinge projecting on one side from the top and bottom. These projections slot into holes cut into the lintel and threshold.

Types of door

WHERE large enough timber is available a door may be made in one piece, but more often it must be assembled from several boards. Rustic doors are constructed from boards laid side by side nailed to two or three others laid at right angles. Diagonal pieces counteract stress and keep the door rigid.

Requiring considerably more skill, the construction of panelled doors involves

Windows

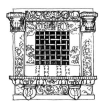

TOP: DOUBLE TOLLA
WINDOW SET INTO
THE WALL, GUJARAT,
INDIA.

ABOVE: CARVED
WINDOW FRAME,
KASHMIR.

TOP RIGHT: ANGLO-
SAXON HINGED
SHUTTER.

WINDOWS ARE set into walls to allow the passage of light and air. In very hot regions, such as the Thar Desert on the borders of India and Pakistan, where shade is prized for its comparative coolness, buildings sometimes have very small windows or none at all to exclude the burning sun. Likewise in regions with cold winters, such as Finland or Siberia, openings are kept small to cut down on draughts. In Islamic and Mediterranean countries it is common practice to build a home around a courtyard with all or most of the windows facing in which protects the family from the prying eyes of outsiders.

Frames

LIKE doors, even the simplest of windows, no more than a hole in a wall, must have a strong member over the top to support the structure above. This may be stone but, as in the case of the double tolla construction of north India, may be of load-bearing timbers. Jambs at the sides fit into the lintel above and a sill across the bottom which usually employs mortise and tenon or bridle joints in combination with mitres. Particularly in Hindu countries, the whole frame may be heavily carved. In Nepal windows are given a great deal of attention – they are constructed with complex joinery and lavishly carved.

Glazing

IN most parts of the world the introduction of glass panes is comparatively recent. In medieval Europe windows were formerly shuttered or covered with cloth or horn. This was cut into suitable lengths and then heated until it became soft enough to flatten out into a sheet. In the East light entered a room

softly through thin sheets of paper. Before the invention of float glass it was only possible to produce panes in small sizes. This old glass often had a distinct distorting ripple, a quality now considered to have greater charm than consistent industrially produced glass. To hold the small panes in place the frame was divided into smaller sections by glazing bars neatly interlocking with a clever variation of the halving joint.

Opening windows

THE majority of windows, collectively known as casements, are hinged on one side and open outwards. The sash

TOP LEFT: *Mexican window protected by a grid of wooden bars.*

LEFT: *Carved and fretted window frame with shutters hung on metal hinges, north-west India.*

RIGHT: *Carved window frame and balcony front, Gujarat, India. The projections lock the frame into the structure of the wall.*

window is an ingenious system in which glazed components, counterweighted with iron weights inside the window frame, open and close by moving up and down. This space-saving design was developed in the Netherlands and came to England during the 16th century when it was used in the building of Hampton Court Palace.

Shutters

WHETHER glazed or open, windows may be secured with wooden shutters to keep out both thieves and the elements. The picturesque appearance of houses with shutters, like those in the Swiss Alps, has a rustic appeal, inspiring the occupants of many sheltered, urban buildings to fit purely decorative, non-functioning shutters to their windows.

ABOVE, LEFT: *Tudor bay window supported by a carved oak panel, Newport, Essex, England.*

ABOVE, RIGHT: *Green shutters outside a small shrine in the Fort at Jodhpur, Rajasthan, India.*

RIGHT: *Vertically opening sash windows in the seaside town of Southwold, Suffolk, England. Sash windows were introduced to Britain in the 16th century.*

BELOW, LEFT: *House front with windows and doors assembled with complex joinery, Patan, Nepal.*

BELOW, RIGHT: *Pair of small windows assembled with mortise and tenon joints and tongue and groove panels, Istalif, Afghanistan.*

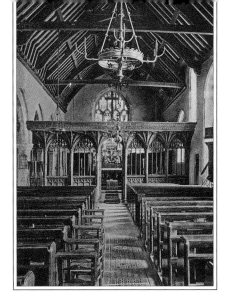

Screens and grills

Neither screens nor grills provide a solid barrier, but only partially block the passage of light and air. In both Muslim and Hindu countries, where many women spend their lives in purdah, secluded from the eyes of men, grills allow them to observe the affairs of the world without being seen. Many techniques are used, from the simple overlapping of thin slats which form a lattice to the assembly of the tiny components forming *moushrabiya* (see below).

Top: *Rood screen, St Michael's, Minehead, Somerset, England.*

Above: *Fretwork grill made in Kapal, Bali.*

Fretwork

In India pierced grills of stone or wood are a feature of many buildings, allowing free ventilation, while cutting down the strength of the sunlight. The technique for making these fretwork screens, known as *jali*, was introduced by Persian craftsmen moving east with the spread of Islam. They exploited the local shesham wood and the walnut they found in Kashmir to carve complex geometric patterns or interlaced vegetation, motifs seen in the work of Muslim craftsmen the world over, wherever the wood is of adequate size and quality. Grills made by Hindus in both India and Bali may include floral designs, and also feature swastikas and images of the gods.

Moushrabiya

In North Africa, because of the paucity of good timber, craftsmen became adept at working with small pieces of wood and devised a method of constructing screens and grills from hundreds or even thousands of small balls and pegs socketed together without glue or nails to allow for distortion. Also used in the construction of some furniture, this technique is called *moushrabiya* which is derived from the Arabic word for 'balcony'. Even today the streets of Marrakesh in Morocco are full of men and boys turning these components on bow lathes. In Kashmir, northern Pakistan and Afghanistan a similar technique is used in which the grills are made from a wooden frame containing slats of wood held apart by decoratively placed spacers fitted into notches.

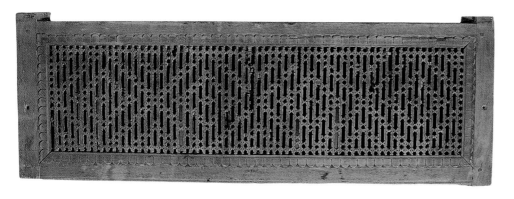

Shoji and hanji

SOFT ambient light filters into Japanese rooms through panels called *shoji* which are covered with paper. Like many other home improvements, they were introduced from Korea where they are known as *hanji*. Some *shoji* panels can be slid back to give a clear view of the world outside and are protected from the elements by removeable rain shutters.

Sliding and folding screens

TRADITIONAL Japanese buildings were constructed in modules divided by sets of sliding doors which could be slid back or even bodily removed to change the internal floor plan, creating open plan or intimate areas as required. The moving sections were of wood covered with paper which was then beautifully painted, often incorporating a background of gold leaf or powdered mica. The spaces could also be divided diagonally with free-standing folding screens, always in pairs, easily moved around for maximum impact, creating either privacy or a dramatic setting.

Folding screens are also made in India – they have jointed frames enclosing carved and pieced *jali* work, while in Europe it is more common to find the wooden frames filled with textiles.

OPPOSITE, BELOW, LEFT: *Ventilated cupboard, north India.*

OPPOSITE, BELOW, RIGHT: Moushrabiya *doorway, Medersa ben Youssef, Marrakesh, Morocco.*

ABOVE, LEFT: *Balcony front constructed from rails with decoratively placed spacers, Afghanistan.*

ABOVE, RIGHT: *Japanese workman replacing damaged paper on* shoji. *More subtle than the net curtains used in the West,* shoji *maintain privacy, while allowing a soft light to permeate a room.*

BELOW, LEFT: *Large Indian frame with fretwork and opening panels held together with mitred mortise and tenon joints.*

BELOW, RIGHT: *Bay with fretwork screens and windows, Mahdia, Tunisia.*

FIVE

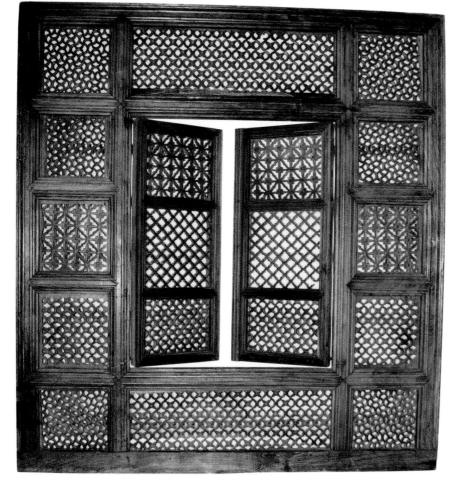

TRANSPORT

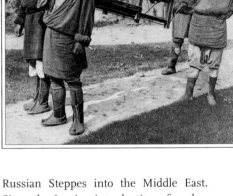

RIGID, STRONG, easily worked and reasonably light, wood has been used since prehistoric times to facilitate the task of moving people and objects, from Chinese wheelbarrows and Hungarian farm wagons to Hittite war chariots.

Sledges

TODAY, the sledge is associated with travel across snow where wheels would become bogged down – the most common are Eskimo sledges pulled by dogs or Russian troikas pulled by horses, but sledges are also used on solid ground. In the past the megaliths used to build Stonehenge in England, the giant Easter Island statues and the stones of the Egyptian pyramids were all pulled on wooden sledges by large teams of men, reducing the friction with rollers. The nomadic peoples of the American Plains transported their goods on a simple A-shaped *travois*, or drag, made of lashed poles. These were originally pulled by dogs, but after the arrival of the European settlers larger frames were fitted to the newly introduced horses.

Litters and palanquins

ANOTHER way to lighten a load is to share it between two or more individuals by placing it on a stretcher or frame. This is a common way of moving injured people, but is also still employed in Dutch towns for carrying large cheeses around the markets. People with wealth

RIGHT: *Nepalese sedan chair.*

BELOW, LEFT: *A crude bullock sledge dragged by bullocks in the fields outside Nadi, Fiji.*

BELOW, RIGHT: *Native American* travois *made by lashing tipi poles together.*

or status may also be carried around in a chair on poles, such as the Indian *doolie*, or European sedan chair. Although potentates may wish to be seen, carried in procession by their inferiors, many litters are completely enclosed for privacy. Among the most magnificent palanquins were the *norimono* employed by Japanese nobility during the 17th century – they resembled a small, heavily lacquered room.

The wheel

THE wheel was used for transport more than 6,000 years ago, first for wagons and then for the horse-drawn chariots which, some time during the 3rd millennium BC, thundered from the Russian Steppes into the Middle East. Since the Iranian introduction of spokes the wooden wheel has changed very little in the last 4,000 years.

In England three kinds of wood are used to make a wheel, elm for the nave or hub, oak for the spokes and ash for the felloes that form the rim. The hub, which will eventually spin on the axle, is turned on a lathe from a large block of elm. A series of mortises are cut into it to house the oak spokes shaped with a drawknife and spokeshave. The rim is assembled from a number of curved pieces of ash

FIVE

called felloes, each long enough to receive two spokes. The spokes again slot into mortises, while the felloes are joined together with oak dowels. Once all the parts of the wheel have been hammered into place a heated iron ring is dropped round the rim, binding the wheel together as it shrinks.

The design of some carts has remained unchanged for millennia and Albanian carts of the early 20th century were almost identical to ox carts from the Indus

ABOVE, LEFT: *Farm cart with solid wooden wheels, California, North America.*

RIGHT: *Ceremonial wooden cart at Wat Doi Sutep, a temple in northern Thailand.*

BELOW, LEFT: *A Norfolk farm wagon painted blue. English agricultural vehicles once sported colours which identified their home county.*

INSET: *Traditional English wheelbarrow. They were probably invented many centuries ago in China.*

Valley civilization, dating from 4,000 years before. The design of English agricultural carts was a matter of great pride – each county had its own design and distinctive paintwork.

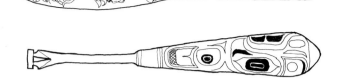

ABOVE: CARVED MAORI HOE FROM NEW ZEALAND AND A PAINTED TLINGIT PADDLE FROM ALASKA, 1878. WHILE CANOES ARE OFTEN COMMUNALLY OWNED, PADDLES ARE FREQUENTLY MADE AND USED BY INDIVIDUALS AND MAY BE HIGHLY DECORATED.

ARCHAEOLOGICAL REMAINS in the Aegean Sea and northern Europe suggest that man first took to the sea in the 8th millennium BC, from which time shipbuilding has been a highly respected craft. In New Zealand war canoes or *waka* were once the most important Maori cultural symbols and the men who built them were often of chiefly rank. Hernán Cortés, during his conquest of Mexico in the 16th century, considered his shipwright, Martin Lopez, the most important man in his force.

ABOVE: *Fijian bank note illustrated with a bamboo raft or* bilibili. *Rafters are widely used on inland waterways, but are less suitable for the open sea.*

RIGHT: *Chinese junk off the coast of Chusan.*

BELOW: *The hull of a large vessel under construction in the shipyard at Essaouira, Morocco. Such boats with raised bow and stern and a deep draught are used for fishing on the Atlantic Ocean.*

Rafts

THE first boats were no more than floating logs propelled by the hands and feet. A more stable vessel can be created by fastening several poles or logs together to form a raft. Quick and easy to build, rafts, such as the Fijian bamboo *bilibili*, can still be seen floating down inland waterways all around the world.

Dugouts

DUGOUT canoes have been used wherever the trees are large enough and are still the most common form of boat in the Pacific, Indonesia, South America and parts of Africa.

Firstly, a tree has to be hollowed out, most often with an adze, but often with the aid of drills and fire. The inside is then filled with water or, in British Columbia, with urine, which is then heated by

dropping in hot rocks. This softens the timber enough to brace and widen it in the middle, leaving the bow and stern higher. The largest dugout ever built was a Maori kauri wood *waka* which was 35.7 m (117 ft) long and was built in 1940 to celebrate the signing of the Treaty of Waitangi. Maori canoes have separate prow, stern and side pieces lashed on to the hull.

Plank boats

HULLS made from planks tied together or nailed to a framework can be constructed in a far wider range of shapes and sizes appropriate to local needs. The largest wooden ship ever was the American built *Rochambeau*, completed in 1872 – it was 115 m (377 ft) long. Noah's Ark, according to the Bible, was 21 m (70 ft) longer! The small plank boats built by the Chumash of California were sewn together from short pieces of driftwood.

Large ships such as those of the British navy during the 18th century required huge timbers that had grown into the right curves. To build a 100-gun warship eighty acres of forest had to be felled. Patriotic English landowners planted thousands of trees, especially oaks, and surveyors travelled the country earmarking boughs and branches for specific projects.

Clinker building, the technique of overlapping planks for greater strength, was developed by the Vikings. Preserved ship burials discovered in Norway at Gokstad and Oseberg were built in the 9th century AD using overlapping strakes fastened with iron rivets. Robust clinker construction has often been used for the fishing boats sailing the rough waters of northern Europe ever since.

Figureheads

From fishing boats in the Solomon Islands to Spanish galleons, a figurehead is often fixed to the prow. Originally these were an invocation to the powers controlling the sea to have mercy on vulnerable sailors or provided the vessel with eyes to help it find its way.

ABOVE, LEFT: *The largest dugout canoe in the world, the Maori war canoe Ngatokimatawhaorua, built from the trunks of three kauri trees. The process of hollowing out trunks for canoes was made easier by stripping bark from one side of the tree to allow decay to set in before felling took place. The war canoe was, before colonial times, an important symbol of tribal identity.*

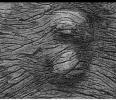

FIVE

TOP: *A sampan, small Chinese river boat. Families of fishermen or traders in South-East Asia still live on their boats.*

ABOVE: *The sternpost of a Maori war canoe, carved with a watchful ancestor figure and lashed to the body of the dugout.*

LEFT: *Two fishing boats with hulls built with butted planks, Isle of Mull, Scotland.*

LEFT: *Detail of a bao board, Zanzibar.*
RIGHT: *Carved Ashante combs, Ghana.*
BELOW, LEFT: *Chinese ruan.*
BELOW, CENTRE: *Ceremonial durbar dais, Rajasthan, India.*
BELOW, RIGHT: *Rajasthani puppet, India.*
BOTTOM: *Didgeridoo sold to tourists in Cairns, Australia.*

SIX

HEART AND SOUL

HEART AND SOUL

ABOVE: *Devotees in a boat making an offering at a shrine in the lagoon near Venice, Italy.*

O F ALL the uses to which wood is put not all are directly related to the basic task of survival. Many are more concerned with the emotional, psychological and spiritual well being of the individual. The oldest known surviving wooden structure is not a house for the living, but a tomb for the dead constructed in around 700 BC in Turkey for the remains of Midas, the legendary king of Phrygia.

EDUCATION

A HUNDRED years ago in Europe and North America school children were equipped with a slate on which to write, but even today Islamic boys' schools in North Africa provide their students with a wooden board on which to copy out verses from the Koran. The mosques and madrasahs of Marrakesh in Morocco and Kohistan in Pakistan are adorned with carved quotations, while in China the aphorisms of Confucius or Lao Tse were once engraved on the walls of temples and schools, to be replaced in the 20th century by the maxims of Chairman Mao. Teaching aids too are made from wood, for instance, the *retablo* used by Catholic priests and missionaries when teaching the Bible to the illiterate or heathen. By far the most important use of wood in education has been as a material for the cutting of blocks for printing books, both sacred and profane.

ABOVE: *Gilded text on the ceiling of the Fuk Tak Chi Temple in Singapore. Such invocations may be raised, intaglio or simply painted.*

BELOW, LEFT: *Arabian children enjoying the 'big wheel', here not ferrous, but wooden.*

ABOVE, LEFT: *Boards used for copying the Koran at a boys school in Mali.*

LEFT: *Berber legal documents recorded on pieces of cedar wood, Morocco.*

ART AND ENTERTAINMENT

W OOD IS employed in many of the arts in a supporting role. For centuries, before canvas became popular, wood was a common choice as a base for paintings and continues to be the preference for icons. It is used as a material for the manufacture of masks and dance accessories, including hand wands and paddles as well as the blocks in the points of ballet shoes. The orchestras of both East and West include many wooden instruments, while once the hillsides of the Balkans and the mountain sides of the Andes both resounded to the trilling of home-made flutes and pipes.

In the West, childhood years and adult leisure hours are filled with wooden toys and games – building bricks, stacking towers and spinning tops, dominoes, skittles, fishing rods, cricket bats or croquet mallets.

CRIME AND PUNISHMENT

To prevent the abuse of trust, marriage contracts among the Berbers of the Atlas Mountains are traditionally recorded on pieces of cedar wood, so that they will not sink in the rivers. Policemen all around the world patrol the streets armed with a hardwood truncheon or solid stick. Once arrested, law breakers may be fitted with wooden yokes to hamper their movements, beaten with sticks or canes, locked in a cage or cell and even strung up from gallows.

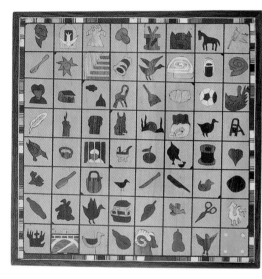

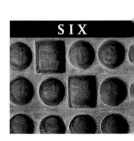

TOP: *Criminal in a wood and bamboo restraint, Thailand.*

ABOVE: *Marquetry game board from Madagascar.*

ABOVE: *Mende men playing wari, Sierra Leone.*

ABOVE, RIGHT: *Nigerian carved dance mask.*

BELOW: *Toy bear from Switzerland.*

SIX

SOUVENIRS

Today, travellers often return home with souvenirs just as pilgrims to sacred places have done for millennia. Christian visitors to Bethlehem are likely to return home with olive-wood crucifixes or donkeys, while Hindu pilgrims may acquire sandalwood carvings of the patron deities of the shrines they have visited. Modern-day tourists bring wooden cockerels from Portugal, bears from Switzerland or Bavaria, clogs from the Netherlands, thistle-topped porridge spirtles from Scotland, boomerangs from Australia and statuettes of Don Quixote from southern Spain.

PRINTING

THE INTRODUCTION of printing meant that information could be disseminated cheaply to the masses. Using an inked-up block of wood or metal upon which images or writing have been cut, thousands of identical printed sheets can be run off in the time that one hand-drawn or written sheet could be produced. The same technique made it possible to produce quickly textiles with repeating patterns such as the printing cloth of Rajasthan. Although metal has now generally become the medium for books, wood is still widely used in the printing of cheap textiles in developing countries and exclusive, prestigious materials in the West.

The history of printing

PREHISTORIC pottery was often decorated with impressed patterns, a technique which led to the first form of writing, cuneiform, developed by the Sumerians 5,000 years ago by pressing a wedge-shaped stylus into a soft clay tablet.

By AD 100 the Chinese were stamping official documents and textiles with seals and blocks carved from wood or ivory and by the end of the 9th century they had used wooden blocks to print the world's first printed book, an illustrated Buddhist scroll called 'The Diamond Sutra'. It was the zeal of missionaries, first Buddhist and later Christian, that encouraged the spread of printing right across Asia and Europe. The Chinese also invented moveable type, but it was in Germany in about 1438 that Johann Gutenberg devised the first printing press, a hand-operated wooden structure inspired by the wine press. Woodblock prints became a high art form with the designs of Albrecht Dürer (1471–1528), but Dürer usually only drew the images, and it was highly skilled craftsmen who copied the designs onto wood and cut the lines.

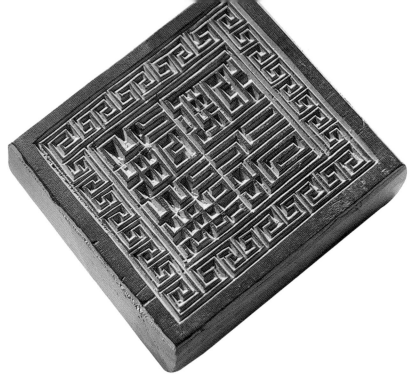

The block

Cutting a block is delicate work and requires wood with a dense stable grain that will not split or splinter. The oldest known European woodblocks were cut from walnut, but more widely used were sycamore and maple or lime, which had been proved to be high-quality materials by 16th-century carvers. The best wood for printing blocks is box as it is slow growing and therefore has a very close grain. Unfortunately this means that it never reaches more than a few inches in diameter and large blocks must be made up from several pieces. The possibilities of cutting into the end grain of box had been tried in Armenia and Constantinople, but reached a new level in the hands of the Englishman, Thomas Bewick (1753–1828), who drew with a cut white line, which he usually drew and cut himself, producing charming, light-filled illustrations of the natural world.

OPPOSITE,; BELOW CENTRE; AND BELOW, RIGHT: upeti, *a board used for rubbing patterns onto barkcloth, Samoa; barkcloth with pattern rubbed on an* upeti.

TOP LEFT: *Wood printing block showing the footprints of the god Vishnu, India.*

TOP RIGHT: *Korean seal with square calligraphy.*

ABOVE, LEFT: *Block-printed Shiah Muslim shrine cloth, Ahmedabad, Gujarat, India.*

ABOVE, RIGHT: *Japanese woodblock print by Kunisada from the mid-19th century.*

Japanese printing

Many of Japan's greatest artists, such as Hokusai, Hiroshige and Utamaro, specialized in the art of the woodblock print which reached the peak of their popularity during the 18th and 19th centuries. These images, cut from a number of carefully registered cherry-wood blocks, one for each colour, employed large areas of flat colour rather than the linear shading and hatching of European work. A distinctive feature of Japanese prints was the subtlety of colour achieved by the printer's careful application of ink to the block.

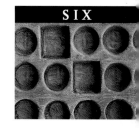

SIX

PERSONAL PRESENTATION

Taking pride in one's appearance is part of human nature. Whether the reason is to display one's wealth and status, to make a statement of tribal identity or to attract a mate, the need to present an image of oneself to others is universal. Items for personal use have always had the most attention lavished on their decoration.

Mirrors

Mirrors come in all shapes and sizes, from ones small enough to slip in a handbag to the pivoted full-length cheval-glass or *psyche* that became popular in the 1800s. The frames are often made of wood, which is probably carved or coloured. Among the most ornate frames were the elaborately carved and gilded fantasies in the Rococo and Chinoiserie styles fashionable in 18th-century France and England. Equally whimsical are the chunky frames of the Yoruba in Nigeria who sometimes endow homely objects with hands and feet.

Hair

In many cultures the hair, the 'crowning glory', receives more attention than other parts of the body, as it is considered a symbol of strength and virility, and the style of a person's coiffure often serves to advertise age, marital status or spiritual commitment. African tribes and the Polynesians are particularly fond of carved and decorated combs for both arranging the hair and holding it in place and among the Asante of Ghana the carving of elaborate combs by suitors is considered a gesture of devotion.

Cosmetics

Powders and paints for decorating the face and body require careful storage to prevent contamination and to keep them suitably wet or dry. Liquids such as perfumes and unguents or kohl, for eyeliner, are kept in a bottle or jar with a thin neck and stopper, while powders are kept in boxes. Boxes, carved in one piece,

Top left: Comb from the Hermit Islands, north of Papua New Guinea, 19th century.

Left: Man's ceremonial comb from Bamu River, Papua New Guinea.

Above: *Comb carved by an Ashante bachelor for his sweetheart with symbols of love and the inscription 1932.*

Right: *Two boxes for camwood powder used as a cosmetic by the Kuba of the Democratic Republic of Congo. In many places items like these, which are carved in one piece, are believed to retain a greater concentration of the life force of the tree from which the wood was obtained. The incised patterns are also found on the raffia textiles of this region.*

Opposite, above, left: *Batak jewelry box from Samosir Island, Sumatra.*

are used by the Kuba of Central Africa to store camwood powder. When required, the powder is mixed into a paste with castor oil using the box's inverted lid for a palette.

Jewelry

Necklaces and earrings of polished wooden beads are found in many places, for instance, of olive wood in the Middle East, ebony in India, purpleheart in Colombia and red-coated carved 'cinnabar' beads in China. Bangles and bracelets carved or turned from wood are widespread, but these allow more surface area for ornamentation than beads and may be inlaid with wire or shell or painted in bright colours.

Accessories

Buttons were invented thousands of years ago in China and since then have often been made from wood. In Japan, where traditional clothes have no pockets, objects are kept in a sleeve or in a bag slung from the *obi* or sash held in place with a *netsuke*, a small toggle carved from wood or ivory. During the rise of the merchant classes during the Edo period (1603–1868) *netsuke* developed into miniature masterpieces depicting mythical beings, astrological animals, human figures and even vegetables.

Near right: *Yoruba mirror with feet, Nigeria.*

Top right: *Pot for kohl, used as eyeliner, Marrakesh, Morocco.*

Inset: *Arranging hair with a comb, Zanzibar.*

SPORT

THE STRENGTH and prowess of Cuchulainn, the youth who later became the greatest of all Irish mythical heroes, was first recognized by Conchobar, the King of Ulster, as the boy was single handedly defeating all his opponents in a game of hurley, a game played with a curved stick and hard ball. Sport has always been, and continues to be, an important part of martial training, developing strength, stamina and quick reflexes. Other 'sports', such as hunting, shooting and fishing, have evolved from the search for food or from the need to move around in difficult conditions. Skiing developed in icy conditions, while pole vaulting evolved from channel-hopping techniques employed in fens and polders.

History

MANY sports were developed out of the warfare training of recruits or the practice exercises of veterans during the winter break in campaigning. Roman soldiers improved their techniques with wooden swords as did the Samurai from whom we have inherited the Japanese sport of kendo. For the Moguls, the crucial fighting force was the cavalry and from their weapons, practice the game of polo was derived. The display of physical prowess was incorporated by the Ancient Greeks into the worship of the gods, giving rise to the original Olympic Games, and, in the form of Funeral Games, accompanied the departure of great heroes and leaders. Sports included javelin throwing, chariot racing and rowing. Rowing competitions can still be witnessed today – the English University boat race, Chinese dragon boat racing and the dashes across Apia harbour in Samoa every evening by fifty-man canoes.

All manner of sporting paraphernalia is made of wood, from hard *Lignum vitae* bowling bowls to tall rugby goal posts, skittles and cricket stumps. Even today many of these products are produced by cottage industries and small family businesses rather than large industrial organizations.

Racquets, mallets and bats

FOR striking a ball the best woods must not fracture easily or transmit the shock of impact to the arm and so the most common choice is hickory in North America and ash in Europe. However, the subtleties of different games may demand woods that are straight, hard or flexible. Synthetic fibres are now widely used in many sports and table-tennis bats are made from plywood, but certain woods have become associated with particular sports. For instance, the heads of golf clubs, although the game was invented in Scotland, are traditionally made from

BELOW: *TUDOR WOODCUT SHOWING CHILDREN PLAYING GAMES, INCLUDING SKITTLES, BOWLS, STILT WALKING AND TOP SPINNING.*

ABOVE, LEFT: *Two American baseball bats made from hickory wood to absorb the shock of impact.*

TOP RIGHT; AND RIGHT: *Croquet mallet with brass reinforcements around the striking faces; willow cricket bat and ash stumps. The handle of the bat is of rubber and rattan cane for shock absorbency.*

LEFT: BOWLS PLAYERS, AFTER
A MEDIEVAL MANUSCRIPT.
THE BEST BOWLING BALLS ARE
MADE FROM HEAVY LIGNUM
VITAE, TURNED ON A LATHE.

persimmon wood with shafts of hickory, polo sticks have ash, sycamore or bamboo root heads and rattan cane handles, while billiard cues are made from straight-grained, attractively coloured hardwoods such as goncalo alves, ebony and purpleheart.

Making a cricket bat

For more than two hundred years cricket bats have been made from the wood of *Salix alba caerulea*, known as the cricket-bat willow and grown especially for this purpose since it is close grained and resilient. Felled trees are cut into lengths and then split into wedge-shaped 'clefts', which are then seasoned for a year before being shaped with a draw knife, spoke-shave and plane into a bat. A triangular slot is cut in the top to receive the handle, which is made separately from a bundle of squared-off canes sandwiched with rubber. A regular coat of linseed oil is applied to keep the bat in good condition.

RIGHT: *The fifty man crew of a racing canoe disembarking after evening practice in Apia harbour, Samoa.*

RIGHT, MIDDLE: *Like many other articles of sporting equipment, fishing tackle is now often made from synthetic fibres. Previously strong but flexible materials such as bamboo were employed for rods and hardwoods were used to make reels like these mahogany Nottingham Starbackreels of 1910 and 1911, so called because of the shape of the brass reinforcement plate on the back.*

BELOW, LEFT: *The ash and beech frame of a tennis racquet strung with gut. When not in use, the heads of wooden tennis racquets were best kept clamped in a frame to prevent warping.*

BELOW, RIGHT: *A Hawaiian surfer. Now an international watersport, surfing was originally developed by Polynesian islanders as a method of crossing the breakers surrounding their coral-encircled islands.*

SIX

GAMES

BELOW, LEFT; AND BELOW, RIGHT: *Balinese chess set from Tampaksiring; English 19th-century turned chessmen.*

BOTTOM: *Wari board from Ghana.*

OPPOSITE, BELOW: *A Tanzanian wari board.*

ABOVE: MONGOLIAN HOROI PIECES.

OPPOSITE, BOTTOM: *Playing backgammon in the Lebanon. Particularly elaborate marquetry backgammon sets are produced in the Middle East and North Africa.*

IN POLYNESIA islanders with time on their hands would compete over a pile of sticks, trying to withdraw one at a time without disturbing any others. The game, spillikins, is now popular in the West and is called 'pick up sticks'. Although this game requires manual dexterity, it is a game of tactics. Games are fun, but they also help to develop powers of thought and concentration. Strategic games have always been particularly popular among generals and rulers, people for whom strategy is an important life skill. In Persia chess was called 'the game of kings'. Some games depend on skill alone, while others have the added factor of chance in the form of dice, spinners or thrown sticks. The 'game' is often seen in allegorical terms as a struggle between good and evil and those about to die are sometimes depicted as playing a last game with the sepulchral figure of death.

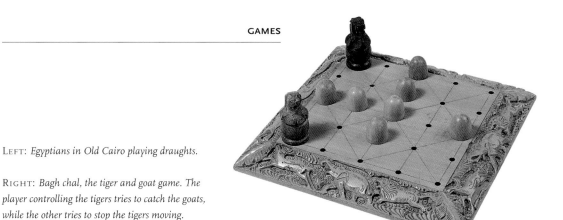

LEFT: *Egyptians in Old Cairo playing draughts.*

RIGHT: *Bagh chal, the tiger and goat game. The player controlling the tigers tries to catch the goats, while the other tries to stop the tigers moving.*

Board games

THE leisure hours of ancient peoples in Mesopotamia and Egypt were often occupied with strategic games. Just as impromptu contests are improvised today, makeshift boards were scratched on the stones of the pyramids and Assyrian gateways and pebbles or odds and ends were used as counters. In Egypt the nobility had sets of ebony and ivory for playing senet, a game in which moves were decided by throwing sticks and counters were moved across a board with thirty squares in an attempt to reach 'the Kingdom of the god Osiris'. The origins of other games such as chess are apocryphal, credit claimed for their invention by the folk heroes of many cultures. Virtually all tactical games are played on a board marked out with lines, squares or hollows in such a way as to define the direction and distance of moves allowed. The layout of these grids may be enhanced with decoration, often marquetry or inlay, exploiting woods of contrasting colours. It has been suggested that the name 'chess' is a corruption of the Latin word 'tesserae' which means 'mosaic tiles'. Counters and pieces are also made from woods of different colours such as box and ebony, but are carved or shaped according to cultural preference, the king in an Indian chess set, for instance, rides an elephant.

Equal and unequal contests

WHEN the players have the same purpose, to eliminate the opponent's 'men' or reach the opposite end, the board is symmetrical and each has the same number of pieces. While chess and its poorer relative chequers or draughts played on a grid of sixty-four squares are now enjoyed all over the world, the premier game in the Middle East and North Africa is backgammon, mapped out with interlocked triangles, and in the Far East the game of go which is played on the intersections of the lines, not the squares. All over Africa the contest takes place over the mancala board, also called oware and wari, a game of strategy in which opponents take turns to move their twenty-four pieces clockwise around the cups in a boat-shaped board, each striving to be the first to reach home.

In another type of competition the opponents have forces of different sizes and different objectives, usually one tries to capture all his opponent's pieces, while the other tries to surround him or block his moves. Among these number the Viking game *hneftafl*, the medieval fox and geese and the Indian game of bagh chal (tiger and goat). Most often the pieces are moved along lines and may peg into holes drilled in the board.

SIX

TOYS

CHILDREN IN ancient times played with toys that were not all that different from toys today and they were mostly made from wood. Dolls, model carts and pull-along animals were enjoyed by young Sumerians and Egyptians 5,000 years ago – the most obvious difference being that they appear to be one-off items that were probably made by a loving parent or friend and not bought from a professional. Fine play things were only owned by the wealthy as they could afford to commission a craftsman to produce bespoke items. One of the oldest known rocking horses, made in about 1610, was inspired by the tilting horse used for medieval jousting practice and was made to be ridden by the future King Charles I of England. However, there were few full-time toy makers before 1800 and it was not until the middle of the 19th century that the first shop selling only toys was opened.

Types of toy

TOYS that move around autonomously such as the clockwork autoperipatetikoi (mechanized walking dolls) of 19th-century North America or the pecking hens and spanking bears made in Russia are not as interesting as interactive toys. The toys that children most enjoy are those that encourage imaginative play and crude improvised objects can provide hours of fun. In the 18th and 19th centuries Western parents were particularly keen that playthings should be 'instructional' or 'improving' and a plethora of educational toys, games and puzzles were churned out to feed the minds of future empire builders. The earliest jigsaw puzzles were constructed in the 1760s from maps mounted on mahogany and sawn into pieces.

TOP LEFT: *German spinning tops with whirling arms.*

TOP RIGHT: *Jigsaw puzzle from Marrakesh, Morocco.*

ABOVE, LEFT: *English acrobatic teddy bear. Squeezing the bottom of the frame tightens the string and makes the figure swing around.*

ABOVE, RIGHT: *Articulated pine wood snake with a leather spine made in the workshop of Ruperto Monsalve, Villarica, Chile.*

RIGHT: *A child-size version of a truck, complete with panelling and painting typical of full-sized vehicles in Afghanistan and Pakistan. Made by the Kabul Toy Company, Afghanistan.*

SIX

150

Imagination

Toys for imaginative play generally represent the adult world in a scaled-down form and provide children with the opportunity to come to terms with the concepts, principles and feelings they will need to understand as they grow. Doll's houses, Noah's Ark sets, toy soldiers and weapons are all played with unconsciously to this end.

Manipulation

Many toys and games enjoyed by both young and old are considered a diverting way of passing the time, while developing coordination. Using a wooden cup to catch a ball attached to it by a piece of string evokes images of idle squires in the Age of Chivalry, but was also popular amongst the eskimos as they waited for spring. Stacking toys and building bricks are loved by the very young of every generation, but the fashion comes and goes for spinning tops, common in Ancient Egypt, or yo-yos, invented thousands of years ago in China.

Moving toys

Pull-along or 'carpet toys' may simply roll on a set of wheels, but since Egyptian times they have been made to flap their wings, snap their jaws or bob up and down as they trundle across the floor. Other moving toys may be stationary and employ gears and handles. These toys have a simple appeal and charm lacking in the sophisticated metal and china automata which were the executive toys of the 19th century, far too fragile and expensive for the hands of children.

ABOVE, LEFT: *Pull along toy bought in England. Back wheels with an eccentric axle cause the rabbit to bob up and down.*

ABOVE, RIGHT: *Painted Noah's Ark set.*

BELOW, LEFT: *A small boy being given a toy boat, Volendam, Holland.*

BELOW, RIGHT: *Toy bears from Bogorodskaya, Russia. Pulling the rods makes the large bear spank the small one.*

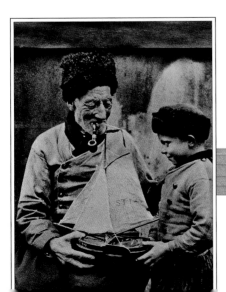

ABOVE: A MAORI
KARETAO, OR
JUMPING JACK, WITH
ARTICULATED ARMS.

DOLLS AND PUPPETS

SOMETIMES NO more than a piece of cloth or a scrap of wood, some dolls and puppets have involved sophisticated craftsmanship with moving parts, and often employ wood, particularly for carved heads and hands. In some form or another they have been found among the debris of virtually every civilization, but their function has not always been limited to that of a toy.

LEFT: *A whittled North American doll, dated 1887.*

BELOW, LEFT: *Turned and painted Russian dolls.*

BELOW, RIGHT: *West African dolls (from left to right, Fante, Ghana; Asante, Ghana; Mossi, Burkina Faso) carried by girls in their waist bands.*

Dolls

THE commonest dolls are intended as playthings for infants, but in the hands of the young they take on the role of companion and confidant. They take part in role play as the child learns and experiments how to interact with the real world. Frequently they become imbued with so much emotional association that they seem real and many folk tales are related in which a doll comes to life and saves the day – for instance, the Russian story of Vasilissa the Beautiful who is confronted with many trials that she overcomes with the aid of a magical doll given to her by her dying mother.

Adults, too, may benefit from the presence of dolls. In Nigeria among the Yoruba, for instance, mothers who, while giving birth, have lost one of a pair of twins have a small wooden effigy made which is called an *ere ibeji*. This little surrogate is washed, dressed, fed and rubbed with oil, indigo and red camwood in the belief that it will bring the family luck. Without doubt, it also helps the mother cope with her bereavement.

Stylized wooden dolls are given to girls in Ghana and Burkina Faso who carry them in their waistbands and care for them. Upon marriage the girls take them to their husband's home in the hope they will aid conception.

Puppets

THE French word poupée actually means doll and a puppet is in essence an animated doll, the word 'animate' means on one level 'to cause to move', but on another, 'to bring to life'. Puppets are used to entertain, but the subject of their performances is often of an epic or religious nature such as the tales of the Paladins recounted in Sicily and the Hindu *Ramayana* enacted in Java.

The simplest form is the glove puppet, often with a wooden head, manipulated by the hand inside. The most famous of this type in the West is the popular English seaside hero Mr Punch, a character derived from the Italian Commedia del Arte.

Rod puppets are manipulated with thin sticks attached to strategic points such as the head and hands. This is the type used in the Wayang Golek performances of central and west Java.

The marionette is controlled with strings attached to expressive parts of the body and has the advantage that life-like movement is made more convincing by the fact that the puppeteer can stand at a distance. There is a long tradition of marionette theatre in Prague in the Czech Republic, and modern puppets are sold all over the city. The most famous performances are by the Spejbl and Hurvinek Theatre which tell tales of the eponymous father and son.

The ultimate puppet was of course Pinocchio, a marionette carved by an Italian toy-maker, who came alive and ran away to become a real boy.

ABOVE, LEFT: *Two figures with articulated heads and limbs made in the Czech Republic.*

ABOVE, RIGHT: *Nepalese marionette, from Bhaktapur, with two faces and four arms, representing a dancer in the Nava-Durga festivities.*

RIGHT: Wayang golek *rod puppet used in Javanese performances of Hindu epics.*

BELOW: *Puppets with mango wood heads for sale in the fort at Jodhpur, Rajasthan, India. Legend has it that the first puppeteer was created by the Hindu god Brahma to entertain his wife, the goddess Saraswati.*

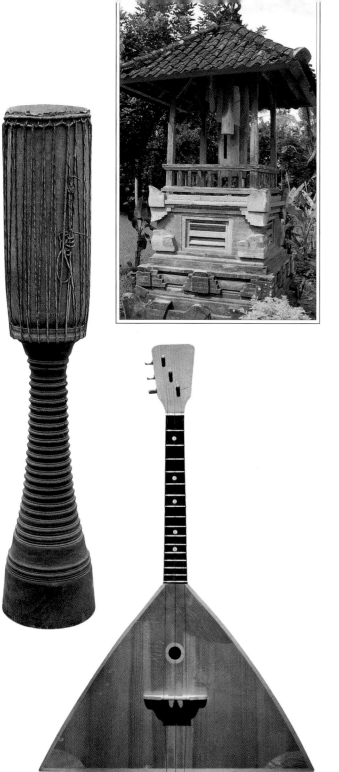

SOUND

SOUND IS transmitted by vibration. The resonance of wood depends on its density. The sound of a clarinet made from mpingo (African blackwood), for instance, is hard and pure, while that of a bamboo flute is soft and fuzzy. The density, colour and stability of hardwoods make them highly desirable for the manufacture of musical instruments, but many are becoming scarce or have even become extinct. As a result a number of leading musicians are now supporting an appeal for the responsible, sustainable management of suitable timber in the hope that future generations will be able to enjoy music played on beautiful instruments.

Warnings

SUPPLEMENTING the explosions of fire crackers at Chinese New Year, the whirring tap of double-headed drums twirled between the hands of the populace to frighten away evil spirits can be heard. Similar practices are to be encountered all over the world – in Japan Shinto processions are accompanied by the sound of tapping sticks and in South America and Australia mysterious humming warnings are given by whirling a bullroarer on the end of a string. Animals, too, may be protected by sound and in the Hindu Kush in Afghanistan and Pakistan wooden bells are hung as amulets around their necks. Just like evil spirits, birds are scared from a farmer's fields with clappers or castanets and Japanese deer are deterred by the clonking of water-powered bamboo scarers.

Summoning and communicating

GONGS and clappers are used to summon both spirits and people. In Bali every village is equipped with a *bale kulkul*, a log of jackfruit wood hung in a tower, sounded to call the community together, while in Africa and Polynesia messages are transmitted over great distances by the beating of 'talking drums' cut from large sections of hollowed tree trunk. Hunters, on the other hand, may attempt to attract ducks or caribou by imitating their calls, blowing through hollow tubes or whistles.

Music

IN some form or other music appears in the arts of every culture, often utilizing instruments made from wood. In the modern world it provides entertainment,

but it has been used in the worship of the gods and as a tool, as with the drum of the Siberian shaman, for the invocation of a trance state.

Percussion instruments such as Australian Aboriginal clicking sticks, Spanish castanets and xylophones all rely on the sound produced by striking a block of resonant wood, but more sophisticated instruments, for instance, slit drums, are hollowed out to increase the reverberations. The greatest range and volume is produced when the wood is completely hollowed and covered with a piece of skin. Goatskin is often used for this, but the Egyptian tabla may be covered with fish skin.

Wind instruments are played by blowing down a hollow tube. As the length of tube down which the air vibrates dictates the pitch, a number of different notes are possible if holes, which can be opened or stopped by the fingers, are drilled at intervals along the length.

Stringed instruments have strings of wire, hair or sinew stretched across a wooden frame. The sounds of the vibrating strings are amplified by a sound bowl, which may be made from a naturally hollow object such as a gourd or turtle shell or constructed like an elegant wooden box.

OPPOSITE, FAR LEFT; ABOVE, RIGHT; CENTRE LEFT; AND CENTRE RIGHT: *Indian long drum, as tall as a man;* bale kulkul, *of jackfruit wood, used for summoning meetings, Ubud, Bali; Russian balalaika with wooden sound board; chip-carved Yugoslavian shepherd's pipe.*

OPPOSITE, BOTTOM LEFT; AND BOTTOM RIGHT: *Playing panpipes, Brazilian Amazon;* Tibetan sarang *with a skin-covered sound bowl.*

LEFT: *Afghan sarang strung with both plucked and sympathetic strings.*

ABOVE, CENTRE: *Wooden bell hung around a buffalo's neck, Bali.*

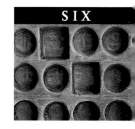

SIX

TOP RIGHT; AND ABOVE, RIGHT: *A slit drum for sending messages, Zomba, Malawi; Aboriginal hardwood clicking sticks, Cairns, Australia. Hardwoods are the most resonant.*

SPIRITUAL WOOD

THE HEATHEN in his blindness, bows down to wood and stone!' said Bishop Reginald Heber (1783–1826), conveniently ignoring the fact that Christian churches are filled with carved images of Christ and the saints. In fact, in lands well equipped with trees, wood may be used in the construction not only of religious images, furniture and paraphernalia, but also in the buildings where worship takes place.

The religious rites of ancient folk such as the Druids and the Greeks took place in groves of oak and olive trees that conquerors hacked and burned in their efforts to stamp out the old beliefs. Even today individual trees may be considered sacred and offerings placed among their roots or in their branches. In Thailand old trees can often be seen with a ribbon around their trunks and in parts of Ireland hawthorns are still festooned with votive strips of cloth.

Churches, temples and shrines

Worship in the open continues all around the world at wayside shrines placed at crossroads, boundaries and other strategic locations. These small raised structures are often humble, containing only a small statue or image, but they are frequently heavily laden with food, flowers and fragrances by respectful passers by. Shrines are often erected in the home or family compound and their tending, for instance in Bali, is an important part of daily life.

Communal worship demands larger buildings and these, particularly in forested lands lacking a good supply of stone, have often been built of wood. Noted types include the Christian stave churches of Norway, the carved mosques of the Hindu Kush in Afghanistan and Pakistan and the Buddhist temples at Nara in Japan. The interiors of these structures are filled with wooden detailing and seating, screens and preaching platforms, whether Christian pulpit or Muslim minbar.

Statues and symbols

Islam abhors the carving of likenesses, but most other sects have no such qualms, filling their holy places with all manner of idols and images. The making of a religious statue is in itself an act of devotion and meditation and may be carried out or commissioned as a penance, an appeal or as a memorial. Any wooden surface can be painted or sculpted with signs and symbols, ranging from depictions of gods and their attributes in Hindu temples to comic allusions on the underside of misericords in the choirs of European cathedrals. Among the most potent of all is the stark image of the cross, featured centrally in Christian churches.

Portable religion

In Japan, Central America, Mediterranean countries and India festivals are celebrated with much shoving and jostling by pulling or carrying the heavy images of

OPPOSITE, TOP LEFT: *Originally placed on the altar in Catholic churches,* retablos *are portable shrines that were often used by missionaries. This Nativity scene from Ethiopia is small enough to be hung around the neck like an amulet.*

OPPOSITE, MIDDLE LEFT: *Peasants seated in front of a large crucifix, Czech Republic.*

OPPOSITE, BOTTOM LEFT: *Afghan folding Koran stand carved from one piece of wood.*

OPPOSITE, CENTRE; AND OPPOSITE, RIGHT: *Painted carving of Lord Krishna, Udaipur, Rajasthan; hardwood carving of the goddess Lakshmi, wife of Vishnu. South India.*

saints or gods on an outing around the town or village. Icons shown to worshippers only on special occasions or *retablos* which may be used to preach and evangelize or to serve as portable shrines are much lighter. *Retablos,* boxed scenes depicting religious stories, were introduced to Peru by the conquistadors in the 16th century to convert the indigenous population to Catholicism, but bear a startling resemblance to the brightly painted *kavadh* employed by itinerant Rajasthani storytellers reciting tales of the Hindu gods in India. More portable still are the rosaries, often of wood, upon which the Christian, Hindu, Buddhist and Muslim faithful count their prayers. In fact, the word 'bead' comes from the Saxon 'biddan' which means to 'pray'.

ABOVE, LEFT: *Painted crucifix cut in one piece, El Salvador.*

ABOVE: *A doulang, stand for offerings of fruit and flowers, used by the Toraja in Sulawesi, Indonesia.*

BELOW: *A Peruvian retablo. The box is wood, but the figures are made from a mixture of plaster and potato paste.*

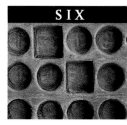

SIX

157

RITUALS AND CEREMONIES

T HE CELEBRATION of significant moments, both public and private, involves countless wooden objects, many of which have become imbued with an aura of significance from generations of use. A block of wood, many believe, is charged with the life force of the tree from which it was cut and so objects used for ritual rather than mundane purposes are imbued with most power when carved from a single piece.

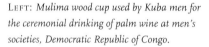

LEFT: *Mulima wood cup used by Kuba men for the ceremonial drinking of palm wine at men's societies, Democratic Republic of Congo.*

Pomp and circumstance

T HE throne of a monarch or chief is a symbol of their status and is often raised on a dais under a canopy. They sit on their throne while others stand or sit on the floor looking up. In Ghana, when the Asantehene (the Asante chief) walks in procession his stool is carried reverently by an appointed stool bearer. The British coronation throne in Westminster Abbey in London is made of wood and for hundreds of years housed the Stone of Scone upon which Scottish kings were crowned. Since the pharaohs sat with their crook and flail – the symbols of their authority – in their hands rulers have flourished their orbs and sceptres, while lesser officials have carried a staff, a baton or a truncheon.

Rites of passage

F ROM birth to death we count the stepping stones of life. On the Indonesian island of Sumba a new born child is ritually bathed in a carved wooden bowl. In Benin entertainers cavort lewdly with huge wooden phalluses during the initiation of Taneka youths. In Marrakesh in Morocco a bride is showered with gifts as she sits in a wooden chair.

Food and drink

M ANY ceremonies involve food and drink as offerings to the spirits, as hospitality or to induce a state of trance or hallucination and sometimes, as in the Potlach of the American North-west or the feasts given by 'men of influence' in Nuristan in Afghanistan, as a sign of

OPPOSITE, TOP RIGHT: *San Jose (Saint Joseph), patron saint of carpenters, carried in procession during Corpus Christi in Cusco, Peru.*

OPPOSITE, CENTRE RIGHT: *Ceremonial food vessel in the form of a life-sized pig, Philippines.*

OPPOSITE, BOTTOM RIGHT: *Basin for ritually washing new born babies, Sumba, Indonesia.*

ABOVE, LEFT; AND ABOVE, RIGHT: *Priest's anthropomorphic dish for drinking kava, Fiji; Tibetan carved and painted prayer table.*

BELOW, LEFT: *Apache Mountain Spirit dancers wearing wooden tablita headdresses.*

BELOW, RIGHT: *Carving on a board for storing a ceremonial kris, a wavy bladed sword, Java.*

wealth. Special spoons, cups and bowls may be required and these may be elaborately fashioned. Today, tourists in Fiji are likely to acquire a copy of a fork used by priests and chiefs at feasts in former times when they ate their enemies. Another popular souvenir in Polynesia is a bowl used for the serving of yaqona or kava, an intoxicating brew prepared with considerable solemnity and formality in a large bowl with feet.

Dances

DANCING often serves a ritual purpose and the dancers may carry symbolic objects. Some, such as English Morris dancing, involve energetic leaping and the whacking of sticks, activities interpreted by experts as being intended to ensure fertility, although quaintly skipping around an enormous wooden maypole may serve the same end. Other dances, like those of the First Peoples of North-east America, may be more warlike and involve the striking of an effigy or 'war post'. Many require the carrying of ornate paddles or, especially in arid regions

such as New Mexico and Arizona, wands representing rain-bringing lightning.

Divination

COMMUNICATING with the Otherworld can be a risky business and so experts stick rigidly to trusted formats and paraphernalia. These include containers for ritual objects and boards or bowls onto which seeds, shells or stones are thrown and the meaning of the resulting pattern deduced.

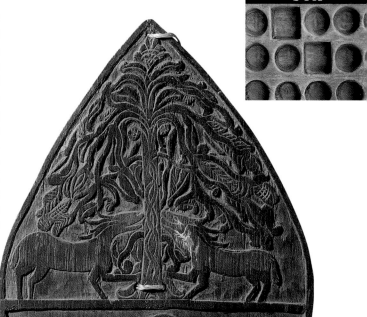

MASKS

IN ANCIENT Greece it was common for a theatre to be packed with over 10,000 spectators, but although acoustics were superb, the facial expressions of the actors could not be seen and so mood and character were conveyed with the help of masks. The Greek for mask was 'persona' from which we derive the English words 'person' and 'personality'. Masks may be made from cloth, leather, metal or papier mâché, but many of the most expressive and spiritually significant are carved from wood.

The origins of masks

CAVE paintings from prehistoric times, such as those at Les Trois Frères in France which are about 15,000 years old, sometimes depict human figures disguised in the skins or heads of animals – usually interpreted as shamans enacting rites to ensure the success of the hunt. These ritual re-enactments and invocations developed into magical and religious ceremonies, plays and dances in which the wearing of costumes or masks has continued to play a part. From these spiritual beginnings activities that serve as a statement of tribal or cultural identity and also as pure entertainment have developed.

The voice of the spirit world

MASKS for spiritual use are treated with great respect. Often the carver must purify himself rigorously before commencing work and remain clean until the task is complete. Specific materials may be prescribed as in the case of the 'false face' masks used in healing ceremonies by the Iroquois in the American North-east. Not only did these have to be carved from living wood, but red masks had to be made in the morning and black masks in the afternoon.

In some cultures, such as parts of West Africa, it is believed that masks may become so imbued with the spiritual power of the character represented that they take on a life of their own and take possession of the wearer. Some of these masks are considered so powerful that they must be carefully locked away when not in use.

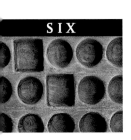

ABOVE, LEFT; LEFT; AND ABOVE, RIGHT:
*Wayang Wong mask, Bali; stylized mask,
Democratic Republic of Congo; Yoruba mask
of the god of Death, Nigeria.*

Types of mask

THE most common form of mask, such as those used in Javanese *topeng* dances or Japanese Noh drama, covers only the face and so allows the wearer considerable freedom of movement and expression. Masks covering only the top of the face allow the actor the clear use of his voice. Some cover the whole head or balance on top and so dictate more limited, stylized movement. This type is usually accompanied by a costume that hides the body completely to convey an otherworldly presence, for instance, the Zangbeto, a spirit believed by the Fon of Benin to guard leaders.

Masks made by the Native Americans of the North-west Coast are sometimes fitted with moving beaks operated with strings. Double-face masks actually open right out to reveal a second face inside.

ABOVE, LEFT: *Mask representing a bearded figure wearing a bronze helmet worn by hunters. Bought in Mali.*

ABOVE, RIGHT: *A Kuba mask from the Democratic Republic of Zaire. Holes around the jaw line were used to attach a straw cape. Many African masks are part of a costume that completely hides the body of the masker which, combined with choreographed movements, create the impression of a creature or being from another dimension.*

LEFT: *Long-faced mask from Mozambique, 1967.*

161

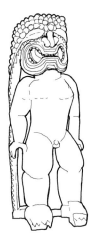

SPIRITS AND ANCESTORS

IN MANY cultures spirits and ancestors may be feared, respected, or even worshipped and are frequently represented in wooden carvings on memorials, buildings and household objects.

Ancestors

THE Navajo of the south-western United States choose not to mention those who have died for fear of invoking the *chindi*, the wrathful element that remains behind, but in most cultures the ancestors are treated with great respect. Making offerings to their statues or memorials, which have been carved or built to provide a 'home', and singing their praises is believed to ensure their goodwill and prevent their dangerous displeasure. Culture heroes and great leaders such as the Chinese master craftsman Lu Ban may even be elevated to divinity.

Highly revered in Angola, the 'civilizing hero' Chibinda Ilunga introduced the ancestors of the Chokwe to metal tools and weapons and after death took on the role of a tutelary spirit. Later rulers commissioned many wooden carvings of him carrying weapons and wearing the royal headdress, thus stating their genealogical link to him and validating their authority.

Intermediaries

IN many places the past is considered a link to the future since the dead once lived in this world, but now live in the next and so, having experience of both worlds and able to travel from one to the other, they are ideally suited to act as intermediaries and intercede for those still alive with the supernatural authorities. In most parts of the world the ancestors are traditionally called upon for help, but for Christians it is the saints and for Buddhists the Bodhisattvas, who all once dwelled in this world, that are invoked.

Spirits

Animism and shamanism are philosophies that existed for millennia before any of the major religions and are still practised today either in an original, unadulterated form or intermingled with a superimposed religion such as the Catholicism of Latin America.

It is believed that all living things have a spirit or life force, as well as the wind, the rain, the rocks and the very earth itself. All these spirits must be treated with respect, especially those that have been adopted by a clan or tribe for their specific virtues. The most potent are those that have appeared to individuals in visions as spirit guides and these are regularly depicted on personal items or carved on portable charms and amulets.

Totem poles

The cedar totem poles of the American north-west are the largest of all wooden carvings but their significance varies from tribe to tribe. Erected at the front of the house, sometimes incorporating the door, a pole proclaimed a family's lineage and status like a coat of arms. The carving of stacked creatures could be a way of invoking the power of totemic animals. At other times the pole might be a memorial marking the giving of a potlatch feast, the assumption of authority or the death of an elder. As a funerary pole it could mark a grave or even hold the bones of the departed.

Opposite, top left; and left centre:
Ancestors carved on panels in a Maori meeting house, New Zealand; Haida memorial pole, British Columbia, Canada.

Opposite, above, right; and bottom:
Colombian 'trouble dolls' kept in a bentwood box; Nigerian dog fetish. In Africa and parts of Indonesia dogs often serve as emissaries to and from the Otherworld.

Above; and right: Ancestor figure, Papua New Guinea; tutelary ancestor figure placed near an altar, a Bambara carving from Segou, Mali.

Near right: Ancestor totems, French New Hebrides.

Above: Hopi
katsina,
New Mexico, USA.

SIX

163

DEATH

THROUGHOUT OUR lives we depend on implements and equipment made of wood to help provide our daily needs, and on death wood may be used to contain our remains and mark our resting place.

Coffins and tombs

THE Egyptians stopped burying their dead in baskets in around 2494 BC and began to lay them flat in wooden caskets of tamarisk or sycamore fig. Wealthy Egyptians had a set of nesting sarcophagi and coffins made from fragrant, imported cedar of Lebanon adorned with paintings and hieroglyphics. In parts of Indonesia members of noble families are traditionally cremated, their bodies enclosed inside a wooden bull; the bones of Maoris were once stored in rotund human-shaped receptacles while, since the 1950s, it has become popular among members of Ghana's Ga people to be buried inside a coffin carved to resemble something related to the deceased's life, an aeroplane for a pilot, a lorry for a truck driver, a giant fish for a fisherman.

Owing to shortages of stone, timber was used during the Megalithic Period for the construction of barrows at Haddenham in England and Sarnovo in Poland. It was, however, common practice among the people of the Steppes to bury notables in wood-lined chambers under the ground such as those at Pazyryk in Siberia and Noin Ula in Mongolia which date back to 500 BC. Tomb-like coffins decorated with superb carving can still be seen exposed

above ground in the rocky valleys of Nuristan in north-east Afghanistan.

The Ship of the Dead

IN many cultures ships and boats are associated with the voyage to the after life. In the Solomon Islands coffins are sometimes shaped like a canoe, while many Sumatran textiles depict the spirits of the dead sailing in wooden ships to the other world. In Ancient Egypt bodies were transported in wooden boats across to the west bank of the Nile for burial and model vessels were often among the grave goods. Viking leaders were laid in a ship which was then buried under a large mound, like the burials at Gokstad in Norway and Sutton Hoo in England, or set alight and sent out to sea in a blaze of glory, a ceremony still reenacted annually at Up Helly A in the Shetland Islands.

Effigies and memorials

CARVINGS or sculptures may be erected on or near a grave or sometimes in the family home as a memorial or as a

TOP LEFT; ABOVE; TOP RIGHT; AND LEFT: *Bone chest carved by Maori woodcarving students in Rotorua, New Zealand; grave at Santa Barbara Mission, California, USA; canoe memorial, Te Puru, Coromandel Peninsular, New Zealand; Warramunga tribesmen at a tree burial, Australia; Araucanian cemetery, Argentina.*

OPPOSITE, LEFT: *'Taotao' effigy figure placed in groups on balconies outside Toraja cliff graves, Sulawesi, Indonesia.*

OPPOSITE, CENTRE: *The carved and inscribed door to a Toraja cliff grave, Sulawesi.*

OPPOSITE, FAR RIGHT: *Pukamani figure traditionally erected on poles at burial sites, carved from ironwood by Tiwi people from the Bathurst and Melville Islands off northern Australia.*

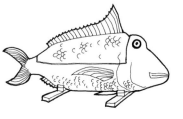

placatory offering. The memorial may take the form of an effigy, as in Sulawesi where the life-like carvings of deceased Torajas watch out from the balconies of burial caves high on the cliffs. At other times memorials are carved with religious or magical symbols to help the spirit on its journey to the after life.

The Tree of Life

DURING the 1990s in England, on the coast of Norfolk, tides washed away mud to reveal a mysterious circle of wooden timbers since named Sea Henge. In the centre was a massive inverted tree trunk, which dendrochronology proved had been felled in 2050 BC, its roots in the air like a giant hand. One theory is that the body of a respected figure had been laid upon the upturned roots. Less than a hundred years ago in parts of Australia and on the plains of North America indigenous peoples continued exposing their dead on a raised wooden platform or safely cradled in the branches of a tree. The tree was a link between the Earth and the Sky, between Life and Death.

SIX

COFFIN FOR A FISHERMAN MADE IN ACCRA, GHANA.

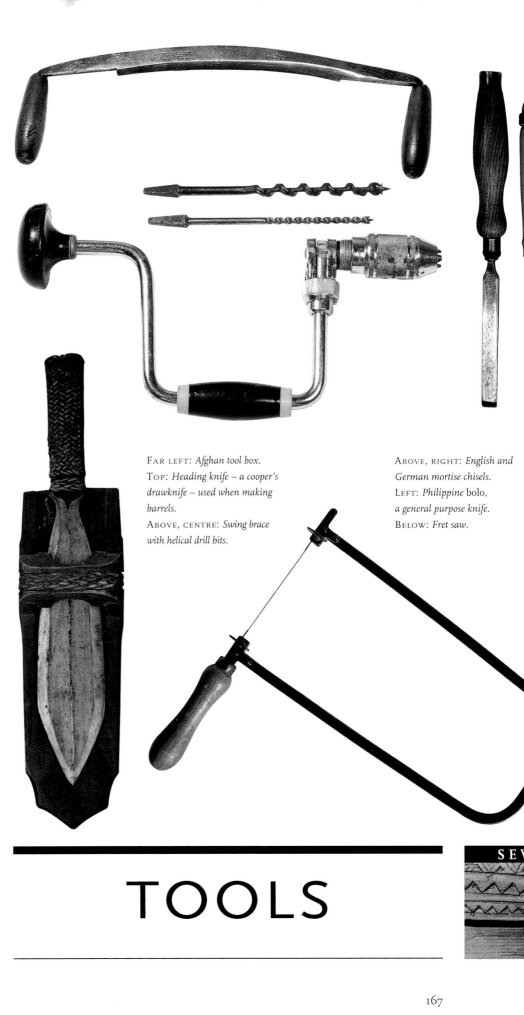

FAR LEFT: *Afghan tool box.*
TOP: *Heading knife – a cooper's drawknife – used when making barrels.*
ABOVE, CENTRE: *Swing brace with helical drill bits.*

ABOVE, RIGHT: *English and German mortise chisels.*
LEFT: *Philippine bolo, a general purpose knife.*
BELOW: *Fret saw.*

SEVEN

TOOLS

TOOLS

OOLS ARE highly revered in many places – designed and constructed by the shaping
and combining of a number of raw materials to perform a specific task. Some birds
are able to winkle insects out of their holes with a stem of grass and sea otters
carry a favourite stone for cracking open shellfish, but it is only the higher primates, with
their large brains and opposable thumbs, who adapt materials to their specific needs –
a chimpanzee will break a stick into a manageable length for breaking nuts. However, it is
only man who designs and constructs tools from scratch. The Maori consider them *tapu*
(taboo), not to be touched by women or unclean people, and the Japanese carpenter treats
them as a Samurai would his sword, they represent his soul.

ABOVE, LEFT: Reconstruction of a knapped flint knife fitted in a wooden handle.

ABOVE: Flint axe head, the sharp edge is achieved by knocking off flakes with a stone or a piece of antler.

LEFT: Flint axe head fitted into a socket in a wooden shaft and bound with rawhide thongs.

LEFT, MIDDLE: Greenstone adze head from Papua New Guinea. A very sharp edge can be achieved by painstakingly rubbing the blade against an abrasive stone surface.

BOTTOM LEFT: Shipwrights using a side axe, chest auger, hammer and axe depicted on the Bayeux Tapestry.

STONE TOOLS

HE EARLIEST known tools, believed to be at least 2.5 million years old, were
discovered in Ethiopia. Designed for cutting, chopping and scraping, they
were made by knocking flakes off one rock with another and were sharp enough
to cut through flesh and bone. By the Late Stone Age the range of implements included
choppers, scrapers, axes, knives, hammers and points. Tools with handles were in use
40,000 years ago as shown by a hafted axe discovered in Papua New Guinea.

Rocks such as flint, quartz or basalt can be shaped by flaking, but others such as
sandstone require painstaking pecking and then grinding against an abrasive surface to
achieve an edge.

METAL TOOLS

THE HIGH temperatures achieved by early potters for firing made it possible to smelt metal from ore. Copper was worked in Turkey about 8,000 years ago, bronze was being worked in the Near East 5,000 years ago and iron was widespread 2,500 years ago. Many regions, however, did not acquire metalworking technology until the arrival of explorers and settlers during the first millennium AD. Metal can be given a keen cutting edge, is hardwearing and can be sharpened easily when required which meant that it became possible to cut and shape wood more precisely, allowing the development of precision carving and sophisticated joinery.

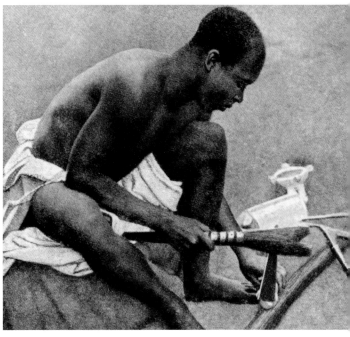

LEFT: *Sakai tribesmen in the Perak Hills of Malaya equipped with stone-headed axes.*

OTHER MATERIALS

MANY NATURAL materials with a hard or sharp edge have been used to make tools. In Papua New Guinea an adze sometimes had a clamshell blade. On the American North-west coast a chisel might once have had a blade of beaver tooth.

Fire has been exploited in many ways – as an aid to felling timber, to hollow canoes, straighten and harden missiles, to drill holes and even, in the craft of pyroengraving or pyrography, to draw delicate patterns on a smooth surface.

ABOVE, RIGHT: *Zande woodworker in the north-west Congo carving with an axe. If the blade is turned ninety degrees the axe becomes an adze.*

LEFT: *A Belgian country craftsman using a side axe to shape sabots, wooden clogs. During riots against industrialization French activists threw their sabots into machines to wreck them, hence the word sabotage.*

RIGHT: *Japanese carved* netsuke *(toggle) depicting a group of woodworkers equipped with hammers, chisel and saws. To a Japanese craftsman, tools are the equivalent of a Samurai's sword and should be treated with great respect.*

SEVEN

MARKING AND MEASURING

THE SECRET of accurate woodworking is the careful measuring and marking of timber before the actual cutting and shaping begins.

TOP: THE EGYPTIAN HIEROGLYPH FOR CUBIT.

ABOVE: GOD CREATING THE UNIVERSE, AFTER AN ILLUSTRATION IN A 13TH-CENTURY FRENCH BIBLE.

The human body

TRADITIONAL Balinese buildings are still laid out using the *Asta Kosali* system in which the units of measurement are based on the body of the building's owner. The basic unit is the combination of the arm span, the distance from the elbow to the tip of the middle finger, and the width of the fist with the thumb extended. Although now generally standardized, many other systems are also anthropocentric. In Britain, before metrification, standard units included the foot and the yard (the distance from the nose to the fingertip). The Egyptian cubit (52.4 cm) was based on the forearm and horses are still measured in hands.

Tools for measuring size

THE basic tool for measuring is a rod of predetermined length. This is marked off in smaller units according to the local system. Rulers and rules may be simply straight sticks, folding wooden devices, tapes or flexible metal strips that withdraw into a case. When a comparison is required, a pair of hinged dividers may be employed or callipers which are designed to measure a rounded form or a gap.

Marking a straight line

DRAWING along the straight edge of a piece of timber or metal with a pencil or metal scribe will normally produce a fairly accurate line. On an uneven surface a common practice is to stretch a chalked line tight and twang it sharply. Japanese carpenters use a *sumi-tsubo* which works on the same principle, coating a thread in ink as it is drawn out.

Marking angles

OFTEN seen as a master craftsman's badge of office, the 'square', a wooden or metal device shaped like the letter L used for measuring right angles, has been used by craftsmen all over the world for centuries. The try square has a metal blade fitted at a right angle into a wooden stock and makes the task easier as it can butt up against the edge of a piece of timber. The mitre square is similar, but has the metal blade set at 45 degrees.

LEFT: *Steel callipers used for comparing sizes.*

ABOVE: *Balinese man demonstrating* Asta Kosali, *the Balinese system of measurement based on the human body. A building is laid out according to the proportions of its owner.*

BELOW: *A retractable steel rule. Turning the handle withdraws the flexible rule into its case.*

Gauges and templates

For rebates or mortises, lines a specified distance from an edge can be marked with a variety of gauges pushed along the side of the work. These have a fixed blade or marking pin and a head that can be slid along the beam to set the size of the required gap.

To ensure that shapes are cut accurately, the woodworker may draw around templates cut from paper, wood, metal or plastic. For some tasks, such as marking dovetails, these can be bought ready made but often, as in the case of boat building, they may be made specifically for the task in hand.

Finding a level

Vertical lines have since time immemorial been checked with the use of a plumb line, a weight hanging on a cord. In ancient times horizontals were checked using pipes of water that quickly found their own level. The modern equivalent is the spirit level which displays a bubble suspended in a curved, oil-filled tube.

Top: *Boxwood ruler fitted with brass hinges, so it can be folded away conveniently when not in use.*

Above: *An English Edwardian gauge for marking mortises; rosewood with brass fittings.*

Right: *A try square with a rosewood stock used for marking lines at a right angle to the edge of a piece of timber.*

Above: A craftsman with his square, after William Caxton, 1483.

Right: *An ebony try square with brass fittings. Before mass production, many individually made tools were items of beauty in their own right.*

Below: *Pocket-sized boxwood spirit level with a brass face plate. Depending on the task for which they are intended, spirit levels vary in size and shape, some are over a metre long.*

Above: Japanese *sumi-tsubu* used for marking straight lines.

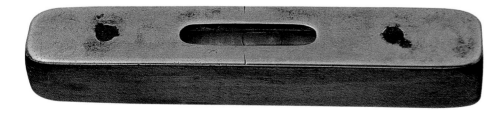

Axes

The axe is one of the most ancient of tools. Originally, stone axes were held in the hand and were used for many chores, including scraping and butchering meat. With the addition of a wooden handle, which enhanced the power behind a blow, they became the archetypal chopping tool. Early axe heads were tied to the haft with sinew or thongs, but by the time of the Minoan culture in Crete it had become common practice to wedge the haft into a socket in the head as we still do today.

RIGHT: MASTER CARVER WITH DIVIDERS AND AXE, AFTER A 15TH-CENTURY MANUSCRIPT.

The versatile axe

With its fearsome chopping power, the axe has been used for millennia to fell both trees and men, and has often been fitted with a double head designed to be swung easily in both directions. The blades were frequently crescent shaped and, taking on an association with the moon, featured in many religious practices and sacrifices. On the walls of the compound built at Knossos in Crete some time around 1600 BC, reputedly by the legendary craftsman Daedalus, there are many depictions of double-headed axes. The Greek for 'axe' was *labrys* from which the word labyrinth is derived. The practical Vikings used their axes for both destruction and construction and some of the old wooden churches, such as the 10th-century Russian buildings in Novgorod, were built and carved with little more than an axe.

The felling axe

Used for chopping down trees and wielded with both hands, the felling axe is the most powerful of woodworking hand tools. Until the end of the 19th century in Europe it had a wedge-shaped blade and a straight handle about 1 metre (3 ft) long, a design basically the same as those depicted in the Bayeux Tapestry. The American axe which superseded it had a convex blade with a bend in the haft called a 'fawn's foot'. This increased the speed of the woodman's swing and therefore the force he could exert.

SEVEN

The hatchet

THE hatchet has a shorter haft than the felling axe and is designed to be used with one hand. It is ideal for trimming fallen timber, for splitting billets and for roughly cutting wood to shape before more precise work begins. The hatchet proverbially buried by Native Americans was a trade item introduced by settlers. Colloquially known as a tomahawk, it had a hollow shaft and a pipe bowl fitted to the back of the head.

The side axe

ALTHOUGH similar to a hatchet, the side axe has a blade sharpened to a bevel on only one side. The handle may also have a sideways curve which allows the axe to be used to pare down wood with a light chopping action without bashing the knuckles.

The thrust axe

THE thrust axe is no longer in use, but it was used in Europe for shaping wood. It resembled a chisel set at right angles to its handle and was employed to slice rather than chop.

OPPOSITE, ABOVE, RIGHT: *Middle Bronze Age axe head of the 'palstave' type designed to fit into the split in a handle; replica made by Dave Chapman from cast bronze.*

OPPOSITE, BELOW, LEFT: *Double-bit axe with straight handle, Pennsylvania, North America. Shock-absorbent woods, such as hickory in North America and ash in Europe, are used for handles.*

OPPOSITE, BELOW, RIGHT: *Short hand axe or hatchet designed for use with one hand.*

TOP: *Czechoslovakian side axe offering a flat face on one side.*

ABOVE: *British shipwright's masting axe for trimming spars.*

RIGHT, CENTRE: *The head of an English shipwright's side axe.*

LEFT: *Roughly shaping a billet of hibiscus wood with a hatchet at the Balinese woodcarvers' cooperative in Mas, near the cultural centre of Ubud. A considerable amount of shaping can be achieved with the axe before chisels and gouges are brought into use.*

RIGHT: *Austrian lumbermen in the Alpine forest, their felling axes on their shoulders.*

ADZES

THE ADZE is very similar to the axe, but the blade is set at right angles to the handle and curves inwards towards it. It is reminiscent of the shape of deer antlers which, known to have been in common usage in prehistoric times, may have provided the inspiration for its design. While the axe is used for chopping, the adze is designed for chipping and slicing away the surface of the wood. In former times it was used to trim planks and boards, to hollow out canoes and to cut the hollows into the seats of Windsor chairs. Some form of adze has been employed in most parts of the world, but it has been the primary tool for carpentry and carving in West Africa, the American North-west, New Zealand and in the Pacific. Such is the reverence for the adze or *toki* in Oceania that it is used as a ceremonial or ritual object, and as a symbol of authority.

Raw materials

THE first adze and axe were very likely the same stone hand tool held at a different angle. Suitable stone, such as flint or obsidian, that could be chipped into an edge was highly prized and traded over great distances. Tools made from stone quarried in the Italian Alps have been found at Neolithic sites as far away as the British Isles. The greenstone or nephrite, called *pounamu* by the Maoris, was first admired for its cutting properties once it had been painstakingly ground to shape and only much later collected for the beauty of its translucent colour.

In Papua New Guinea and parts of the Pacific shell blades made from the thick calcareous material at the heart of conch shells were once common. The adze of the Chumash in California was fitted with a blade made from sharpened pismo clam shell.

TOP: *Panel created by smoothing a board with an adze; replica Anglo-Saxon chair with adze marks.*

ABOVE; AND FAR LEFT: *Adzes with stone blades, secured with basketry ring, Sepik River, Papua New Guinea; shipwright's adze and small cooper's adze.*

The adze was among the first tools cast in metal by the Egyptians, while the axe was introduced to them by the Greeks or Romans more than 1,000 years later.

The elbow adze

THE best known form of the adze is the elbow adze, so called because of the bend formed where the blade joins the long handle. The craftsman stands on or over his work and swings the adze down in a series of rhythmic cuts which create a distinctive pattern. Varying force and blades of different curvature can be used to remove chips of different sizes, large chips when hollowing out a canoe, but small when shaping the seat of a chair. A smaller one-handed adze can be employed to great effect for carving or for work in a confined space such as the inside of a barrel. Seldom found in the tool kit of Western amateurs, the adze continues to be an essential part of the stock in trade of specialist woodworkers such as barrel makers, chair makers and shipwrights and is still considered indispensable by craftsmen in Africa and around the Pacific.

The D-adze

THE D-adze is an implement mainly employed by Native American carvers in the North-west. It consists of a blade attached to a d-shaped handle designed to fit the hand and, depending on the curvature of the blade, can be used to remove large chips or for finishing work. Formerly the blade might have been stone or bone, but is now normally made from recycled car leaf springs or old files to suit the individual carver's needs.

ABOVE: D-ADZES FROM THE AMERICAN NORTH-WEST COAST.

LEFT: AZTEC WOODCARVER WITH ADZE, AFTER A 16TH-CENTURY CODEX.

BELOW, LEFT: *Elbow axe with a greenstone blade lashed in place with cord, Highlands, Papua New Guinea. Good stone for cutting edges was once a valuable trading commodity, but has now been largely replaced by recycled metals.*

BELOW CENTRE: *The prow of a Samoan canoe hollowed out with innumerable blows with adzes of various sizes.*

TOP: *A ceremonial adze with chip-carved handle and elaborate coconut-fibre bindings for the basalt blade, Mangaia, Cook Islands.*

ABOVE, INSET: *Zande carver working with an adze, Democratic Republic of Congo.*

SEVEN

KNIVES

SINCE EARLY man chipped and ground the first sharp blades, working men and women around the world have kept a knife in their belts or pockets. Other tools might be carried when required for a specific task or kept in a workplace, but the knife is easily transported and can serve many purposes – whether it is used for eating, basketmaking, horticulture or woodworking.

Machetes

IN country covered with dense forests the tool of choice is a long, sword-like knife that can be used to hack and slash offending vegetation or enemies. In Spanish-speaking countries it is called a machete and in South-East Asia a parang. Although not a precision implement, in skilled hands it is often used for rudimentary carpentry.

Drawknives

THE drawknife is fitted with a handle at each end and pulled across the work, which is often clamped in a shave horse. Although seldom seen today, drawknives were once stock in trade for shipwrights, coopers, chair makers and many other specialized craftsmen. The scorp is a European one-handled drawknife with a deeply curved blade for hollowing spoons and bowls.

Curved knives

ORIGINALLY made from the incisors of beavers in Canada and North America the curved, bent or crooked knife is the primary carving tool. Never produced commercially, these knives are still made from suitable recycled steel such as files or circular saw blades, which are ground to shape, heated until they turn a purple colour and then bent to the desired curve by pressing against

TOP LEFT; FAR LEFT; AND NEAR LEFT: *Samoan warrior carrying a nifo'oti, traditional Samoan weapon with a hooked blade; 'Welsh love spoon' with linked chain; jack knife with blades that fold back into the handle.*

BELOW, LEFT; BOTTOM; AND BELOW, RIGHT: *Thunderbird carved with a curved knife, Nishga tribe, British Columbia, Canada; Fijian* sele, *machete; sharpening stakes with a* sele.

a piece of wood. Usually gripped under-hand for cutting towards the body, curved knives are still used for carving the totemic patterns on houses, poles and containers on the North-west coast and for under-cutting the grooves on kerf-bent boxes.

Folding knives

Blades that can be folded back into the handle are both useful and portable as shown by the number of variations and names including pen knife, pocket knife and jack knife (jack is an Old English word for the common working man). An old name for the large clasp knife is 'whittle' which is derived from the Old English word thwitan which means to cut.

Whittling

Technically, whittling is the art of carving with a knife carried out in the free time of working men. The most common whittled objects are toys, whistles and love tokens such as spoons, which in Wales traditionally feature virtuoso details such as chains and moving balls. In Africa the knife is the usual tool for all carving after roughing out with an adze. In Japan some craftsmen specialize in *itto-bori* (one-knife carving) – a skill learned from the indigenous people of the north, the Ainu. With this technique a bird is carved in one piece with its plumage suggested by careful slivering with a large knife.

ABOVE: Bent knife made from an old file blade, Ojibway tribe, Minnesota, North America, 1870.

TOP: *Woodcarving knife, or* pongutik, *Bali. Like most tools, Balinese craftsmen make these knives for their own use.*

ABOVE: *A short bladed knife designed for the stabbing cuts used in chip carving, England.*

LEFT: *A Balinese craftsman in Mas trimming a carving of Ganesh with a* pongutik, *wood-carving knife.*

RIGHT: *Comb for a loved one, carved with a knife by an Asante man, Ghana. The symbolism of keys and padlocks, similar to Welsh love spoons, refer to the unlocking of the heart.*

SEVEN

Hammers

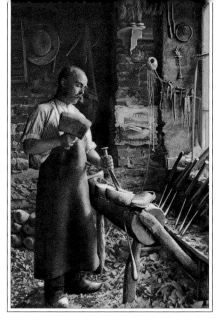

A SIMPLE TOOL, employed by many craftsmen, jewellers, cobblers, stonemasons, blacksmiths and woodworkers, the hammer has become a symbol of creative masculine force. Because of the ringing blows struck by the craftsman it has become associated with the gods of thunder – in a similar way, the Scandinavian god Thor was considered the protector of peasants and ordinary working folk. Miolnir, Thor's hammer, was a potent weapon that returned to his hand after he had thrown it at his enemies, but also had the power to revive the dead. Weddings were sanctified with the sign of the hammer and it was popular as a talismanic pendant around the necks of Vikings. In Japan a magic mallet is the attribute of Daikoku, the god of wealth, and is endowed with the power to grant wishes and confer wealth. In the 20th century, accompanied by the sickle of agricultural labourers, the hammer was adopted by communist nations as a symbol of the might and rights of the working masses.

ABOVE: *Belgian craftsman hollowing sabots with a gouge struck with a wooden mallet.*

BELOW, FROM LEFT TO RIGHT: *Lightweight cross-peen pin hammer; general purpose cross-peen hammer made in China; adze-eye claw hammer for driving in nails and levering out bent ones.*

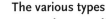

The various types

ANY heavy, solid object such as an antler, a rock or a block of wood may be used to augment a blow with the hand and many prehistoric artefacts, obviously designed for this function and worked to fit the hand comfortably, have been discovered. Later examples are often grooved which suggests that they were lashed to a wooden handle. This would lengthen the swing, increasing the leverage and enhance the impact. Experience has shown that woods such as ash or hickory are most suitable for handles as they absorb some of the shock of the impact. Power, however, is achieved at the cost of accuracy and so, over the millennia, especially since the

BELOW, LEFT: *European-style cross-peen hammer.*

SILVER PENDANT AMULET OF THOR'S HAMMER, FROM A VIKING GRAVE.

LEFT: EGYPTIAN
CRAFTSMAN USING
A MALLET, AFTER
A TOMB PAINTING.

development of metallurgical skills, hammers have evolved with varying lengths of handle and a selection of different heads.

Woodworking hammers range from the lightweight pin hammer, used for driving small nails or pins, to heavy hammers for large nails. The striking face of continental European hammers is square, while on British and American hammers it is round. Projecting to the rear is the 'peen'. This may be a wedge-shaped cross-peen for nails or a domed-ball peen. The peen of heavier hammers are sometimes shaped like a claw for levering out bent nails.

Mallets and mauls

Woodworkers around the world may use a metal hammer for driving nails, but prefer to use a wooden mallet for striking chisels and gouges. This may be a simply shaped block of hardwood such as *Lignum vitae* or a head on a shaft. In Europe carpenters favour a squared-off block of beech with a separate handle that is tapered so that every blow drives the head on more firmly. Carvers, on the other hand, prefer rounded wooden mallets that can be used to strike a blow from any angle. Mallets of differing sizes may be used according to the scale of the work.

When considerable force is required, specialists such as coopers will employ gigantic two-handed mallets called mauls or beetles which may have a head reinforced with metal bands.

ABOVE, LEFT: *Cutting fine detail with a mallet and chisel, Mas, Bali. In the hands of an experienced carver short blows with a mallet can offer more precise control than the pressure of the hand.*

RIGHT: *English beech wood carpenter's mallet with slightly tapered faces.*

LEFT, INSET: *Using mallet and gouge to carve a seat from a tree root, Banue, Philippines.*

LEFT: *Ash-handled mallet with the rounded head preferred by carvers of both wood and stone.*

SEVEN

CHISELS AND GOUGES

EVEN BEFORE the development of metal, chisels and gouges of stone, shell or bone were an essential part of the woodworker's tool kit and were used for shaping and trimming, and for carrying out the most intricate work. The design of blade varies according to culture and function and professional carvers may have hundreds of gouges and chisels of assorted sizes and shapes. The shape of the handle also varies – it is dictated particularly by the method of pressure exerted, whether hand or hammer. Both chisel and gouge are frequently used head on, but precision work is carried out with a slicing motion with the blade at an angle to the work.

Chisels

A CHISEL is essentially a long piece of metal, squared off at the end and most often sharpened on only one face. Long handles are used for turning and domed handles that fit the palm are used for fine carving and cutting printing blocks, both intended to give the best grip for the specific job. The handles of firmer chisels, intended for cutting mortises, are reinforced with a metal ring to protect them from the blows of hammers, and a leather washer between the handle and blade absorbs the shock. In many places, such as Bali, where craftsmen make their own tools this problem is avoided by not fitting the blade with a handle at all.

Gouges

GOUGES resemble chisels except they are rounded in section which makes them ideal for cutting curves or hollows. Like chisels, gouges vary considerably in size, but the cutting edge or 'sweep' is always a true radius curve. An 'out-cannel' gouge has the bevel or edge ground on the outside, while an 'in-cannel' gouge is sharpened on the inside.

ABOVE: ANDEAN
CHISEL WITH WOOD
HANDLE AND COPPER
BLADE.

OPPOSITE, TOP: *Long-handled wood-turning gouges.*

OPPOSITE, ABOVE, LEFT: *Balinese carver using a* pungancha, *chisel.*

OPPOSITE, BELOW, LEFT: *Mike Wickam using a long-handled wood-turning gouge.*

OPPOSITE, CENTRE: *Two old gouges and a chisel with different types of handle.*

FAR LEFT: *Japanese chisels, the one on the right is for cutting the soles of clogs.*

NEAR LEFT: *Three turning chisels with skewed cutting edges.*

RIGHT: *Balinese* pungancha *chisel with no handle, made by a carver for his own use.*

BELOW: *Small V-shaped gouges for fine detail, designed to fit in the palm.*

Veiners and parting tools

IN section, veiners are U shaped with straighter sides than a gouge and parting tools are V shaped. Both are designed for cutting grooves which may be used to define a shape or, as in the case of Maori 'hae hae' lines that snake and spiral across their carvings, may be a decorative feature in their own right.

Spoon bends, dog legs and back bends

CHISEL and gouge blades are sometimes curved along the shank in order to reach awkward places such as the hollow of a bowl or spoon. They may be spoon bent with a concave curve, dog leg with a concave crank, or back bent with a convex curve.

Japanese chisels

THE reputation of the Japanese chisel has spread far beyond Japan. Unlike Western chisels, which are mass produced and stamped out by drop forging, a traditional Japanese chisel is handmade by a blacksmith who forges two separate pieces of steel together with repeated hammering. One piece is of hard steel to produce an edge that will stay sharp for a long time and the other piece, of softer steel, makes a resilient backing. These chisels cut very clean and have been an important factor in the development of Japanese precision joinery.

Planes

Possibly invented in Ancient Greece, the plane, like many other tools, had developed by Roman times into a form very similar to the modern version. The wooden type, sometimes with a sole of hard *Lignum vitae* or brass, has become less common in Europe and North America since the first metal designs were patented in North America in 1827. Planes are used to shave away a roughly worked wooden surface, shaping and smoothing it closer to its final form.

Plane design

All planes consist of a box or frame in which a metal blade is set at an angle. In older designs the blade is held in place by a wooden or metal wedge, while later designs use a screw or powerful spring mechanism. The depth of cut and thickness of shaving is controlled by the size of an adjustable gap between the metal blade and the body of the plane. For the application of extra force the body is often fitted with knobs or handles, making it easier to push it or, in the case of Japanese planes, to pull it across the surface of the work.

Types of plane

Bench planes, wood and metal, are the standard levelling tool and range in size from smoothing planes, around 22.5 cm (9 in.) long, designed for finishing, up to try or jointing planes around 60 cm (24 in.) long which are ideal for planing a straight edge when a shorter one might follow the undulations of the work. In between is the general-purpose jack plane. The scrub plane, used diagonally across the grain, is fitted with a convex cutting edge to remove wood quickly.

Intended for one-handed use, the smaller block plane cuts at a shallow angle

Above: The Workshop of Joseph of Nazareth *by William Lance. Joseph is using a block plane.*

Below, left: *Modern metal planes, a smoothing plane and small bull-nose rebate plane.*

Below, middle: *A 19th-century cooper's chiv for trimming the inside of barrels.*

Below, right: *An 'old woman's tooth', a simple form of router made in the 19th century.*

SEVEN

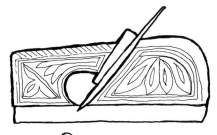

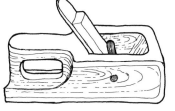

TOP; AND ABOVE: PLANE FROM SWAT, PAKISTAN; ROMAN METAL-FACED PLANE.

and, unlike the bench plane, has the bevel on the upper side of the blade. It is most often employed for smoothing end grain, working from the edges to the centre.

Rebate planes are used by joiners for cutting a rectangular recess or rebate along the edge of the work. To facilitate this they are fitted with a blade that extends the full width of the sole.

There are many specialized variations of planes, some designed for trimming curved surfaces and others, like the router, for hollowing out. Plough and combination planes can be fitted with a number of interchangeable blades for cutting grooves and mouldings, a task that until the beginning of the 20th century was accomplished with a set of moulding planes, one for each shape required – reeds, flutes, ovolos and ogees. These are also the tools required to make tongue and groove joints.

The spokeshave

Working on the same principle as a plane is the spokeshave, so named because of its use in the trimming of spokes by wheelwrights. It is a two-handed tool with an adjustable blade set into the handle at an angle that takes a shaving as it is pushed away from the body. Designs vary considerably according to the specific requirements of its owner, whether cooper or wheelwright.

TOP: *Two wooden bench planes with the blade secured with a wooden wedge. The older is an English 19th-century tool and the other one was made in Holland for the contemporary market.*

ABOVE: *A 19th-century moulding plane fitted with a shaped blade. Cabinet makers once possessed a number of these for cutting different shapes – for reeding, fluting, ogees and ovolos.*

BELOW: *The plane is a descendant of the drawknife which was a sharp blade with a handle at each end used for cutting shavings. The spokeshave (illustrated here) is a more refined version fitted with a shorter blade. By opening or narrowing the gap between blade and handle, the thickness of the shavings is kept consistent.*

Saws

Accoording to Greek myth, it was Talos, the nephew of the master craftsman Daedalus, who invented the saw. One day while wandering along the seashore he picked up a fish spine and, idly drawing it back and forth, discovered that it could cut a stick in half. On returning home he produced a version in metal and showed it to Daedalus who, in a fit of jealous pique, pushed the unfortunate youth off the roof to his death.

A saw consists of a row of teeth that cut a groove or 'kerf' into a piece of timber. Although simple saws had been made by chipping teeth on the edge of a piece of flint, it was not until the development of metal-working skills that really effective blades were produced. However, by Roman times all the main types of saw had been invented, with the exception of power tools such as the chain saw.

Teeth

Usually, to maximize their cutting power, the teeth of a saw, or points as they are often called, are set alternately slightly to left and right. When sharpened at the front they will cut on the push stroke and when sharpened at the rear they will cut on the pull. A saw with large teeth will cut quickly, but crudely, leaving a ragged edge and so small teeth are used for the finest work. A fret saw might have thirty-two teeth to the inch, while a log saw might have only three or four.

TOP: *The* dozuki, *a Japanese back saw for joint making, which cuts on the pull stroke.*

TOP RIGHT: *Cutting logs with a frame saw, Luxembourg.*

ABOVE, RIGHT; AND INSET: *Metal-framed coping saw for cutting curves; small cabinet maker's frame saw tensioned with a screw action at the top. The blade can be turned in the frame.*

ABOVE, LEFT: *Fret saw at work cutting a tight curve.*

Rip saws have teeth sharpened at the end so they cut like tiny chisels, which is ideal for cutting with the grain of the wood, but rips and tears if used across the grain. Instead, a cross-cut saw should be used with its teeth sharpened at the edges – they can be used with the grain, but are less effective than rip saws. Panel saws have fine cross-cut teeth for cutting man-made boards. The largest cross-cut saws, intended for cutting large timbers or logs, have a handle at each end and are operated by two men taking turns at pulling the saw towards them.

Maintaining tension

THE simplest form is the 'hand saw', a metal blade with teeth along one edge, used to cut straight lines. Early Egyptian hand saws resembled bread knives with a simple wooden handle, but modern handles are slotted at right angles to the blade. The Egyptian saw was pulled as it was inclined to buckle on the push stroke, but better quality steel is now used and hand saws more often cut on the push. Miniature versions include the pad saw or keyhole saw used to pierce and cut shapes in the middle of a board.

For cutting joints finer saws such as the 'tenon' and 'dovetail' are employed. To keep these rigid they are fitted with a reinforced strip of brass or steel at the top edge and are therefore referred to as 'back saws'.

A Roman solution to the buckling blade was to keep it under tension, like a bowstring, with a bent stick. This principle of the 'bow' saw has since been used in the design of Swedish tubular steel log saws and fine coping saws and fret saws that are capable of cutting tight curves.

The Romans also used 'frame' saws that tensioned the blade in a wooden frame which could be tightened with a tourniquet. Small frame saws have swivelling blades, ideal for cutting curves, while large versions may have the blade in the middle for ripping planks or even have multiple blades for cutting veneers.

ABOVE: *Swedish-style bow saw with a cross-cut blade, used for cutting logs.*

ABOVE, INSET: *Cutting pieces for pianos using an electric jigsaw.*

BELOW: *Cheap plastic panel saw that can be bought for less than the cost of sharpening a higher quality tool.*

BOTTOM: *A tenon saw with reinforced back.*

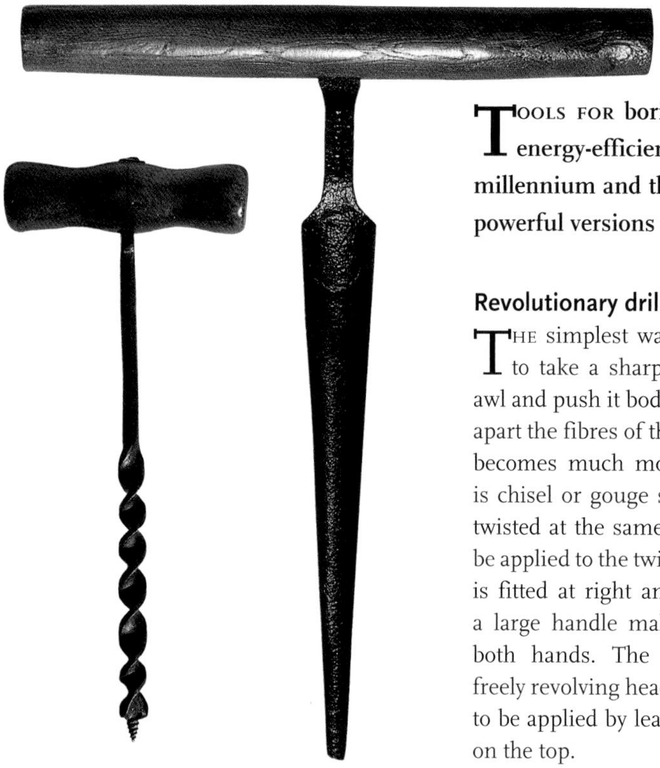

Tools for boring holes have existed since prehistoric times, but the modern, energy-efficient hand drills we know today were only developed in the last millennium and these, more than any other tools, have largely been superseded by powerful versions driven by electricity.

Revolutionary drill design

The simplest way of making a hole is to take a sharp implement called an awl and push it bodily downwards to force apart the fibres of the wood, a process that becomes much more effective if the tip is chisel or gouge shaped and the tool is twisted at the same time. More force can be applied to the twisting action if a handle is fitted at right angles, like a letter T – a large handle makes it possible to use both hands. The addition of a loose, freely revolving head allows extra pressure to be applied by leaning the chest or chin on the top.

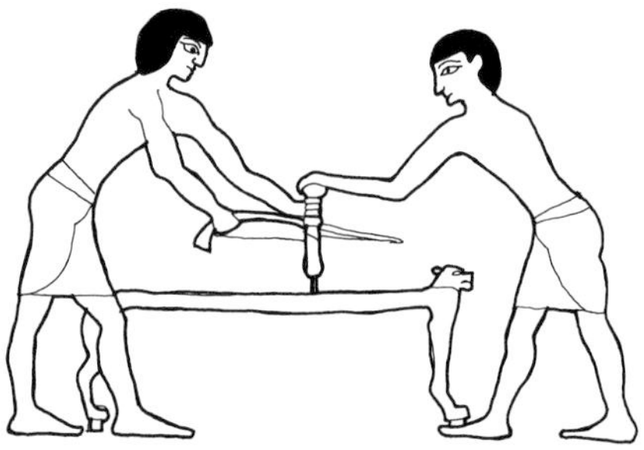

LEFT:
EGYPTIAN
CRAFTSMEN
USING A
BOW DRILL.

Bow and pump drills

Although less pressure can be applied, small bits can be rotated at greater speed with the aid of a bow, a principle well established over 4,000 years ago. The string of the bow is wrapped around the shaft of the bit, pressure exerted on a revolving headpiece and the bow is then pulled rapidly back and forth, causing the bit to turn. The shaft can also be turned by wrapping the cord several times around it and pumping the bow up and down which makes the twisted cord rotate. Another method of pumping employs a hand piece that engages with a spiral groove cut in the shaft, so that as it is pushed down the shaft is forced to revolve.

The brace

The Greek genius Archimedes investigated the use of levers and gears

Left: Pomo Indian pump drill from California, North America.

Opposite, far left: *Wooden pump drill, from Lombok, turned by pushing the cord-wrapped ring up and down. The bit has no screw.*

Opposite, above, second from left: *Twisted with one hand, the gimlet has a helical screw to cut and remove waste.*

Opposite, above, right: *Wheelwright's auger with tapering, gouge-shaped blade, twisted with both hands.*

Opposite, below: *Two hand drills driven by turning a geared wheel. The drill bit is secured in the metal chuck which is tightened in the upper drill using a chuck key and in the lower by hand.*

Above: *Using a bow drill on olive wood, Jerusalem.*

Below: *Dyaks in Sarawak hollowing out a blowpipe using a long metal rod. The second man pours in water to float out the chips.*

in around 230 BC, but it was probably not until the late 14th century that the knowledge was applied to drills. European craftsmen invented the brace by introducing a crank in the handle, so that greater leverage could be applied by swinging the handle. More sophisticated still is the wheel brace, invented in the mid-19th century, which is equipped with a handle at right angles to the actual direction of turning. Ideal for work in tight spaces, this drill is geared so that one full rotation of the handle will turn the bit four times.

Cutting-edge technology

The earliest drills were fitted with chips of hard stone, shell or metal fitted into a wooden shaft. Early metal bits had a triangular tip, but during the Dark Ages large holes were being cut using gouge-shaped 'spoon bits'.

From sometime around the 10th century the auger and the diminutive gimlet, both with T-shaped handles, were improved with the added sophistication of a helical groove running up them which removed waste as the tip dug in. This was the prototype of all modern drill bits which are now mass produced in a variety of metals suitable for penetrating wood, metal or stone, with single or double helical twists and a wide range of sizes designed for making holes up to 7.5 cm (3 in.) in diameter.

Top right: *Swing brace. While one hand swings the handle, pressure can be exerted with hand pressure or body weight on the round handle at the rear.*

Above centre: *Metal bits with square shanks for secure clamping in the chuck of a swing brace.*

Above, right: *A bradawl which makes a hole by forcing the wood fibres apart.*

187

Lathes

Thousands of years ago ingenious woodworkers realized that an enormous amount of time and muscle power would be saved if a piece of wood was made to move against a blade rather than the other way round. They achieved this by fixing a piece of roughly shaped wood between two fixed points, or centres, taking a turn around the wood with a cord and then pulling the cord back and forth to make the wood revolve.

ABOVE: *A basket of turned bobbins and a pile of shavings beneath the frame of a pole lathe.*

LEFT: *The reciprocating motion of the pole lathe. The craftsman presses the pedal with his foot and the work spins towards his chisel. He releases the pressure and the pole springs back up. The cut is made only as the pedal is pressed. Although electrically powered lathes are fast and efficient, many craftsmen in the West also enjoy the intimate experience of using this simple technology which offers a more integrated involvement with the turning process and very little noise.*

BELOW: *Using a bow lathe in Marrakesh, Morocco. One hand controls the revolution of the work with the bow, while the other hand holds the chisel.*

The bow lathe

In Asia and North Africa many woodworkers continue to use a small lathe in which the cord is attached to a bow, just like those used in the time of the pharaohs. The turner sits on the ground pulling the bow back and forth with one hand and holding a chisel to the work with the other, while his feet hold the lathe or chisel steady. As a limited amount of force can be applied and only one hand is free to ply the chisel – unless an assistant operates the bow – most work turned on a bow lathe is small and simple, like the peg and ball components of *moushrabiya* work. Only short chisels can be used because of the confined position.

The pole lathe

In northern Europe the traditional lathe is powered with a springy pole. Another word for pole is 'lath', possibly the origin of the word 'lathe'. The cord wrapped around the work is attached to the pole above and to a pedal below. As the turner pushes the pedal down the work is turned towards him for the cutting stroke, and as he releases the pedal the tension in the pole pulls the cord back up. Pole lathes and turned items have been found in the remains of Iron Age lake dwellings in both England and Scotland.

Perpetual motion

A cut can only be made as the top revolves towards the turner and so the reciprocal motion, back and forth, of the bow and pole lathe means the blade must be withdrawn during the return stroke. A continuous spin in one direction, and therefore uninterrupted cutting, became possible in the 17th century when craftsmen in workshops began using a foot-powered treadle. With the increase in industrialization, many lathes were driven with a band looped around a shaft driven by a waterwheel. However, the pole lathe could easily be set up in a wood or coppice and so continued in woodland use until the middle of the 20th century.

In the developed world electric lathes are now used by most professional and amateur turners. Speeds are often

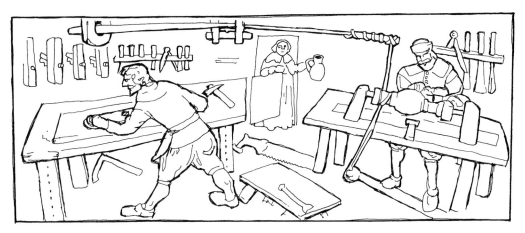

Above, left:
Workshop with a pole
lathe in action, after
a Tudor woodcarving.
A selection of tools
are arranged in racks
on the wall.

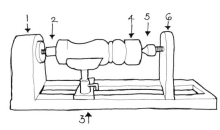

Parts of a lathe: 1. headstock; 2. drive
centre; 3. tool rest; 4. the work; 5. back or
dead centre; 6. tail stock or poppet head.

adjustable, slow for softwood and fast for
hardwood. The motor is housed in the
headstock, driving one centre, while the
centre in the tail stock is said to be dead,
having no power, merely holding the work
in place. This means work need only be
attached to the driving centre, making the
turning of hollowed forms much easier.

Above, right: *Foot-operated lathes in a
Tunisian workshop.*

Above centre: *Electric lathe. Long-handled
chisels and gouges are ready for use in the rack
beneath.*

Near right: *A small electric lathe used by an
amateur turner.*

Far right: *Teenage professional turner in the
souk, Marrakesh, Morocco.*

SMOOTHING TOOLS

THERE ARE occasions when the texture left by tooling with a chisel or adze may be considered attractive, but a smooth finish is often preferable as it is more flattering to the wood, showing the grain to advantage. A smooth surface provides a more suitable base for paint or polish and handling will not cause splinters.

Scrapers

PLANES and chisels cut into the work and raise a shaving, but a metal edge dragged across the work will only remove dust or very fine shavings. Any straight metal edge such as a chisel or a knife can be used in this way, but the best results are achieved with scrapers. These are filed and honed before stroking the edge with a burnisher to raise a hook-like burr ideal for scraping surfaces smooth, especially when the grain is irregular.

Rasps, files and rifflers

METAL rasps are often employed by carvers in the preliminary shaping of wood. They are covered in hundreds of teeth that scour coarsely, leaving a rough surface in just the same way as the pieces of coral once used in Fiji for shaping war clubs. Files have sharpened ridges that remove less wood, but leave a smoother surface. Both files and rasps are available flat or rounded and in large and small sizes. Rifflers are small double-headed tools for reaching into awkward places and have rasp or file heads.

ABOVE: *A wood rasp covered with metal teeth.*

RIGHT: *Two wood files with sharp ridges that remove less wood, but leave a smoother surface.*

BELOW, LEFT; AND BELOW, RIGHT: *Contemporary Surform file which operates like a grater; workman with a sanded panel for a moushrabiya screen, Marrakesh, Morocco.*

OPPOSITE, ABOVE, LEFT: *Scouring rush once used in Europe and Japan.*

OPPOSITE, TOP RIGHT: *Sandpapers coated with garnet, aluminium oxide and silicon carbide.*

OPPOSITE, MIDDLE RIGHT; AND OPPOSITE, BOTTOM: *Sandpaper wrapped around the fingers, Sierra Leone; scraping with a flint blade.*

Abrasives

Scouring with a rough object such as a stone is an ancient technique used by the Ancient Egyptians and rubbing with rottenstone, pumice, charcoal or other gritty substances has been a widespread practice throughout time. In North America the Hopi of Arizona continued to polish their carved katsina dolls with pieces of sandstone well into the 20th century. A more flexible material is easier to manipulate as the Romans, who polished their woodwork with the coarse skin of the skate, discovered. Sharkskin or dog-fish skin were used by the Chumash of southern California, and in New Zealand and Polynesia. In Europe and Japan fine abrasion was for centuries carried out with the scouring rush or Dutch rush, *Equisetum hyemale*, a primitive plant related to the mare's tail, which contains large quantities of glassy silica absorbed from the sandy soils in which it thrives.

Today, we use the term sanding to describe the final smoothing process as it is accomplished with sandpaper, a material invented in Bristol, England, during the 19th century for finishing pianos. The term sandpaper is loosely used to cover a range of abrasive papers ranging from fine to coarse and including glasspaper, garnet paper, aluminium-oxide paper and silicon-carbide paper. In essence, all are based on the fish-skin principle and consist of gritty

particles glued to a paper or cloth backing. For the smoothest sanded finish the paper should be wrapped around a block of wood or cork, although the modern Hopi wraps it around his fingers.

Burnishing

Even the finest sandpaper leaves tiny scratches, but rubbing with a smooth piece of bone, stone or metal presses the grain flat and imparts a slight sheen. Over time, the smoothest of finishes is achieved by the rubbing of hands and fingers.

SEVEN

HOLDING WORK STEADY

IF WORK with any degree of sophistication or accuracy is to be produced the timber must not move around under the craftsman's hands, but must be held securely in place.

The body

THE simplest, cheapest and most readily available tools for holding work steady are the hands, chest and feet, and these are in constant use by every woodworker. To this day, carvers in many developing countries work seated on the ground holding a piece of wood between their feet or in their laps. Although it may not be possible to use as much force, in this position the carver has the advantage of being more sensitive to the stress exerted on the fibres of the wood.

Supports and jigs

IT is often enough to have a frame upon which a piece of timber can be rested for sawing or marking and the simple trestle or saw horse is found all around the world. The legs of this may be extended upwards to form an inverted V to cradle the work more securely.

Stops or pegs are sometimes inserted into a workbench to stop movement under the thrust of a plane or chisel. A more sophisticated tool is the bench hook used for sawing. A block fitted to the underside holds it against the workbench, while a block on top restrains the work.

Frames or jigs may be constructed for many specific tasks in which one or more pieces of wood must be kept in a specific position. For instance, the delicate task of cutting mitres is made easier with a mitre block or box, an open-ended structure with slots cut in the sides to guide a saw at the correct angle.

The shave horse

IN Europe many woodland and traditional crafts employ the shave horse, a narrow bench the craftsman sits astride. A spar is hinged through the bench and attached to a heavy block above and a pedal below. When the pedal is pushed with the feet the block comes down and clamps the work in place.

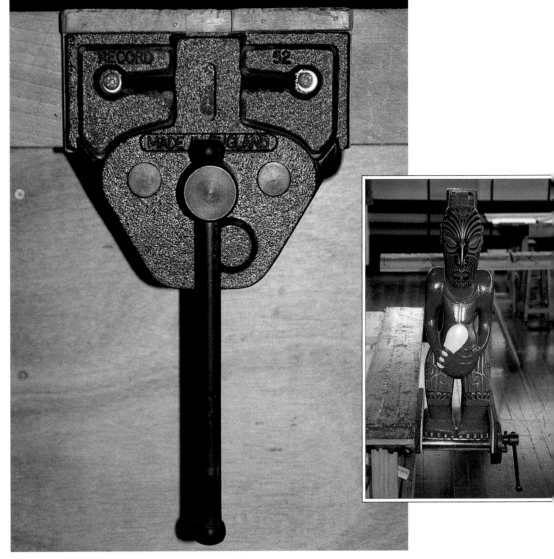

RIGHT; AND FAR RIGHT: *Heavy metal vice permanently attached to a work bench for securing timber while work is in progress; a* poutokomanawa *figure clamped in a vice at the carving school at the New Zealand Maori Arts and Crafts Institute in Rotorua.*

Vices

THE invention of the screw by the Greeks in the 5th century BC eventually led to the development of the wine press and the vice. Normally attached to a workbench, metal and wooden vices squeeze together like a pair of jaws when the screw is turned. The strongest vices are made of metal, but are often padded with wooden blocks to avoid damaging the surface of softer materials.

Cramps

CRAMPS or clamps are essentially portable vices most often used to apply pressure while glue is setting. They may consist of a bar with jaws that can be slid up and down or they may be shaped like the letter G with a screw to close the gap. Some, like the mitre cramp, may employ more than one screw to hold separate pieces in place.

It is harder to cramp curved surfaces such as chair legs and this has traditionally been accomplished with a rope tied tightly. One recent development, the web cramp, consists of a length of nylon webbing pulled tight by a ratchet mechanism.

SEVEN

Sources of Illustrations

The following abbreviations have been used: *a*, above; *b*, below; *c*, centre; *i*, inset; *l*, left; *r*, right; *t*, top.

Unless otherwise stated all drawings are by Bryan Sentance

James Austin, 5, 9*bl*, 14*tr*, 18*tl*, 19*b*, 21*tr*, 25*r*, 28*bl*, 28*bc*, 31*bl*, 32*br*, 33*tr*, 35*br*, 39*tl*, 39*tr*, 45*t*, 45*bl*, 49*t*, 50*c*, 51*r*, 52*bl*, 52*bc*, 52*br*, 54*l*, 54*c*, 54*r*, 56*t*, 56*cl*, 57*bl*, 58*b*, 70*tr*, 74*b*, 75*t*, 77*br*, 78*tl*, 78*tr*, 81*bl*, 82*bl*, 83*t*, 83*b*, 84*br*, 85*bl*, 85*br*, 87*l*, 89*tl*, 91*tl*, 91*b*, 97*b*, 99*b*, 100*c*, 101*tl*, 101*cl*, 102*tl*, 103 1st, 2nd, 3rd and 7th from left, 104*b*, 105*tl*, 107*b*, 111*tr*, 111*cr*, 111*b*, 112*bl*, 114*b*, 115*cl*, 116*b*, 117*b*, 118 all, 119 all, 120*tr*, 121*tl*, 121*tc*, 121*tr*, 125*t*, 125*bl*, 126*l*, 129*r*, 133*tl*, 140*cl*, 141*tr*, 143*bl*, 144*t*, 144*cr*, 144*b*, 145 all, 148*b*, 150*tr*, 150*cl*, 151*br*, 152*br*, 153*tl*, 153*tc*, 153*r*, 154*br*, 155*l*, 155*tc*, 156*bl*, 156*bc*, 157*tr*, 158*cr*, 158*bl*, 159*tr*, 159*br*, 160*tl*, 160*r*, 161*tl*, 161*tr*, 162*b*, 163*r*, 165*l*, 165*tc*, 167*t*, 167*c*, 174*br*, 182*l*, 183 all, 184*t*, 186*l*, 186*b*

John Gillow, 36*r*, 41*cl*, 71*cr*, 72*tl*, 86*tr*, 133*br*, 179*bi*, 191*cr*

Polly Gillow, 8–9, 9*tc*, 9*tr*, 10*bl*, 12*tl*, 25*l*, 39*b*, 42*cl*, 44*tr*, 47*tr*, 59*b*, 64*bl*, 69*bl*, 78*b*, 79*tr*, 79*br*, 84*tl*, 87*bl*, 87*br*, 88*tr*, 89*tr*, 97*tl*, 97*tr*, 113*br*, 128*tl*, 129*tl*, 131*bl*, 137*cr*, 153*bl*, 162*t*, 188*l*, 188*c*

Bryan Sentance, 1, 2, 3, 6 all, 7*t*, 7*r*, 9*tl*, 9*cr*, 9*br*, 10*tl*, 10*tr*, 11 all, 12*tr*, 12*r*, 12*bl*, 13*tl*, 14*bl*, 15*t*, 16*bl*, 17*tr*, 17*br*, 18*tr*, 18*bl*, 18*br*, 19*t*, 20–21, 21*tl*, 21*ac*, 21*c*, 21*b*, 22 all, 23*tr*, 23*bl*, 24 all, 26*tr*, 26*al*, 26*br*, 27 all, 28*tl*, 28*tr*, 28*br*, 29 all, 30 all, 31*t*, 31*cr*, 31*br*, 32*tr*, 32*bl*, 33*tl*, 33*bl*, 33*br*, 34*al*, 34*bl*, 34*br*, 35*tl*, 35*tr*, 36*cl*, 37*cr*, 37*bl*, 37*br*, 39*cl*, 39*cr*, 40*tl*, 40*tr*, 41*tl*, 41*cr*, 42*tr*, 42*bl*, 42*br*, 43 all, 44*tl*, 44*bl*, 44*br*, 45*c*, 45*br*, 46 all, 47*tl*, 47*tc*, 47*b*, 48*tl*, 48*ar*, 48*br*, 49*bl*, 49*br*, 50*tr*, 50*b*, 51*tl*, 52*tl*, 52*tr*, 53 all, 54*bl*, 55 all, 56*b*, 57*tl*, 57*tr*, 57*br*, 58*tr*, 59*tl*, 60–61, 61*tl*, 61*c*, 61*bl*, 61*br*, 62 all, 63*tl*, 63*cl*, 64*tl*, 64*br*, 65*tr*, 65*cr*, 65*bc*, 65*br*, 66 all, 67*l*, 67*tr*, 68 all, 69*t*, 69*cl*, 69*cr*, 69*br*, 70*tl*, 70*tc*, 70*bl*, 70*br*, 71*tl*, 71*tr*, 71*bl*, 72*cl*, 72*bl*, 72*br*, 73*tr*, 73*bl*, 74*t*, 75*c*, 75*b*, 76–77, 77*tl*, 77*tr*, 77*cl*, 77*cr*, 77*bl*, 79*tl*, 79*tc*, 79*bc*, 80 all, 81*tr*, 82*tr*, 82*br*, 83*c*, 84*l*, 85*tr*, 86*c*, 86*bl*, 87*tr*, 88*tl*, 88*cr*, 88*bl*, 89*br*, 90 all, 91*tr*, 92 all, 93 all, 94 all, 95 all, 96*tl*, 96*c*, 96*bl*, 98–99, 99*tl*, 99*tc*, 99*tr*, 99*cr*, 100*t*, 101*bl*, 101*br*, 102*bl*, 103 4th, 5th and 6th from left, 104*t*, 104*al*, 104*c*, 105*tr*, 105*b*, 106*l*, 106*b*, 107*tl*, 107*tr*, 108*bl*, 110*bl*, 111*cl*, 112*tl*, 112*r*, 113*tl*, 113*tr*, 113*bc*, 114*tl*, 114*cl*, 115*tl*, 115*cr*, 115*br*, 116*l*, 117*tl*, 117*tr*, 120*b*, 121*bl*, 122 all, 123*tl*, 123*tr*, 123*bl*, 124*bl*, 125*br*, 126*tr*, 126*b*, 127*tl*, 127*tr*, 127*cr*, 127*br*, 128*bl*, 128*bcl*, 128*br*, 129*c*, 131*tl*, 131*tr*, 131*c*, 131*br*, 132*c*, 132*br*, 134*bl*, 135 all, 136*bl*, 137*tl*, 137*b*, 138–39, 139*tr*, 139*cl*, 139*cr*, 139*b*, 140*tl*, 140*cr*, 141*cl*, 141*b*, 142*bc*, 142*br*, 143*tl*, 143*tr*, 146 all, 147 all, 148*cl*, 148*cr*, 149*tr*, 149*b*, 150*tl*, 150*tc*, 150*b*, 151*tl*, 151*tr*, 152*t*, 152*bl*, 154*t*, 154*al*, 154*cl*, 154*cr*, 155*cr*, 156*tl*, 156*br*, 157*tl*, 157*b*, 158*tr*, 158*br*, 159*tl*, 160*b*, 161*b*, 162*r*, 163*tl*, 164*tl*, 164*tr*, 164*c*, 165*tr*, 166–67, 167*tr*, 167*bl*, 167*br*, 168 all, 170 all, 171 all, 172 all, 173 all, 174*t*, 174*r*, 174*bl*, 175*b*, 175*bi*, 176 all, 177 all, 178 all, 179*t*, 179*r*, 179*b*, 180 all, 181 all, 182*c*, 182*r*, 184*l*, 184*c*, 184*ri*, 185 all, 186*tc*, 186*tr*, 187*tr*, 187*ar*, 187*c*, 188*tr*, 188*br*, 189 all, 190 all, 191*tr*, 191*cl*, 191*b*, 192 all, 193 all

Rob Sentance, 63*b*, 67*br*

Mike Waterman from the Mary Butcher Collection, 81*tl*

Reproduced with kind permission of Abbey St Bathans Sawmill, Duns, Berwickshire, 37*tl*

Reproduced with kind permission of the Auckland Institute and Museum, Auckland, New Zealand, photographs by Kryzysztof Pfeiffer, 16*l*, 110*c*, 124*br*, 125*cl*, 175*t*

Reproduced with kind permission of Peter Barton, 86*br*

Reproduced with kind permission of the Gordon Reece Gallery, London, 7*b*, 40*bl*, 48*bl*, 61*tr*, 65*bl*, 73*br*, 78*c*, 101*tr*, 108*tr*, 108*cl*, 109*tl*, 109*tr*, 110*br*, 113*bl*, 130*bl*, 130*br*, 132*bl*, 133*bl*, 139*c*

Reproduced with kind permission of the National Trust, 38–39

Courtesy of UBC Museum of Anthropology, Vancouver, Canada, photographs by Bill McLennan, 39*c*, 59*tr*, 110*tr*, 162*cl*

All other photographs are from the collection of the author.

Glossary

artesonado Spanish word for interlaced cedar wood ceilings in the Moorish style, also found in North Africa.

banding A decorative inlaid strip.

barge board Board running along the edge of a house gable.

bark stripping Removing bark from felled wood. The bark is sometimes then used in tanning leather or for making dye.

bas relief Relief carving in which forms project less than half their true proportion from the background.

bench plane General purpose plane for shaving and smoothing work to its final dimensions.

blockboard Man-made board made up of blocks of timber sandwiched between thin layers of plywood.

bow drill Hand drill which is made to revolve using a bow with its string wrapped around the shaft.

bow lathe Lathe in which the work is made to revolve by employing a bow with its string wrapped around it.

bow saw Saw kept in tension by a bow-shaped frame.

bridle joint Used for T or corner joins. One member is trimmed down to fit between 'jaws' cut into the end of the other member.

bure Traditional Fijian wooden house.

burnishing Polishing by rubbing with a hard, smooth tool.

butt joint Simple join using no interlocking elements; requires reinforcing.

calabash Sub-Saharan African word for a dried gourd used as a container.

carving in the round Three-dimensional work intended to be looked at from all sides.

charpoy Indian bed consisting of a wooden frame strung with twine or rawhide.

chipboard Man-made board composed of bonded wooden chips.

close grain Wood with closely packed fibres, most common in hardwoods.

cooper Maker of barrels and other items with a stave construction.

cross-cut saw Saw intended for cutting at right angles to the grain.

cruck Architectural framework based on the natural curve of tree trunks.

D-adze Adze with a D-shaped handle used with one hand.

double-bit axe Axe with two cutting edges facing in opposite directions.

dovetail joint Strong joint in which two members are cut with interlocking wedge-shaped projections and housings.

drawknife Long, sharp blade with a handle at each end, used for trimming and shaving.

elbow adze Adze with the handle at an angle to the blade, resembling a bent arm or the letter L.

'fairy writing' Dark markings in timber resembling calligraphy, caused by the early stages of decay.

fale Traditional Samoan open-sided building.

featheredge Timber boards with a pronounced lateral taper, used for cladding.

felling axe Large, two-handed axe for cutting down trees.

figure The pattern on the surface of a piece of wood.

file Metal tool for shaping and smoothing, composed of sharp ridges.

frame saw Saw with a metal blade kept under tension by a wooden frame.

fret saw Fine-bladed saw with a deep-bowed frame used to cut tight curves.

fretwork Openwork designs cut with a fine saw.

fumed oak Oak exposed to ammonia fumes before polishing to imitate antique wood.

gesso Smooth undercoat, applied to furniture, made from chalk or plaster of Paris mixed with rabbit-skin glue.

grain The direction in which wood fibres lie.

halving joint Join created by interlocking two members, each of which has had half its thickness cut away.

hanji Korean window panels glazed with paper.

hatchet Small axe for chopping, used with one hand.

heartwood Old wood near the centre of a trunk or bough.

housing joint Join created by fitting one member into a groove cut in the other.

intarsia European tradition of pictorial marquetry, most popular in the 15th and 16th centuries.

jali Indian fretwork screen made of stone or wood.

katsina The spirits revered by the Hopi of Arizona and often represented by dolls of carved cottonwood root.

kerf Slot left in timber by the action of a saw. Also a groove cut with a knife or chisel to facilitate bending.

lap joint Join in which the plain end of one member is set into a rebate cut into the other.

limed wood Wood treated with lime which raises the grain, creating a weathered look.

linenfold Low-relief motif resembling folded cloth.

livery cupboard Medieval cupboard for storing food, with pierced openings for ventilation.

low-relief carving Relief carving in which forms project less than half their true proportion from the background; also known as bas relief.

lumber Timber sawn into planks or otherwise roughly prepared.

masting axe Large bladed axe used by shipwrights for trimming masts and spars.

mate South American word for a dried gourd used as a container.

mitre A joint in which the ends of both members are cut at an angle, usually 45 degrees.

mortise Recess cut into one member to receive another member trimmed to match.

moulding plane Specialist plane with a shaped blade used to create mouldings.

moushrabiya Technique of constructing screens from a large number of interconnected pegs and balls, common in North Africa and the Middle East.

mueble enconchado Peruvian method of decorating large pieces of furniture with mother-of-pearl veneer.

netsuke Carved toggle used to secure small articles to the waistband of traditional Japanese costume.

ochre Clay rich in iron oxide used to make yellow and red pigment.

ormolu Cast bronze fittings, gilded to resemble gold.

panel saw Saw with relatively fine teeth designed for cutting man-made boards.

pataka A Maori storehouse raised off the ground.

peg dolls Small dolls made from dressed clothes pegs.

plywood Man-made board comprising layers of wood veneer set alternately at right angles.

pole lathe Ancient form of lathe propelled by a cord attached at one end to a pedal and at the other to a springy bough.

pyroengraving Drawing with a hot point that leaves behind a scorched and darkened line.

rasp Metal tool for shaping and smoothing, covered with sharp teeth.

retable (Spanish *retablo*) Originally a shelf, ledge or frame behind the altar in a Christian church, but later a box containing sacred images.

rifflers Small double-ended tools with file or rasp heads, designed for working in tight spaces.

rip saw Large hand saw for cutting with the grain.

rosmalning ('rose painting') Norwegian floral peasant style of painted furniture.

sapwood Layers of young wood around the circumference of a trunk or bough.

scarf joint Join formed by two members meeting end to end.

Shakers A celibate American religious sect that flourished in the mid-19th century, calling themselves 'The United Society of Believers in Christ's Second Coming'. They produced distinctive furniture stripped of extraneous decoration.

shave horse A large clamp for holding work, operated with the feet.

shiplap Boards used for cladding with trimmed edges so that each board will overlap the next.

shoji Japanese window panels glazed with sheets of paper.

side axe Hand axe with offset head and sharpened on one side only, used for shaving boards.

spalting Pattern of dark lines in wood caused by deterioration.

spokeshave Tool with a blade in the centre and a handle to each side, for shaving curved work.

stick chair Chair with all four legs plugged into the underside of the seat, while back and arms plug into the top.

swing brace A hand drill turned with an offset crank to provide greater leverage.

tekoteko Carved figure on the roof apex of a Maori building.

tenon Projection cut to fit into a mortise.

tenon saw A back saw used for joint making.

ther Massive wooden temple carriage pulled in procession through the streets of south India.

'thrown' chair Chair made from components turned on a lathe.

thrust axe Tool resembling an axe, but used like a chisel with a slicing rather than chopping action.

timber Wood, before or after felling, intended for use in construction projects.

tongue and groove Method of joining boards in which one member has a groove cut into its edge to receive a projection on the other member.

treenail or **trunnel** A wooden peg or dowel used for securing joints.

trireme Ship from the Classical period with three banks of oars.

try square L-shaped tool for marking right angles.

whittling Carving with a knife, removing wood in small slices and shavings.

yurt or **ger** Central Asian nomad's dwelling consisting of a wooden lattice topped by a roof of bentwood spars and covered in sheets of felt.

Museums and Places of Interest

Australia

Adelaide
South Australian Museum
North Terrace
Adelaide
South Australia (5000)
Tel. (08) 82077500
Aboriginal, Oceanic and South-East Asian collections

Bali

Ubud
Neka Art Museum
Ubud
Gianyar 80571
Bali, Indonesia

Belgium

Dilsen-Stokkem
Maaspark Negenoord
Rechtestraat 7
3650 Dilsen-Stokkem
Tel. (01) 1755016
Open-air museum

Tervuren
Musée de l'Afrique Centrale Royal
13 Steenweg op Leuven
3080 Tervuren
Brabant
Tel. (02) 7695211

Brazil

Rio de Janeiro
Museu do Indio
Rua das Palmeiras 55
Botafogo
Rio de Janeiro 22270–070
Tel. (021) 2862097
Brazilian Native American collection

Canada

Brantford
Kanata
440 Mohawk Street
Brantford
Ontario N3T 5L9
Tel. 519 752 1229
17th-century Iroquoian village

Gatineau
Canadian Museum of Civilization
100 Laurier Street in Hull
Gatineau
Quebec
Tel. 819 776 7000
Native American crafts

Toronto
Royal Ontario Museum
100 Queen's Park
Toronto
Ontario M5S 2C6
Tel. 416 586 5549
Canadian and worldwide collection

Vancouver
Museum of Anthropology
c/o University of British Columbia
6393 Marine Drive NW
Vancouver, British Columbia V6T 1Z2
Tel. 604 822 5087

Victoria
The Royal British Columbia Museum
675 Belleville Street
Victoria
Vancover Island
British Columbia V8W 9W2
Tel. 888 447 7977
Prestigious collection of totem poles and Pacific North-west art

China

Beijing
Museum of the Cultural Palace of National Minorities
Changan Street
100 000 Beijing
Hill-tribe collection

Guiyang
Guizhou Provincial Museum
Beijing Road
Guiyang
550 000 Guizhou
Miao, Dong and Shwe collection

Colombia

Bogotá
Museo Etnografico de Colombia
Calle 34
No. 6–61 piso 30
Apdo. Aéreo 10511
Bogotá
Colombian folk collection

The Czech Republic

Prague
Náprstkoro Muzeum asijskych, africkych a americkych kultur (Náprstkoro Museum of Asian, African and American Culture)
Betlemské nám 1
11000 Prague
Tel. (02) 22221416

The Democratic Republic of Congo (formerly Zaire)

Kinshasa
Museum of Ethnology and Archaeology
Université National du Congo
B.P. 127, Kinshasa

Denmark

Copenhagen
Nationalmuseet
(National Museum)
Prinsens Palais
Frederiksholms Kanal 12
1220 Copenhagen
Tel. 33134411
Ethnographic collections

Fiji

Suva
Fiji Museum
Suva
Viti Levu
Tel. 679 331 5944

France

Paris
Fondation et Musée Dapper
50 avenue Victor Hugo
75016 Paris
Tel. 01 45 00 01 50

Musée de l'Homme
Palais de Chaillot
17 place du Trocadéro
75116 Paris
Tel. 01 44 05 72 72
Worldwide ethnographic collection

Musée National des Arts d'Afrique
et d'Océanie
293 avenue Daumesnil
75012 Paris
Tel. 01 44 74 84 80
African and Oceanic collection

GERMANY

Berlin
Museum für Völkerkunde
Staatliche Museen zu Berlin –
Preußischer Kulturbesitz
Lansstrasse 8
14195 Berlin
Tel. (030) 2660
Worldwide ethnographic collection

Beverungen
Korbmacher-museum
Dalhouse der Stadt Beverungen
Lange Reihe 23
37688 Beverungen
Tel. 05645 1823

Munich
Staatliches Museum für Völkerkunde
München
Maximilianstr 42
80538 Munich
Tel. 089 21 01360
Ethnographic collection

Stuttgart
Linden-Museum Stuttgart-Staatliche
Museum für Völkerkunde
Hegelplatz 1
70174 Stuttgart
Tel. (0711) 2022408
Central Asian and Oceanic collection

HUNGARY

Budapest
Néprajzi Múzeum (Ethnographic Museum)
Kossuth Lajos tér 12
1055 Budapest
Tel. (01) 3326340
Hungarian ethnographic collection

Kecskemét
Szórakaténusz Játékmúzeum
(Szórakaténusz Toy Museum)
Gáspar András ú 11
6000 Kecskemét
Tel. (076) 481469

JAPAN

Osaka
Kokuritsu Minzokugaku Hakubutsukan
(National Museum of Ethnology)
10–1 Senri Banpaku Koen
Suita-Shi
Osaka 565–8511
Tel. 06 876 2151

MALAYSIA

Kuching
Sarawak Museum
Jalan Tun Haji Openg
93566 Kuching, Sarawak
Tel. (082) 44232
Iban crafts

MEXICO

Mexico City
Museo Nacional de Artes e Industrias
Populares del INI
Avenida Juárez 44
06050 Mexico City
Tel. (05) 5103404
*Important collection of Native American
traditional crafts*

MOROCCO

Marrakesh
Dar si Saïd Museum
Rue de la Bahia
Riad Ez-Zaïtoun El Jadid
Marrakesh
Tel. 44 24 64

Palais de la Bahia
Signposted from Riad Ez-Zaïtoun El Jadid
Marrakesh

THE NETHERLANDS

Leiden
Rijksmuseum voor Volkenkunde
(National Museum of Ethnology)
Steenstraat 1
2312 BS Leiden
Tel. (071) 5168800
Indonesian and South-East Asian collections

Rotterdam
Museum voor Volkenkunde
(Museum of Geography and Ethnology)
Willemskade 25
3016 DM Rotterdam
Tel. (010) 2707172
Indonesian and South-East Asian collections

NEW ZEALAND

Auckland
Auckland Institute and Museum
Auckland Domain
Auckland 1000
Tel. (09) 3090443
New Zealand and Oceanic collection

Rotorua
The New Zealand Maori Arts and Crafts
Institute
PO Box 334
Hemo Road
Rotorua
Tel. 64 7 348 9047
Maori meeting house and carving school

Waitangi
Waitangi National Reserve
Waitangi National Trust
PO Box 48
Paihia
Tau Henare Drive
Waitangi
Bay of Islands
Tel. 649 402 7437
*Maori meeting house and Ngatokimatawhaorua
war canoe*

Wellington
Te Papa, Museum of New Zealand Te Papa
Tongarewa
Cable St
Wellington 6020
Tel. (04) 3817000
New Zealand, Hawaii and Oceanic collection

Papua New Guinea
Port Moresby
National Museum and Art Gallery
Waigini
Port Moresby

Peru
Lima
Museo Nacional de Antropologia y
Arqueologia
Plaza Bolivia s/n
Pueblo Libre
Lima
Tel. (01) 635070

Philippines
Manila
National Museum of the Philippines
P. Burgos St
Rizal Park
1000 Manila
Tel. (02) 5271215
Philippine folk and tribal collection

Poland
Warsaw
Muzeum Azji i Pacyfiku (Asia and Pacific
Museum)
ul. Solec 24
00–467 Warsaw
Tel. (022) 6296724

Portugal
Lisbon
Museu Etnográfico da Sociedade de Geografia
de Lisboa (Ethnographical Museum)
Rua Portas de Santo Antão 100
1150–269 Lisbon
Tel. 213425401
Asian, African and South American collections

Russia
St Petersburg
Muzej Antropologii i Etnografii im.
Petra Velikogo (Peter the Great Museum
of Anthropology and Ethnography)
Universitetskaja Nab 3
199034 St Petersburg
Tel. 812 3280712
Asian collection

Samoa
Apia
Falemataaga-Museum of Samoa
Beach Road
Apia, Upolu
Tel. 63415
Small, but excellent, Polynesian collection

South Africa
Cape Town
South African Cultural History Museum
49 Adderley St
PO Box 645, Cape Town
Tel. (021) 4618280
African, Asian and European collection

Spain
Barcelona
Museu Etnològic (Ethnography Museum)
Parque de Montjuic
08038 Barcelona
Tel. 934246402
Worldwide ethnographic collection

Madrid
Museo Nacional de Etnologia
(Ethnography Museum)
Alfonso XII, 68
28014 Madrid
Tel. 915306418
Worldwide ethnographic collection

Sweden
Gothenburg
Etnografiska Museet (Ethnography Museum)
Norra Hamngatan 12
41114 Gothenburg
*African, South American, Lapp and South-East
Asian collections*

Kalmar
Kalmar Läns
Skälby gård
392 38 Kalmar
Tel. (048) 012111
Ethnographic collection

Karlstad
Värmlands Museum
Sandgrund
651 08 Karlstad
Tel. (054) 143100

Luleå
Norrbottensmuseum
Storg 2
951 08 Luleå
Tel. (0920) 243500
Sami ethnography

Stockholm
Folkens Museum Etnografiska
(National Museum of Ethnography)
Djurgårdsbrunnsvägen 34
102 52 Stockholm
Tel. (08) 51955000
Worldwide ethnographic collection

Friluftmuseet Skansen
(Skansen Open Air Museum)
Djurgården
115 93 Stockholm
Tel. (08) 4428000
*Open-air museum with reconstructed
buildings*

Nordiska Museet
(The National Museum of Cultural History)
Djurgårdsv. 6–16
115 93 Stockholm
Tel. (08) 51956000

Umeå
Västerbottens Museum med Svenska
Skidmuseet
Gammlia
906 03 Umeå
Tel. (090) 171800

THAILAND

Bangkok
Kamthieng House
The Siam Society
131 Soi Asoke
Sukhumvit Road 21
Bangkok 10110
Tel. (02) 66164707
Traditional Thai farming and fishing implements

Chiang Mai
Hill-tribe Museum and Research
Rama 9 Park
Chotana Road
Chiang Mai
Tel. 210872, 221933
Thai hill-tribe crafts

UNITED KINGDOM

Bath
The American Museum in Britain
Claverton Manor
Bath BA2 7BD
Tel. 01225 460503
Chairs, mostly Native American

Cambridge
Cambridge and County Folk Museum
2–3 Castle Hill
Cambridge CB3 0AQ
Tel. 01223 355159

Cardiff
Museum of Welsh Life
St Fagans
Cardiff CF5 6XB
Tel. 02920 573500
Includes reconstructions and re-creations of buildings dating from Celtic times onwards

Castel, Guernsey
Guernsey Folk Museum
Saumarez Park
Castel
Guernsey
Channel Isles GY1 7UJ
Tel. 01481 55384
Traditional domestic and agricultural collection

Dereham
Norfolk Rural Life Museum
Beech House
Gressenhall
Dereham
Norfolk NR20 4DR
Tel. 01362 860563

Edinburgh
Museum of Childhood
42 High Street
Edinburgh EH1 1TG
Tel. 0131 529 4142/4119

Farnham
Rural Life Centre
Reeds Road
Tilford
Farnham GU10 2DL
Tel. 01252 792300

Glastonbury
Somerset Rural Life Museum
Abbey Farm
Chilkwell Street
Glastonbury BA6 8DB
Tel. 01458 831197

Gloucester
Gloucester Folk Museum
99–103 Westgate Street
Gloucester GL1 2PG
Tel. 01452 526467

Halifax
Bankfield Museum
Akroyd Park
Boothtown Road
Halifax HX3 6HG
Tel. 01422 354823

Kenmore
The Scottish Crannog Centre
Kenmore
South Loch Tay
Aberfeldy
Perthshire PH15 2HY
Tel. 01887 830583
Iron Age lake dwelling

Kew
Department of Economic Botany
Kew Palace and Museums of the Royal
Botanic Gardens
Kew TW9 3AB
Tel. 020 8940 1171
Collection of ethnographic items illustrating plant use

Lincoln
Museum of Lincolnshire Life
Old Barracks
Burton Road
Lincoln LN1 3LY
Tel. 01522 528448

London
Bethnal Green Museum of Childhood
Cambridge Heath Road
London E2 9PA
Tel. 020 8983 5200

The British Museum
Great Russell Street
London WC1B 3DG
Tel. 020 7636 1555
Worldwide ethnographic collection formerly housed at the Museum of Mankind in London

Horniman Museum
100 London Road
Forest Hill, London SE23 3PQ
Tel. 020 8699 1872
Worldwide ethnographic collection

Victoria and Albert Museum
Cromwell Road
London SW7 2RL
Tel. 020 7942 2000

Luton
Luton Museum
Wardown Park, Luton LU2 7HA
Tel. 01582 746722

Stockwood Craft Museum and Gardens
Stockwood Park
Farley Hill, Luton LU1 4BH
Tel. 01582 38714

Oxford
Pitt Rivers Museum
South Parks Road
Oxford OX1 3PP
Tel. 01865 270927
Extensive ethnographic collection (take a torch!)

Peterborough
Flag Fen Prehistoric Fenland Centre
Fourth Drove
Fengate, Peterborough PE1 5UR
Tel. 01733 313414

Reading
Museum of English Rural Life
Whiteknights
Reading RG6 2AG
Tel. 0118 931 8660

Stowmarket
Museum of East Anglian Life
Abbot's Hall
Stowmarket IP14 1DL
Tel. 01449 612229

UNITED STATES OF AMERICA

Augusta, Maine
Maine State Museum
Library-Museum-Archives Bldg
State House Complex
Augusta, ME 04333–0083
Tel. 207 287 2301

Cambridge, Massachusetts
Peabody Museum of Archaeology and Ethnology
11 Divinity Av
Cambridge, MA 02138
Tel. 617 496 1027

Cherokee, North Carolina
Cherokee Indian Reservation
Cherokee, North Carolina

Chicago, Illinois
Field Museum of Natural History
Roosevelt Road at Lake Shore Drive
Chicago, IL 60605
Tel. 312 922 9410

Denver, Colorado
Denver Art Museum
100 W 14th Av Pkwy
Denver, CO 80204
Tel. 303 640 4433

Dragoon, Arizona
The Amerind Foundation
2100 N Amerind Road
Dragoon, AZ 85609
Tel. 520 586 3666

Eureka, California
The Clarke Memorial Museum
240 E Eureka St
Eureka, CA 95501
Tel. 707 443 1947

Flagstaff, Arizona
Museum of Northern Arizona
3101 N Fort Valley Road
Flagstaff, AZ 86001
Tel. 520 774 5213

Goldendale, Washington
Maryhill Museum of Art
35 Maryhill Museum Drive
Goldendale, WA 98620
Tel. 509 773 3733

Haines, Alaska
Sheldon Museum
11 Main St
Haines, AK 99827
Tel. 907 766 2366

Honolulu, Hawaii
Bishop Museum
1525 Bernice Street
Honolulu, HI 96817–0916
Tel. 808 847 3511

Klamath Falls, Oregon
Favell Museum of Western Art and
Indian Artifacts
125 West Main St
Klamath Falls, OR 97601
Tel. 541 882 9996

Los Angeles, California
Southwest Museum
234 Museum Drive
Los Angeles, CA 90065
Tel. 213 221 2163

New York
American Museum of Natural History
Central Park West at 79th Street
New York, NY 10024
Tel. 212 769 5100

Brooklyn Children's Museum
145 Brooklyn Avenue
New York, NY 11213
Tel. 718 735 4402

National Museum of the American Indian
Smithsonian Institution
George Gustav Heye Center
1 Bowling Green
New York, NY 10004
Tel. 212 514 3700

Norris, Tennessee
Museum of Appalachia
Hwy 61
Norris, TN 37828
Tel. 423 494 7680

Phoenix, Arizona
The Heard Museum
2301 North Central Avenue
Phoenix, AZ 85004
Tel. 602 252 8840

Santa Fe, New Mexico
Wheelwright Museum of the American Indian
704 Camino Lejo
Santa Fe, NM 87505
Tel. 505 982 4636

Second Mesa, Arizona
Hopi Cultural Centre
Second Mesa
Hopi Reservation, AZ 86043
Tel. 520 734 6650

Sitka, Alaska
Sheldon Jackson Museum
104 College Drive
Sitka, AK 99835
Tel. 907 747 8981

Spokane, Washington
Cheney Cowles Museum
2316 First Avenue
Spokane, WA 99204
Tel. 509 456 3931

Tucson, Arizona
Arizona State Museum
University of Arizona
Tucson, AZ 85721–0026
Tel. 520 621 6281

Ukiah, California
Grace Hudson Museum and the Sun House
431 S Main Street
Ukiah, CA 95482
Tel. 707 467 2836

Window Rock, Arizona
Navajo Nation Museum
Window Rock
Navajo Reservation, AZ 86515
Tel. 520 871 6673

Yosemite, California
Indian Cultural Museum
Museum Bldg, Yosemite National Park
Yosemite, CA 95389
Tel. 209 372 0281

USEFUL ADDRESSES

The Convention on International Trade in Endangered Species of Wild Fauna and Flora (CITES)
CITES Secretariat
15 Chemin des Anemones
1219 Chatelaine
Geneva
Switzerland
Tel. 4122 797 3417
www.wcmc.org.uk/CITES/eng/index.shtml

Fauna & Flora International
Great Eastern House
Tenison Road
Cambridge CB1 2TT
UK
Tel. 01223 571000

3490 California Street
Suite 201
San Francisco, CA 94118
USA
Tel. 1 415 346 7412

www.fauna-flora.org
Projects include SoundWood and the Global Trees Campaign

Forest Stewardship Council
Avenida Hidalgo 502
68000 Oaxaca
Mexico
Tel. 52 951 5146905
www.fscoax.org/index.html
Non-profit organization supporting environmentally appropriate and socially beneficial management of the world's forests. Their website lists working groups around the world.

IUCN
The World Conservation Union
World Headquarters
Rue Mauverney 28
1196 Gland
Switzerland
www.iucn.org

The Smartwood Programme
Goodwin-Baker Building
65 Millet Street
Richmond, VT 05477
USA
Tel. 1 802 434 5491
www.smartwood.org
Awards a seal of approval to responsible forest managers

The Tree Council
51 Catherine Place
London SW1E 6DY
UK
Tel. 020 7828 9928
www.treecouncil.org.uk
Disseminates knowledge about trees and encourages planting

The Tree Register
77a Hall End
Wootton, Bedford MK43 9HP
UK
www.tree-register.org
Database of Britain's most notable trees

The Wilderness Society
1615 M St, NW
Washington, DC 20036
Tel. 1 800 843 9453
www.wilderness.org

The Woodland Trust
Autumn Park
Dysart Road
Grantham NG31 6LL
UK
Tel. 0800 026 9650
www.woodland-trust.org.uk
Charity managing forests for conservation in the UK

BIBLIOGRAPHY

GENERAL

Bahn, Paul G., ed., *The Atlas of World Archaeology*, London and New York, 2000

Blandford, Percy W., *Wood Turning*, London, 1953

Book of Woodworking, London, 2001

Bramwell, Martyn, ed., *The International Book of Wood*, London and New York, 1976

Chinn, Gary, and John Sainsbury, *The Carpenter's Companion*, London and Sydney, 1980

Coghlan, H. H., *Notes on the Prehistoric Metallurgy of Copper and Bronze in the Old World*, Oxford, 1975

Edlin, Herbert L., *What Wood Is That?: A Manual of Wood Identification*, London and New York, 1977

Farrelly, David, *The Book of Bamboo: A Comprehensive Guide to this Remarkable Plant, Its Uses, and its History*, London and San Francisco, 1996

Ganeri, Anita, *From Reed Pen to Word Processor: The Story of Writing and Printing*, London, 1995

Griswold, Lester, *Handicraft: Simplified Procedure and Projects*, 9th edn, New York, 1952

Hayward, Helena, ed., *World Furniture: An Illustrated History*, London and New York, 1967

Hooper, Steven, ed., *Robert and Lisa Sainsbury Collection, Volume II: Pacific, African and Native North American Art*, New Haven and London, 1997

Jackson, Albert, and David Day, *Collins Complete Woodworker's Manual*, London, 1996

Knowles, Sir Francis H. S., *Stone-Worker's Progress: A Study of Stone Implements in the Pitt Rivers Museum*, Oxford, 1976

Lewington, Anna, and Edward Parker, *Ancient Trees: Trees That Live For A Thousand Years*, London and New York, 1999

Love, George, *The Theory and Practice of Woodwork*, London, 1969 and 1981

Mactaggart, Peter and Ann, *Practical Gilding*, Welwyn, 1995

Naylor, Rod, *Woodcarving Techniques*, London, 1979

Petch, Alison, *Hunting for the Right Weapon*, Oxford, 1994

Spring, Anselm, *Holz: Das Fünfte Element*, Munich, 1999

Walker, Philip, *Woodworking Tools*, Princes Risborough, 2000

AFRICA

Jereb, James F., *The Arts and Crafts of Morocco*, London and San Francisco, 1995

Phillips, Tom, ed., *Africa: The Art of a Continent*, Munich, London and New York, 1996

Shaw, Ian, and Paul Nicholson, *British Museum Dictionary of Ancient Egypt*, London, 1995

Sieber, Roy, *African Furniture and Household Objects*, Bloomington, Indiana, and London, 1980

Trowell, Margaret, *African Design*, New York, 1971

ASIA

Barnard, Nicholas, *Arts and Crafts of India*, London, 1993

Cooper, Ilay, and Barry Dawson, *Traditional Buildings of India*, London and New York, 1998

Cooper, Ilay, and John Gillow, *Arts and Crafts of India*, London and New York, 1996

Davison, Julian, and Bruce Granquist, *Balinese Architecture*, Hong Kong, 1999

Dawson, Barry, and John Gillow, *The Traditional Architecture of Indonesia*, London and New York, 1994

Heineken, Ty and Kiyoko, *Tansu: Traditional Japanese Cabinetry*, New York and Tokyo, 1998

Impey, O. R., *Japanese Netsuke in Oxford: From the Ashmolean Museum, Pitt Rivers Museum and the Museum of the History of Science*, Oxford, 1987

Kalter, Johannes, *The Arts and Crafts of the Swat Valley: Living Traditions in the Hindu Kush*, London and New York, 1991

Munan, Heidi, *Sarawak Crafts: Methods, Materials and Motifs*, Oxford, Singapore and New York, 1989

Saint-Gilles, Amaury, *Mingei: Japan's Enduring Folk Arts*, Rutland and Tokyo, 1989

Seike, Kiyoshi, *Japanese Joinery*, New York and Tokyo, 1999

Sulaiman Othman, Dato Haji, et al., *The Crafts of Malaysia*, Singapore, 1997

Warren, William, and Luca Invernizzi Tettoni, *Arts and Crafts of Thailand*, London, 1994, and San Francisco, 1996

Watson, William, *Early Civilisation in China*, London, 1966

Watson, William, ed., *The Great Japan Exhibition: Art of the Edo Period, 1600–1868* (exhibition catalogue), London, 1981

Wheeler, Sir Mortimer, *Civilizations of the Indus Valley and Beyond*, London and New York, 1966

AUSTRALASIA AND THE PACIFIC

Archey, Gilbert, *The Art Forms of Polynesia*, Auckland, 1974

Blackwood, Beatrice, *The Technology of a Modern Stone Age People in New Guinea*, Oxford, 1964

Lewis, David, and Werner Forman, *The Maori: Heirs of Tane*, London, 1982

Mead Moko, Hirini, *Te Toi Whakairo: The Art of Maori Carving*, Auckland, 1999

Meyer, Anthony J. P., *Oceanic Art*, Cologne, 1995

Morphy, Howard, and Elizabeth Edwards, eds, *Australia in Oxford*, Oxford, 1988

Mullins, Barbara, and Douglas Baglin, *Aboriginal Art of Australia*, Marleston, 1999

Pownall, Glen, *Know your Maori Carving*, Paraparaumu, 1994

Simmons, D. R., *Te Whare Runanga: The Maori Meeting House*, Auckland, 1997

Starzecka, D. C., ed., *Maori Art and Culture*, London, 1996

CENTRAL AND SOUTH AMERICA

Braun, Barbara, ed., *Arts of the Amazon*, London and New York, 1995

Davies, Lucy, and Mo Fini, *Arts and Crafts of South America*, London and San Francisco, 1994

McEwan, Colin, Cristiana Barreto and Eduardo Neves, *Unknown Amazon: Culture in Nature in Ancient Brazil* (exhibition catalogue), London, 2001

Sayer, Chloe, *Arts and Crafts of Mexico*, London and San Francisco, 1990

Villegas, Liliana and Benjamin, *Artefactos: Colombian Crafts from the Andes to the Amazon*, New York, 1992

EUROPE

L'Art populaire de Hongrie: Collections du Musée d'Ethnographie de Budapest, Woodcarving Magazine, Budapest, 1972

Esterly, David, *Grinling Gibbons and the Art of Carving*, London, 1999

Gloag, John, *Guide to Furniture Styles: English and French, 1450–1850*, London, 1972

Kilby, K., *The Village Cooper*, Princes Risborough, 1998

Miles, Archie, *Silva: British Trees*, London, 1999

Sparkes, Ivan G., *Woodland Craftsmen*, Princes Risborough, 1997; exhibition catalogue, 1972

Traditional Crafts in Britain, Woodcarving Magazine, London, 1982

The Woodcarvers, Woodcarving Magazine, Lewes, 1997

NORTH AMERICA

Bromberg, Erik, *The Hopi Approach to the Art of Katchina Doll Carving*, West Chester, Pennsylvania, 1986

Coe, Ralph T., *Sacred Circles: Two Thousand Years of North American Indian Art* (exhibition catalogue), London, 1976

Feder, Norman, *American Indian Art*, New York, 1995

Horsham, Michael, *Shaker Style*, London, 2000

Hunter Whiteford, Andrew, *Indian Arts*, New York, 1973

King, J. C. H., *First Peoples, First Contacts: Native Peoples of North America*, London and Cambridge, Mass., 1999

McNeese, Tim, *The Illustrated Myths of Native America: The Southwest, Western Range, Pacific Northwest and California*, London and New York, 1999

Miller, Bruce W., *Chumash: A Picture of their World*, Los Osos, California, 1988

Shadbolt, Doris, *Bill Reid*, Vancouver, Toronto and Seattle, 1986

Taylor, Colin F., ed., *The Native Americans: The Indigenous People of North America*, London, 1991

Thom, Ian M., ed., *Robert Davidson: Eagle of the Dawn*, London and Seattle, 1993

ACKNOWLEDGMENTS

WITHOUT POLLY GILLOW's help writing this book would have been harder and much less exciting. I would also like to express my gratitude to the following people for their generosity in providing information and allowing photography: Abbey St Bathans Sawmill, Berwickshire, Peter Barton (guitar maker), Botanicus Ubiquitus Ltd, Paul Butterworth, Chakib, D. W. Chapman and his Bronze Age Foundry, Chanel Clarke and Roger Neich at the Auckland Museum Institute, staff at the City of Ely Community College, Lucy Davies at Tumi, Gary Edwards and Jonathan Todd at Flag Fen, Frog End Aquatics, Nicky Froggatt, Lisa Geller, John Gilbert, John Gillow, Peter Gillow, Reda Gillow, Yvonne Gillow, Michael Graham-Stewart, Hatton Park Primary School, Housebait, The Alastair Hull Gallery in Haddenham, Joel Jaffey, Kay Johnson, Paul Jordan, Jim Kingshott, Heok-Jae Lee, Clive Loveless, Donna Lum at the Kuluk Gallery in Ubud, Sue and Nigel Melville, The Rainbow Serpent Aboriginal Arts and Crafts, Gordon Reece Galleries in Knaresborough and London, Pam Robinson at Moulin Antiques in Grandtully, Alan and Joan Sentance, Christine Sentance, Robert Sentance, Stephen Seymour (Vintage Sports), Kutut Sutapa, Tony Thompson, Waysale Tora, Goodie Vohra, Waterbeach Primary School, Jennifer Webb at the Museum of Anthropology in Vancouver, Ian West, Mike Wickham and the Village Turners.

Index